To Isobel an[d]
Merry Christmas F[rom]
Barbara

CW01647694

Around Staveley

IN OLD PHOTOGRAPHS

DAVID MATTHEWS

In collaboration with
Derbyshire County Council

Alan Sutton Publishing Limited
Phoenix Mill · Far Thrupp · Stroud
Gloucestershire · GL5 2BU

DERBYSHIRE
County Council
We're proud of Derbyshire.

First Published 1995

British Library Cataloguing in Publication Data.
A catalogue record for this book is available from the British Library.

ISBN 0-7509-0872-6

Typeset in 9/10 Sabon.
Typesetting and origination by
Alan Sutton Publishing Limited.
Printed in Great Britain by
Ebenezer Baylis, Worcester.

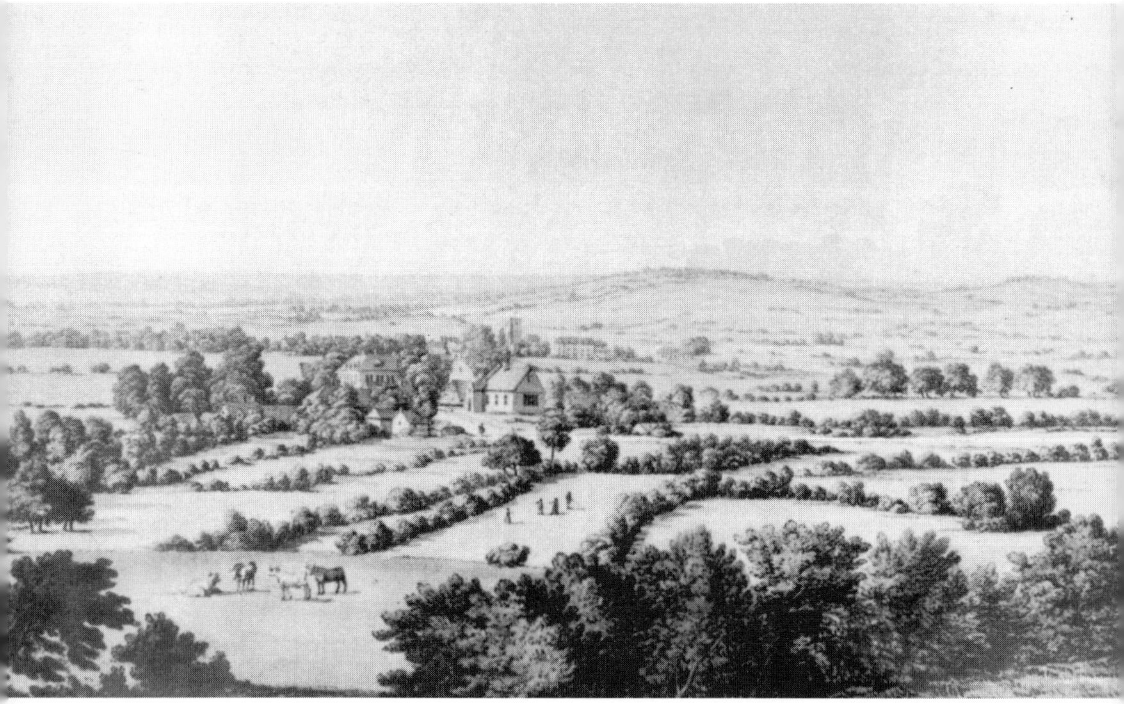

A print of Staveley as seen from Woodthorpe, 1785. Netherthorpe School, almost the only building, stands out together with the roof of what may be Netherthorpe Hall to the left. The church and rectory are just visible at the rear.

Contents

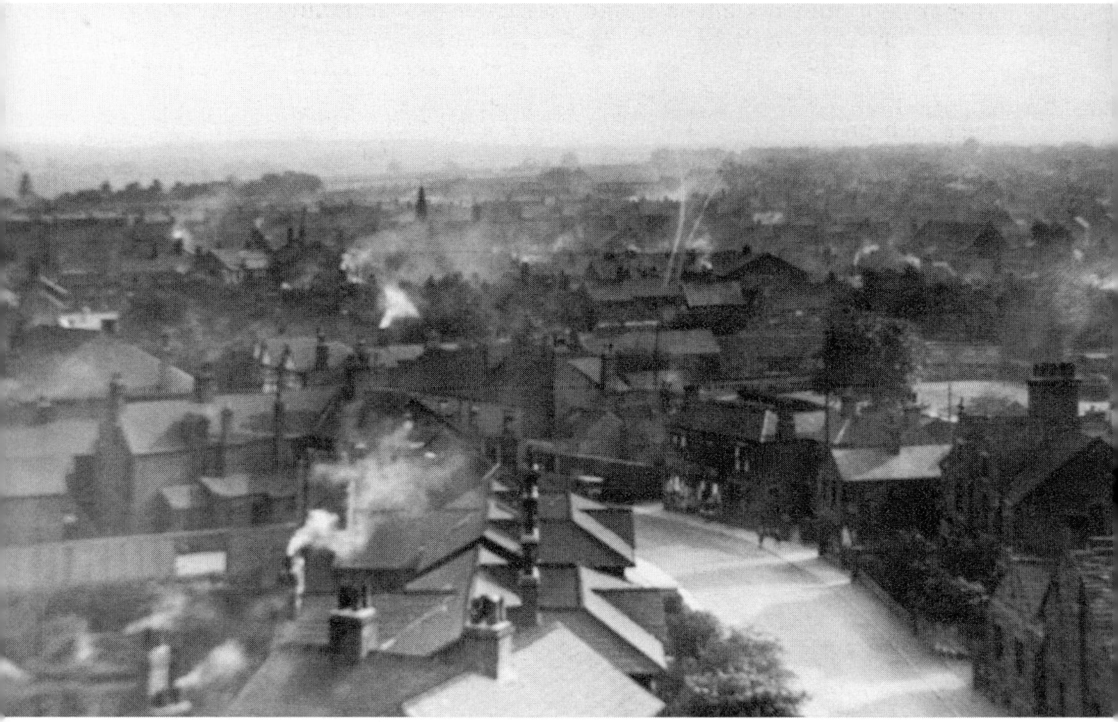

A smoky view south from the church tower, 1950. High Street winds left through the shopping centre, past the Markham Hall, its spire showing above the smoke, and so on to Chesterfield Road on the extreme right.

Introduction

The Manor of Stavelie, which is mentioned in the Domesday Book, belonged to Hacon the Saxon. After the Norman Conquest it was given to a Norman knight named Ascuit Musard. Upon the death of Baron Musard, through the marriage of one of his sisters, a share of the manor came to the Frecheville family. The Frechevilles also came over to England with William the Conqueror and in 1544, via a circuitous route, a Sir Peter Frecheville acquired the rest of the manor. Thus Staveley became for many years the chief seat of the Frecheville family. There are still many reminders of this in Staveley, such as Frecheville Street, and a Frecheville house name for the pupils at what was the Grammar School, which was founded in 1572 by Margaret Frecheville, and many monuments and a chapel dedicated to the family in the parish church of St John the Baptist. By 1681 the Duke of Devonshire had become the principal landowner, having bought the manor and estate from Lord Frecheville of Staveley, another Peter who had been created a peer in 1644.

Although predominantly a rural community, by the early 1800s a variety of small businesses were serving a population of around 3,000: brush manufacturers Fletcher & Son, boot- and shoemakers George Bagshaw and Benjamin Fox, maltsters John Chester at Norbriggs, James Birkett the miller at Staveley Mill, tailors Benjamin Furniss and Thomas Parkin, and of course the wheelwrights and blacksmiths essential for the care of the horses, wagons and carts. Well endowed with taverns and beerhouses, and a selection of shops catering to most needs, the village of Staveley, along with the outlying hamlets of Woodthorpe, Marsden Moor, Netherthorpe, Poolsbrook and Barrow Hill, were quite self-sufficient.

By the mid-1800s this was all beginning to change. The ironworks and the collieries were slowly transforming Staveley into an industrial town and by 1900 Staveley was thriving. The railway and the canal ran through the centre of town, passing very close by the ironworks, and so distributed the products of these industries to all parts of the country. By 1950 probably 90 per cent of Staveley's workforce was employed in the mines or at Staveley Works. The collieries have since been shut down and demolished, foreign companies have taken over what was the iron and steel business to produce chemicals, and small industrial units seem to be the shape of things to come.

During the 1960s the Staveley of old began to disappear. There were no longer the little short cuts – a quick nip down Devonshire Street into Duke Street, pop up New Street and you cut the long High Street/Market Street corner, down past Buttermilk Row and under the Arches to Railway Cottages. The little rows that were a feature all around Staveley, such as Renshaw's Row, Gregory's Row, Netherthorpe Row, Bent Lane, The Poplars, Prospect Place, all made way for more modern housing and new shopping facilities. At one time there seemed to be a public house every few yards: the Crown, where the Staveley Feast was held in the field at the side, the New Inn in New Street, the Devonshire Arms on High Street, and the Canal Tavern, handy for the strollers on the canal path, all vying for customers with the ones that have survived until the present. And do you remember the shops? Frisby's shoe shop on the Cross, Woodhead's Drapery, Bowmer's the tobacconist, the big Co-op on High Street, all the little sweet shops, wool shops, hat shops, chip shops, and not forgetting the ironmonger 'Sonky' Sales where anything could be 'got for the morrow'.

It's good to look back occasionally to how we used to be, when life moved at a slower pace; but perhaps we endow things with a rosy hue that hides just how hard that life sometimes was. Yet there were also the good times, the big celebrations, the church and chapel festivities, the parades and band concerts, the football and the Staveley Feast.

I have tried to include a little of everything in the following photographs, which together with my 'potted history' will I hope give some idea of the people and places that made Staveley the town it once was. I have not used the more well-known views, but I am sure the reader will be able to look and say 'I remember that!'

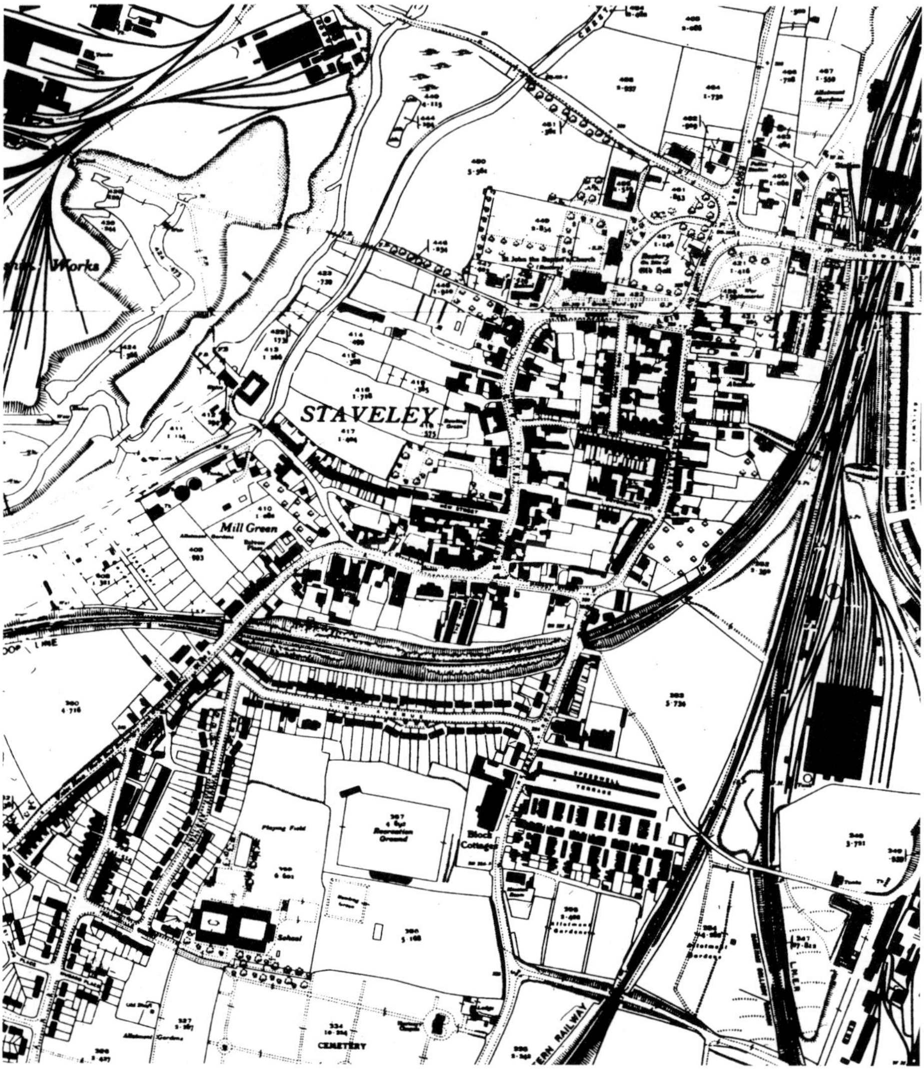

A map of Staveley centre in 1921, showing the area from Chesterfield Road to the Central Railway at Lowgates.

SECTION ONE

Staveley Town

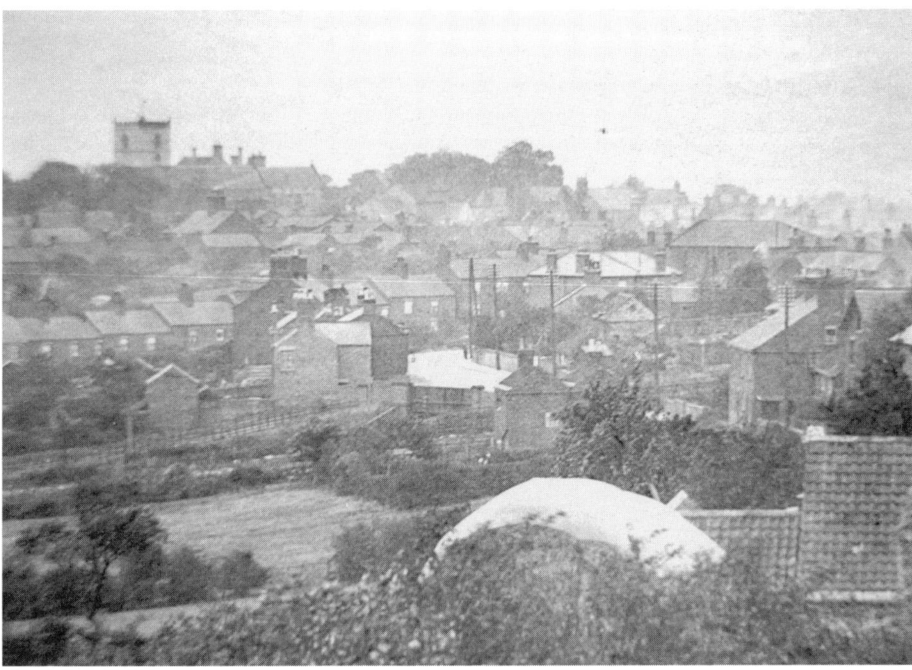

A general view of Staveley from the Mount, 1902. Passing the covered haystack in the farmyard on the left, the road crosses the iron railway bridge by the Nag's Head public house. The houses of Mill Green march up to join Market Street where the road turns to the right.

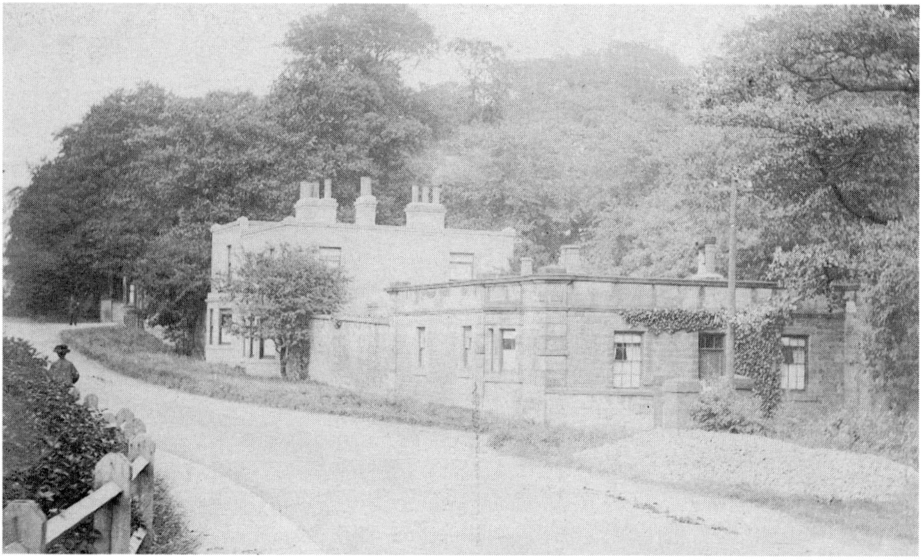

The upper and middle lodges of Ringwood Hall, 1916. The home of Mr Charles Paxton Markham, chairman of Staveley Company (the entrance can just be seen to the left of the newly built middle lodge). This quiet scene is unrecognizable as the now busy main Chesterfield to Worksop road.

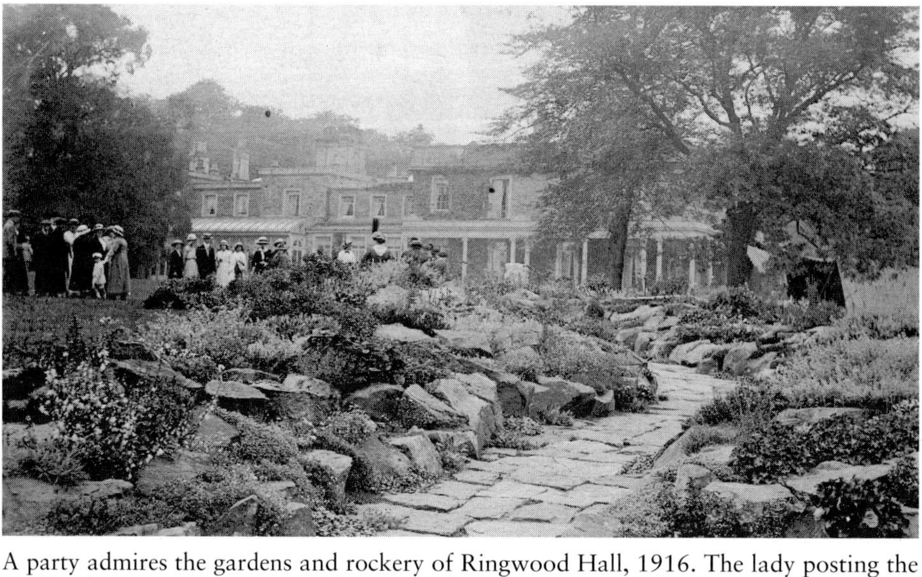

A party admires the gardens and rockery of Ringwood Hall, 1916. The lady posting the card had written, 'It is a beautiful place and the flowers are very lovely.'

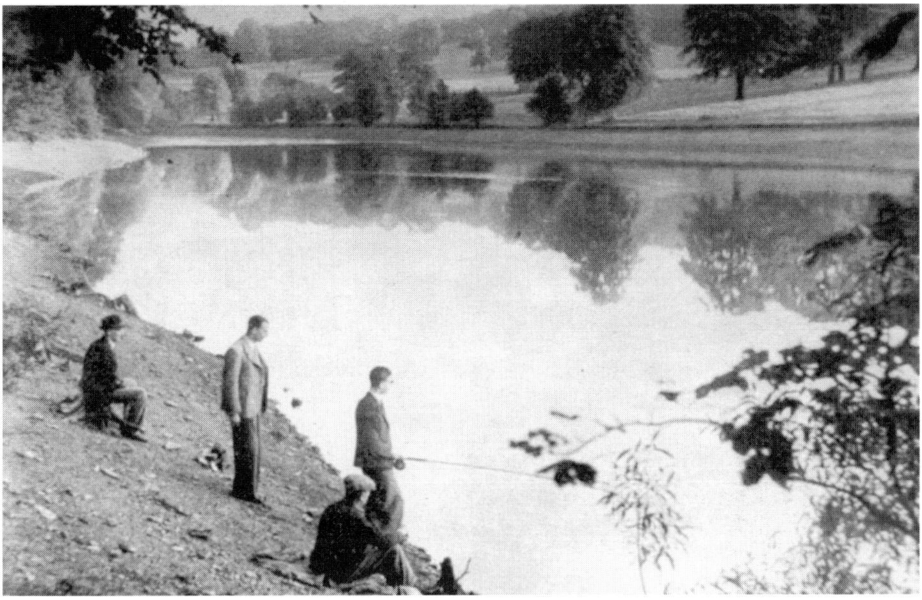

A tranquil picture of fishermen at Ringwood Park lake, 1955. After the deaths of the original owners, the Barrow family, the Hall fell into disrepair until Mr C.P. Markham came to live there in 1911. After his death the Hall and park were presented to the Staveley Company for use as a staff club.

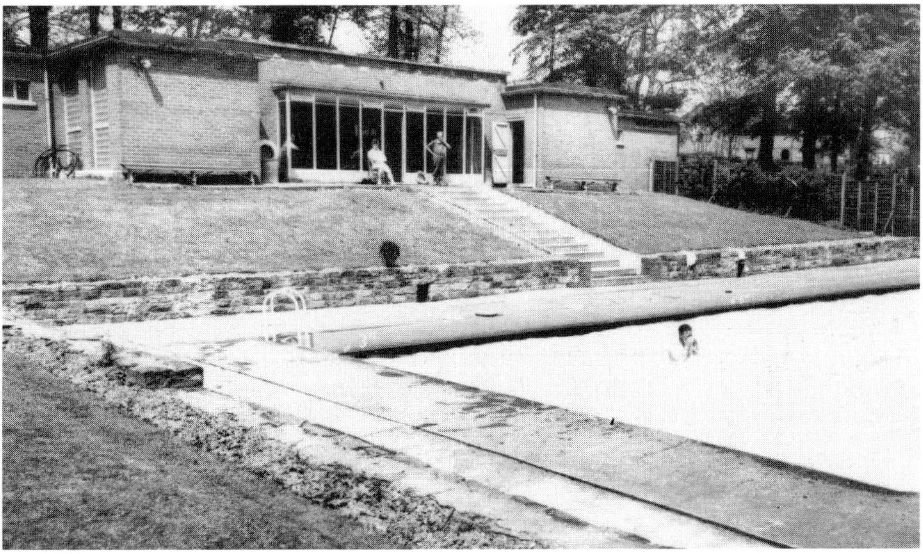

The open-air swimming baths at the lower end of Ringwood Park, 1960s. Although open to the elements the baths were always well patronized, especially by the local children. They were also used for swimming instruction by the nearby schools. The pool and cubicles were demolished in 1994.

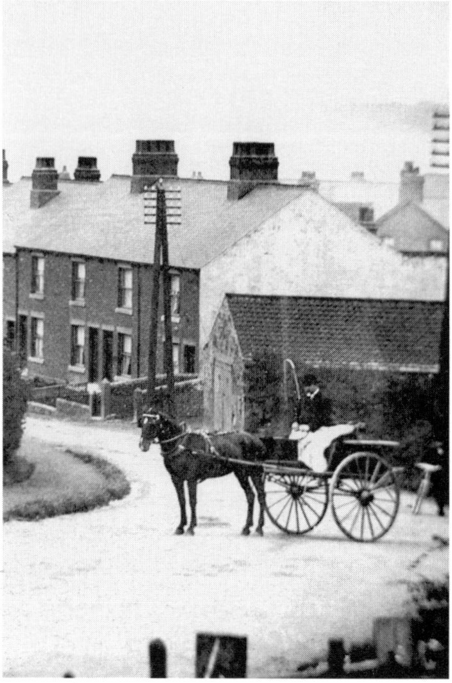

Chesterfield Road, 1902. Taking over from Dr Thomas Hale, Dr Blight, the surgeon from the Barrow Hill practice, halts his trap on The Mount hill. The row of houses to the left are still standing but the old garage at the entrance to Immingham Grove has gone.

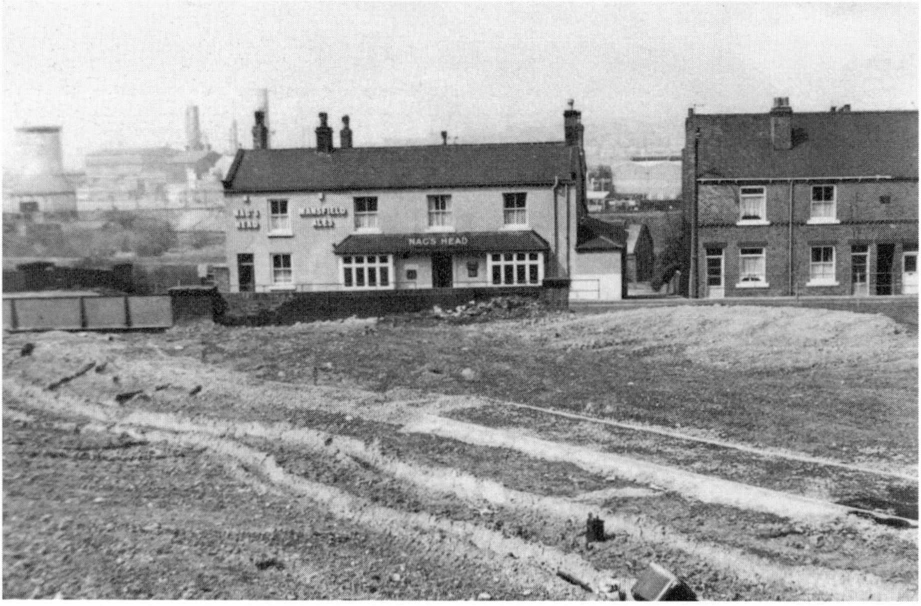

The Nag's Head, Chesterfield Road, in 1964, showing the close proximity of the Devonshire Works. The iron railway bridge on the left would shortly be demolished; the tracks had already been removed.

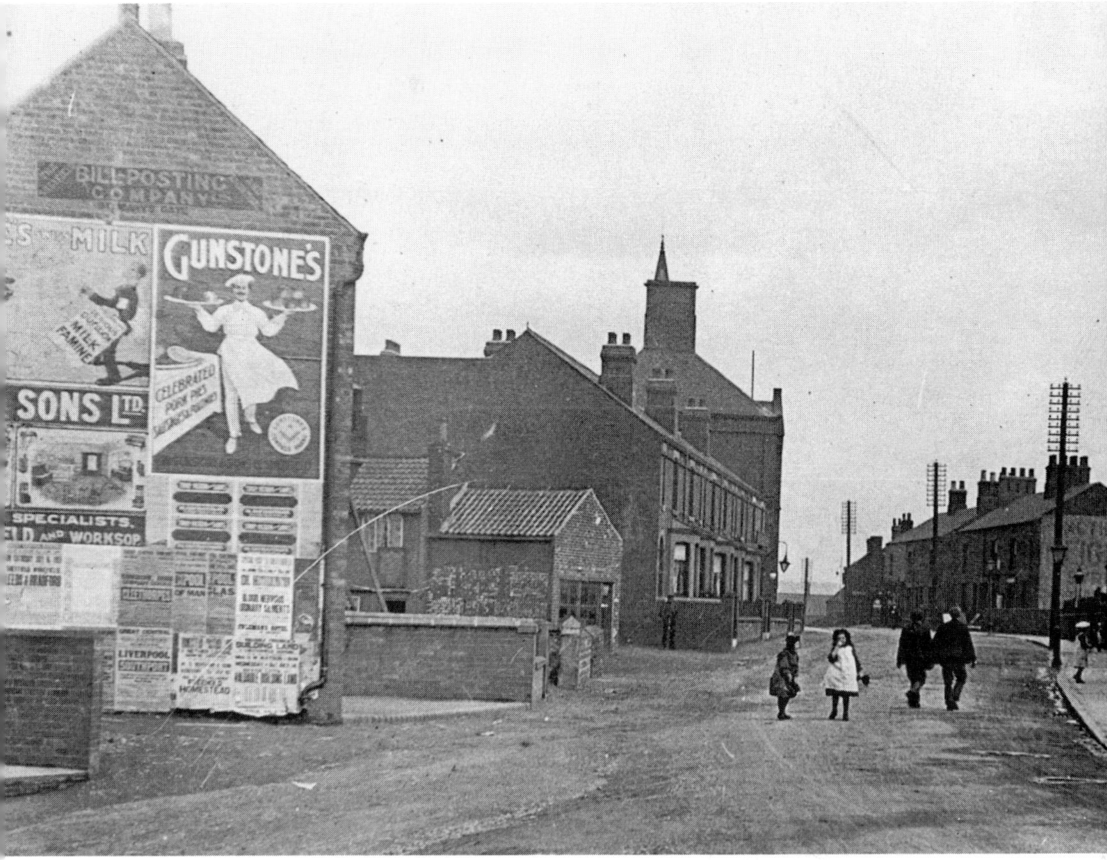

Chesterfield Road, early 1900s. This road has since been renamed Market Street, perhaps to denote the fact that the market was held each Friday in the Markham Hall (the tall building with the spire, in the centre of the picture). The Hall was built in 1893 by Mr Charles Paxton Markham in memory of his father Charles Markham, the director of Staveley Coal & Iron Company. The Friday market, still carried on today, had at that time a variety of stalls: Mr Wragg a tool trader, Mrs Worthington's sweet stall, a Mrs Watts had a 'fent' stall selling drapery goods, Ted Smith with his groceries; there were also butchers and the basket maker Mr Haywood, who also kept the shop across the road. During the week the Territorial Army used the Hall as a gym room. Upstairs was used as a concert hall and dance room and could seat five hundred. The Markham Hall and the house on the left, which is being used as an advertising board, are the only buildings that survive today. The latter was a butcher's shop but is now an insurance broker.

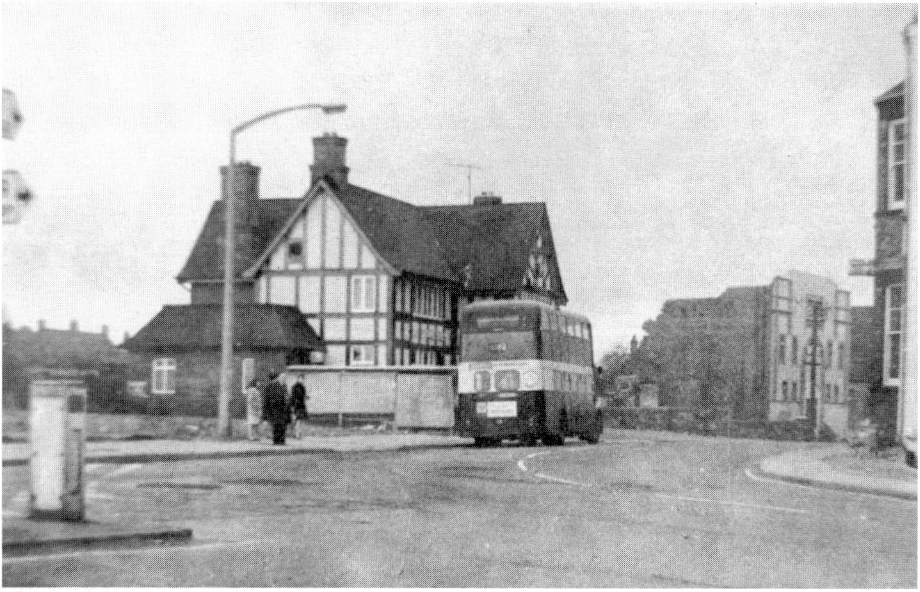

Market Street, 1969. The no. 32 Chesterfield Corporation bus moves past The Foresters Inn towards the Empire Cinema, the back of which has been knocked down. The vacant land around the public house would eventually contain blocks of flats.

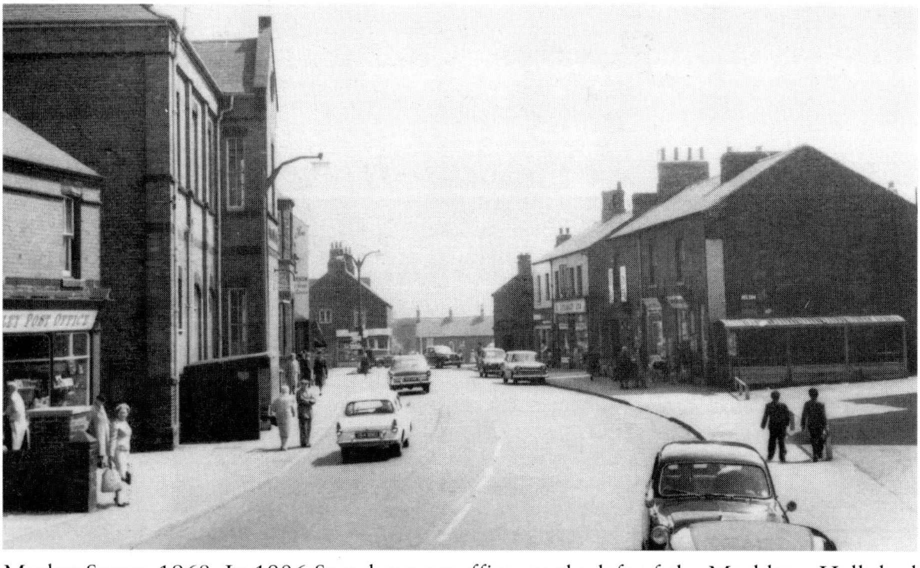

Market Street, 1960. In 1906 Staveley post office, to the left of the Markham Hall, had been used by the Globe Tea Company as a general grocers until it was destroyed by fire. After standing derelict, A. & S. McCabe opened it as a fruiterer's, but changed its use once again when Mrs McCabe became postmistress in 1928.

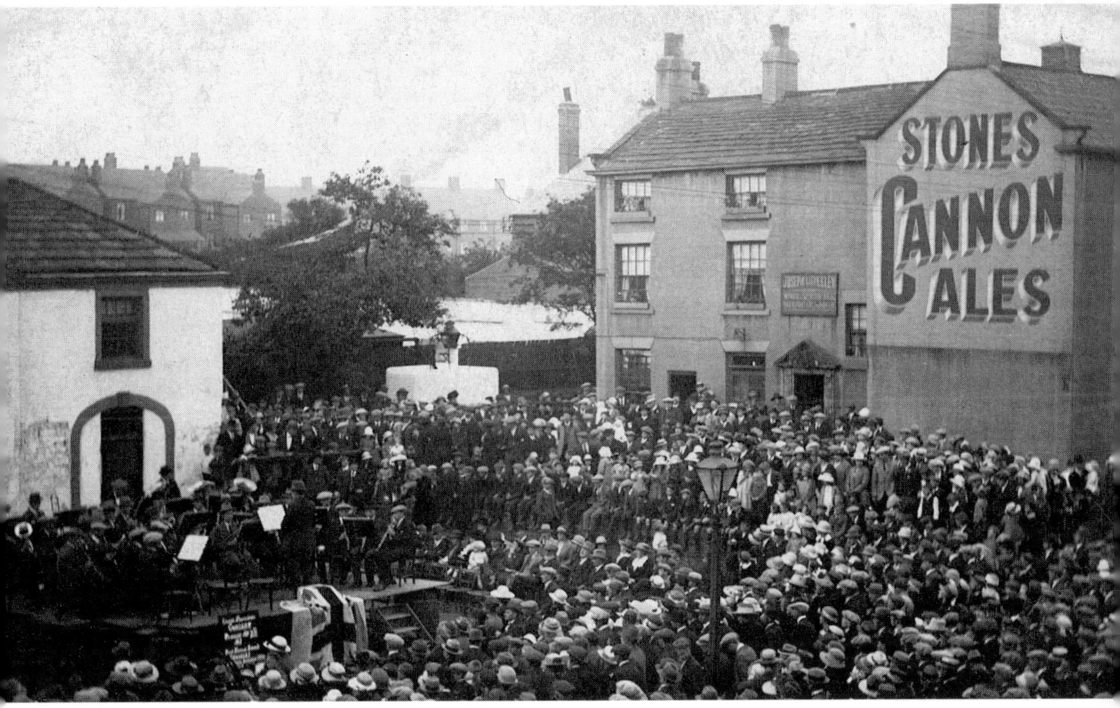

Staveley Feast Sunday, 18 June 1922. One of the great social events of the year, the annual feast was always held on the nearest Sunday to 21 June. Preparations would begin in the week beforehand, with spring-cleaning and lots of food cooked to last over Feast Week: hams boiled, ox tongues boiled and pressed, and fruit cakes baked. The local traders and publicans stocked up ready for the many visitors who would come for the fair. During the preceding week the fair would arrive: the folk in their horse-drawn caravans, the roundabouts and side-shows, with all the heavy equipment conveyed by large steam traction engines. Flying chairs, cake walks, Noah's Ark roundabout, dodgems, coconut shies, fat ladies tents, boxing booths, were all set up in the Crown field to the side of the Crown public house. Feast Sunday was the day of the church parade, which was watched by everyone not taking part. It was led by the rector and the Staveley Military Band, followed by the police force, ambulance and fire brigades, Territorial Army, Girl Guides and Boy Scouts, and the Salvation Army Band. Later the Military Band would give a concert in The Foresters Inn yard. The week finished with a *soirée* in the Markham Hall where Hodson's Band played for the dancing. Everyone had a good time; the children loved the rides and the excitement, saving up their pennies for weeks beforehand, and the adults enjoyed the company of relatives and friends who had visited especially for the feast.

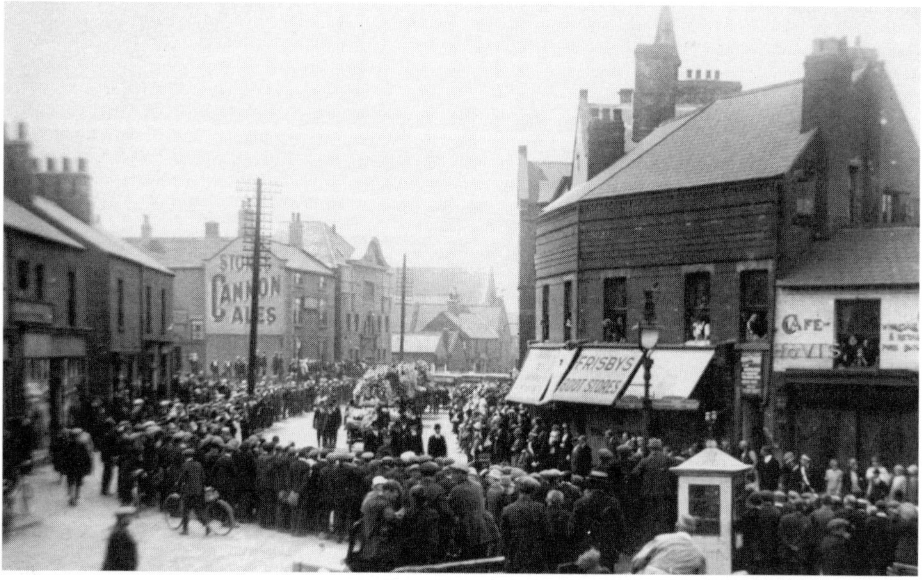

Market Street, 1926. This photograph and the two that follow show the people of Staveley lining the street to watch the funeral cortège of Mr C.P. Markham. Held in high esteem by everyone, the sudden death of the chairman of Staveley Company shocked workers and the public alike.

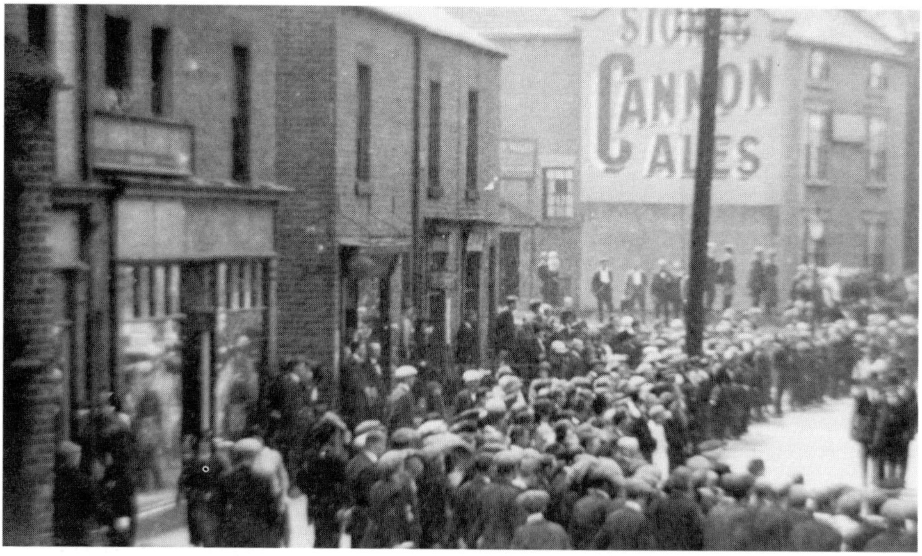

A closer look at the above scene shows the Grand Clothing Hall on the immediate left, at the corner of the entrance to the Poplars – a double row of terraced houses; Thomas Higginbottom's fruit shop occupies the opposite corner. Mrs Hannah Kirk's newsagent's shop is next door, with Charles Haywood's basket making and picture framing business on the end.

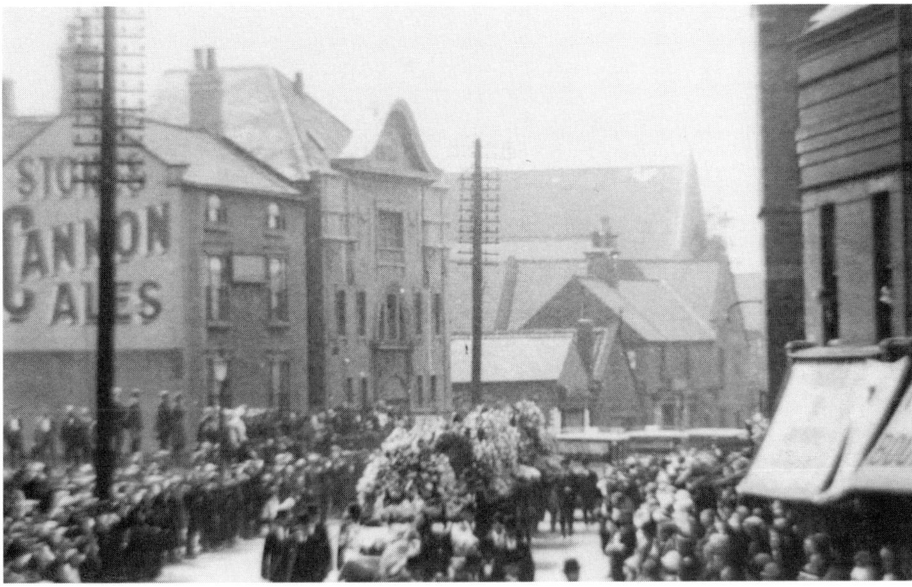

Continuing along Market Street, past the old Foresters Inn, the Empire Cinema is seen more clearly. Both this theatre and the Central Cinema in New Street were originally lit by gas. The Empire was built on the site of Dawson's shop, which was destroyed by fire in 1911. Whitam's pork butcher's next door was built on part of Marples sweet shop and was demolished in 1969.

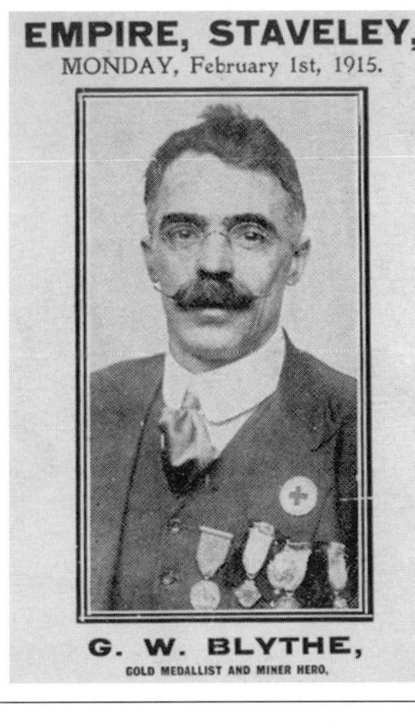

A postcard advertising the recently opened Empire, Staveley, 1915. The Empire Picture and Variety Palace, under manager Arthur Holmes, was in competition with the Central Cinema in New Street belonging to the Kendall Brothers. The Empire was soon acquired by them and the Central closed down.

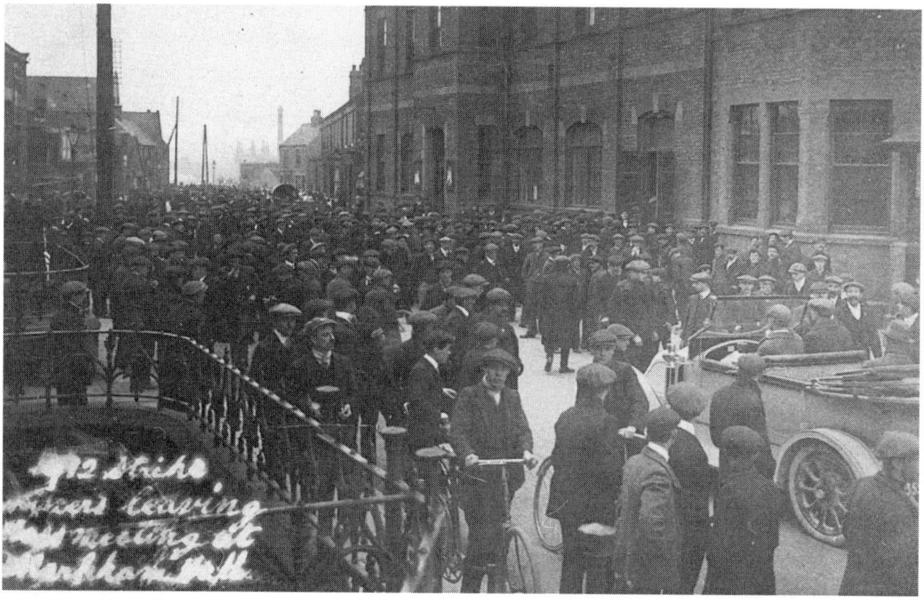

Miners leaving a mass meeting held at the Markham Hall during the 1912 miners' strike. The men at the eight pits in the area owned by the Staveley Company were asking for a recognized daily wage of 5*s*. The open-topped car must have been a rare sight in Staveley.

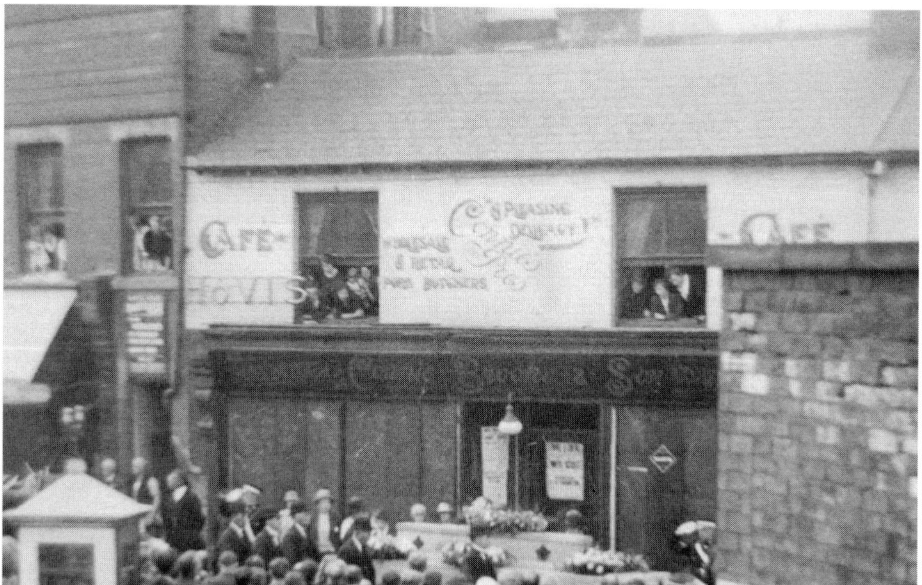

The Cross, 1926. A last glimpse of C.P. Markham's funeral passing Connie Brooke's butcher's and pie shops. More spectators are leaning out of the upper windows of the café. The bakehouse stood at the rear of these shops.

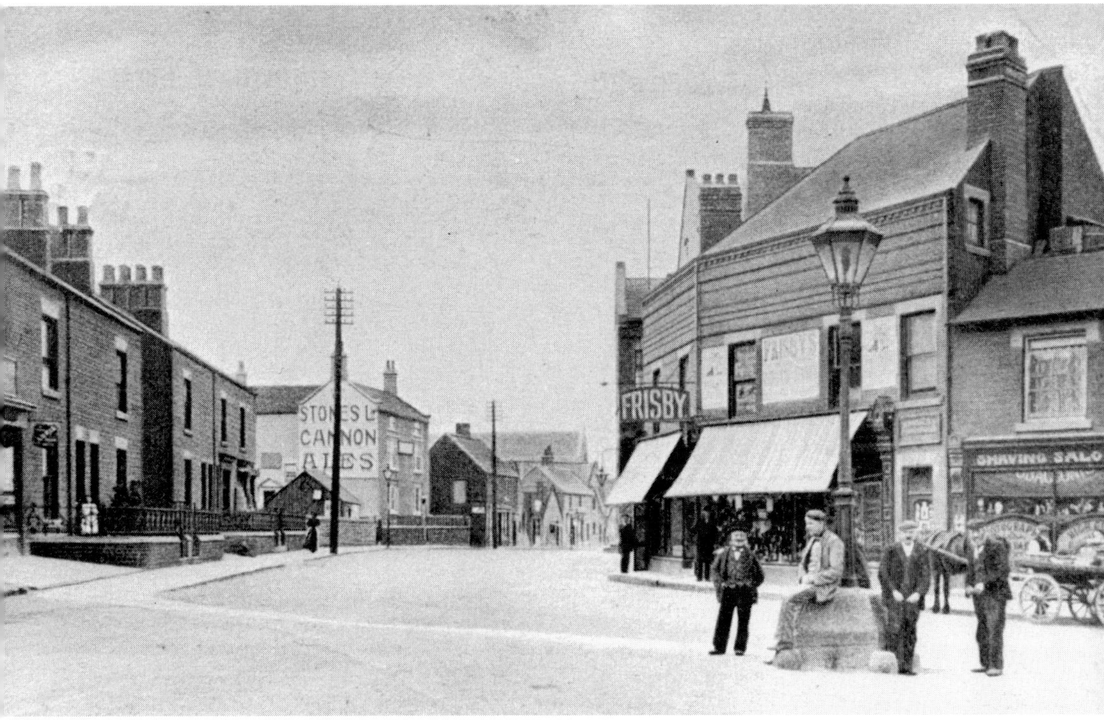

Staveley Cross, 1905. It has been suggested that the old cross that stood in the churchyard was once established here. During the thirteenth and fourteenth centuries a cross, usually situated in the centre of the village, was used as a rallying and preaching point for the local population. Joe Frisby, first mentioned in 1899 as a local bootmaker, is now well established in the shop on the corner and traded here until the whole line of shops was demolished in the 1960s. A little entry passage to the right of Frisby's led to the shop manager's house. The high roof in the centre of the picture, beyond the old Foresters Inn and Dawson's shop, is the newly built Wesleyan chapel. All the houses to the left of the inn would eventually be used as shops.

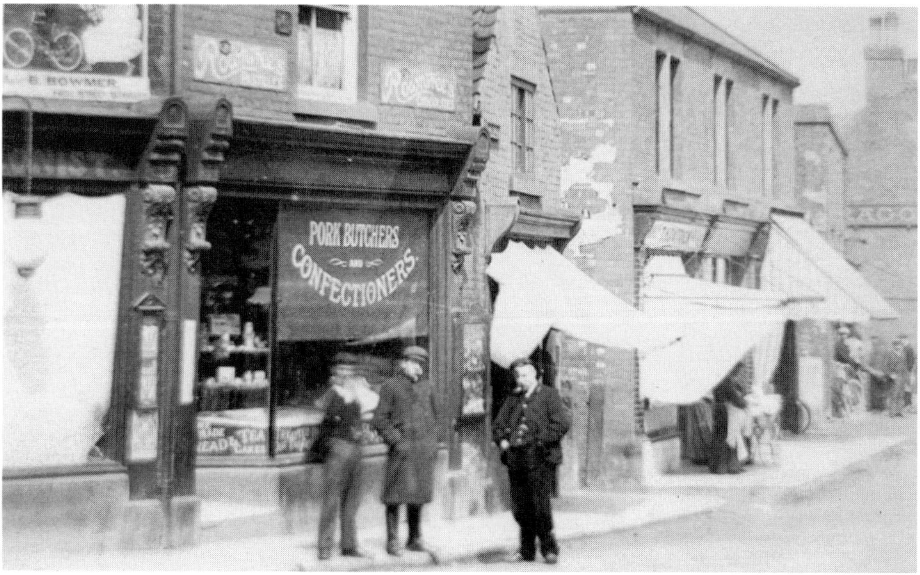

High Street corner, 1906. The gentlemen facing the camera are standing in front of Connie Brooke's pork butcher's shop. E. Widdowson to the right and T.H. Patrick across the alleyway were also butcher's shops. Perhaps because of its largely farming community Staveley was pretty well endowed with butchers! Patrick's and the next two shops were altered to become the Central Staveley Co-operative Store.

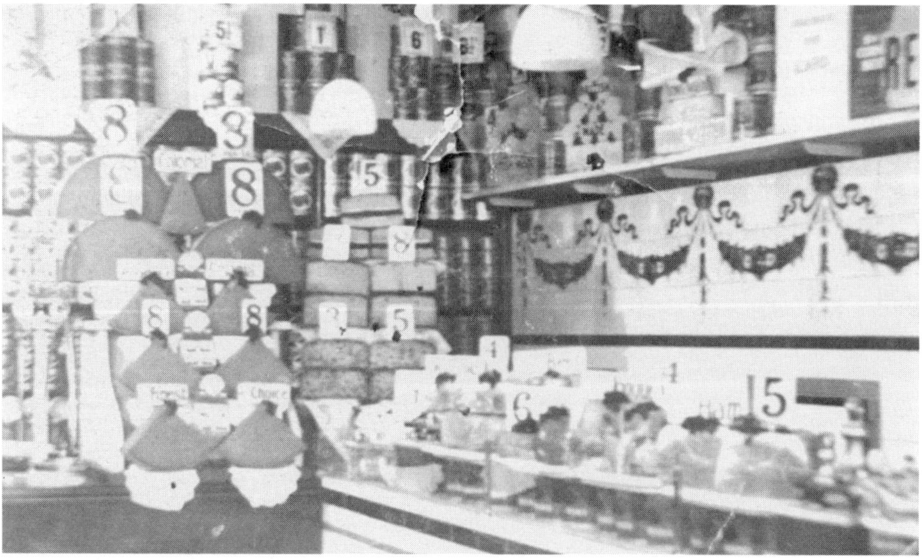

The interior of Melias grocery between 1932 and 1938. Under the name British Traders and Melias this provision merchant took over the premises just visible at the left of the above photograph. The manager was Mr Ernest Hill, with assistants Violet Greenwood and Miss Peabody.

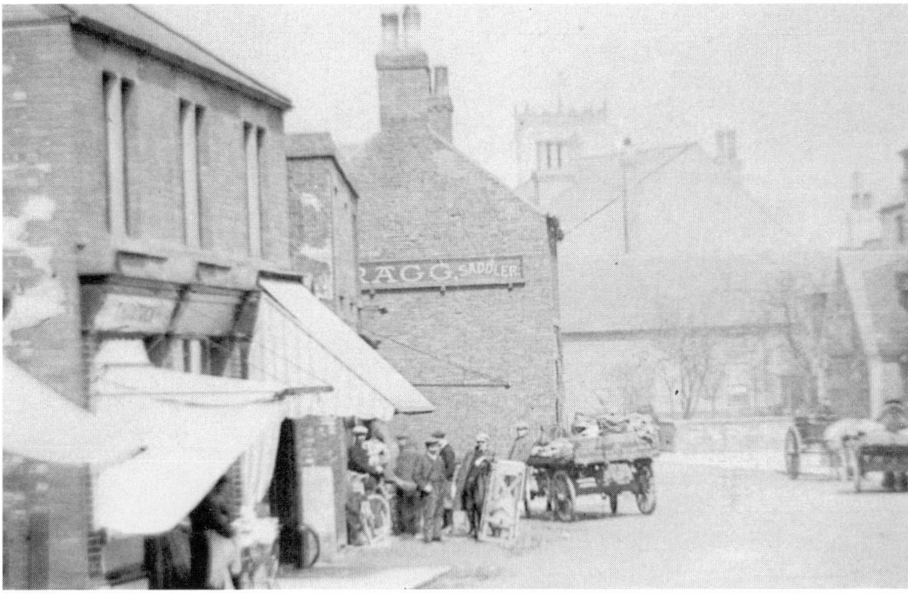

A busy scene on High Street, 1906. The gentleman standing at the pavement edge has a pig inside his crate, possibly on its way to Widdowson's slaughterhouse nearby. Elliot's grocer's cart is just passing the bottom of New Street where H.P. Cragg, a saddler and harness maker, also ran the post office.

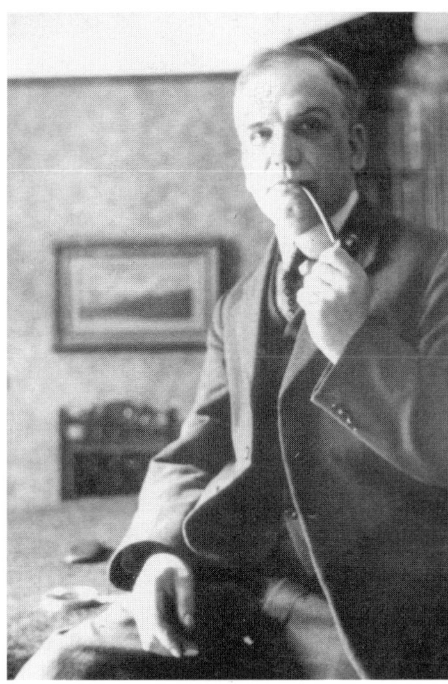

Mr F.W. Cragg, one of the Cragg brothers who owned the stationery and printing business carried on in the building in the top photograph, 1930. This is the gentleman we have to thank for many of the photographs and postcards of old Staveley in circulation.

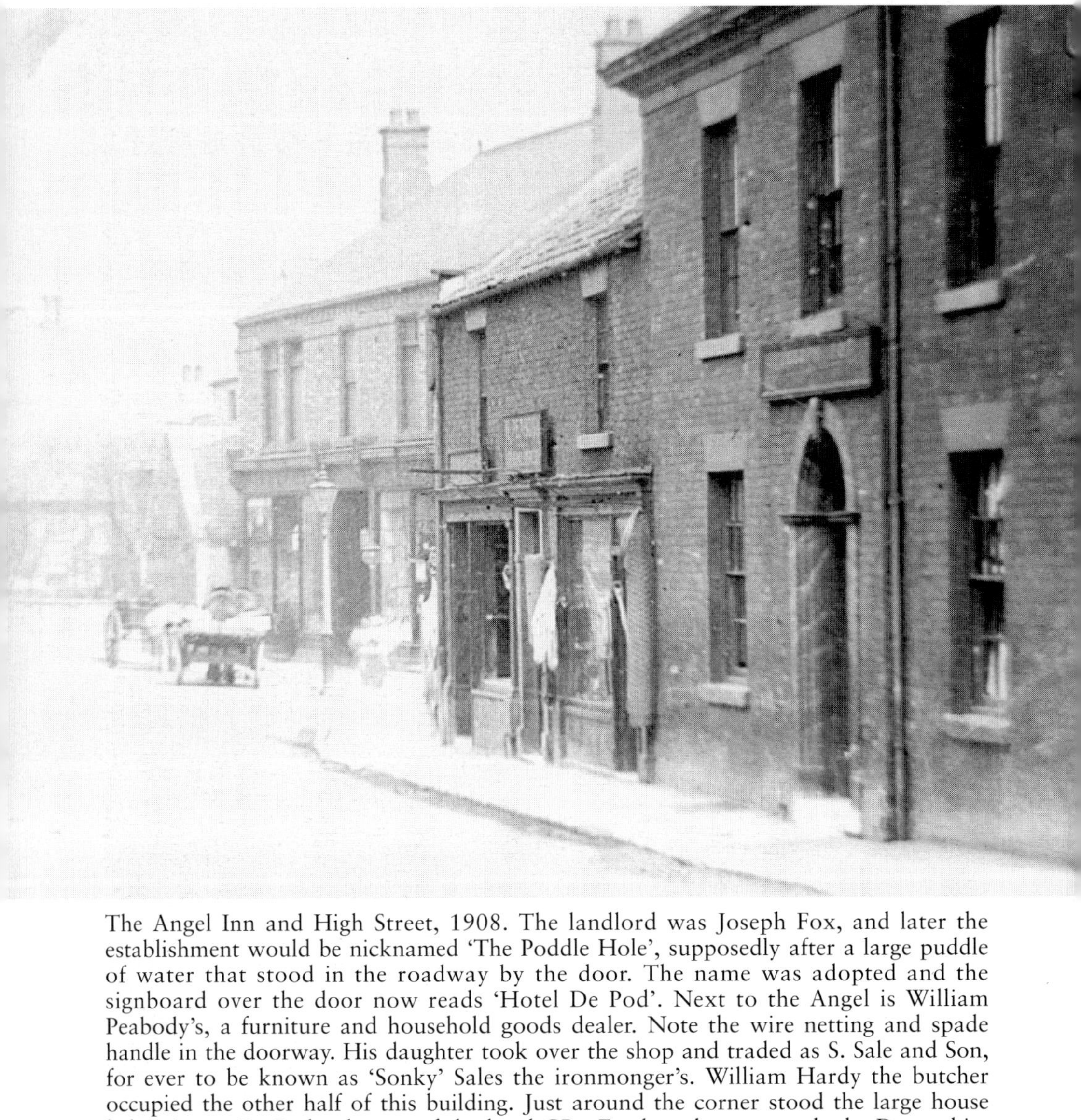

The Angel Inn and High Street, 1908. The landlord was Joseph Fox, and later the establishment would be nicknamed 'The Poddle Hole', supposedly after a large puddle of water that stood in the roadway by the door. The name was adopted and the signboard over the door now reads 'Hotel De Pod'. Next to the Angel is William Peabody's, a furniture and household goods dealer. Note the wire netting and spade handle in the doorway. His daughter took over the shop and traded as S. Sale and Son, for ever to be known as 'Sonky' Sales the ironmonger's. William Hardy the butcher occupied the other half of this building. Just around the corner stood the large house belonging to Dr Badcock, one of the local GPs. Further along towards the Devonshire public house a Midland Railway cart stands outside Herbert Cooper's grocery store. Apart from the two shops by the side of the Angel Inn, which have been knocked down, this part of High Street has been modernized and survives today.

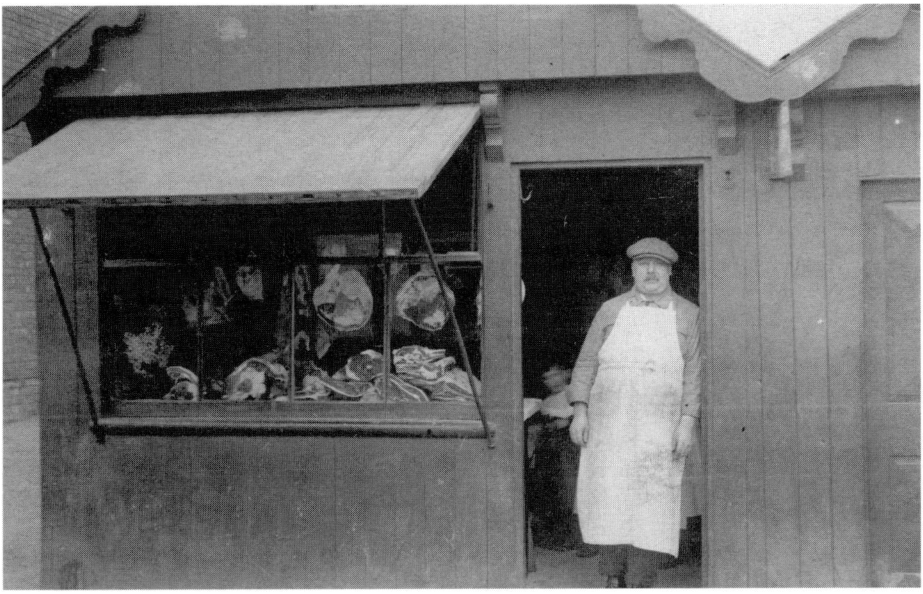

Billy Hardy's wooden butcher's shop, with the man himself standing in the doorway, 1922. The shop was situated on the Cross, just by the entrance to Collier's Row where Lowton's Tripe Box stood at the side of the Angel Inn.

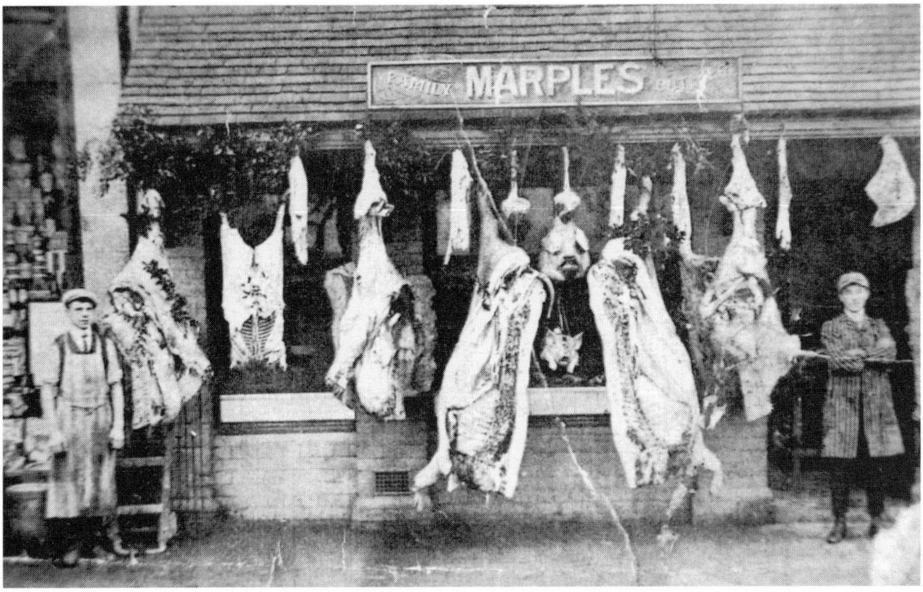

Marples family butcher's, another of Staveley's many butchers, 1910. The two assistants proudly show off their wares at this shop belonging to Paul Marples, which was sandwiched between Robinson's, the grocer and wine merchant to the left, and the Marples family residence to the right.

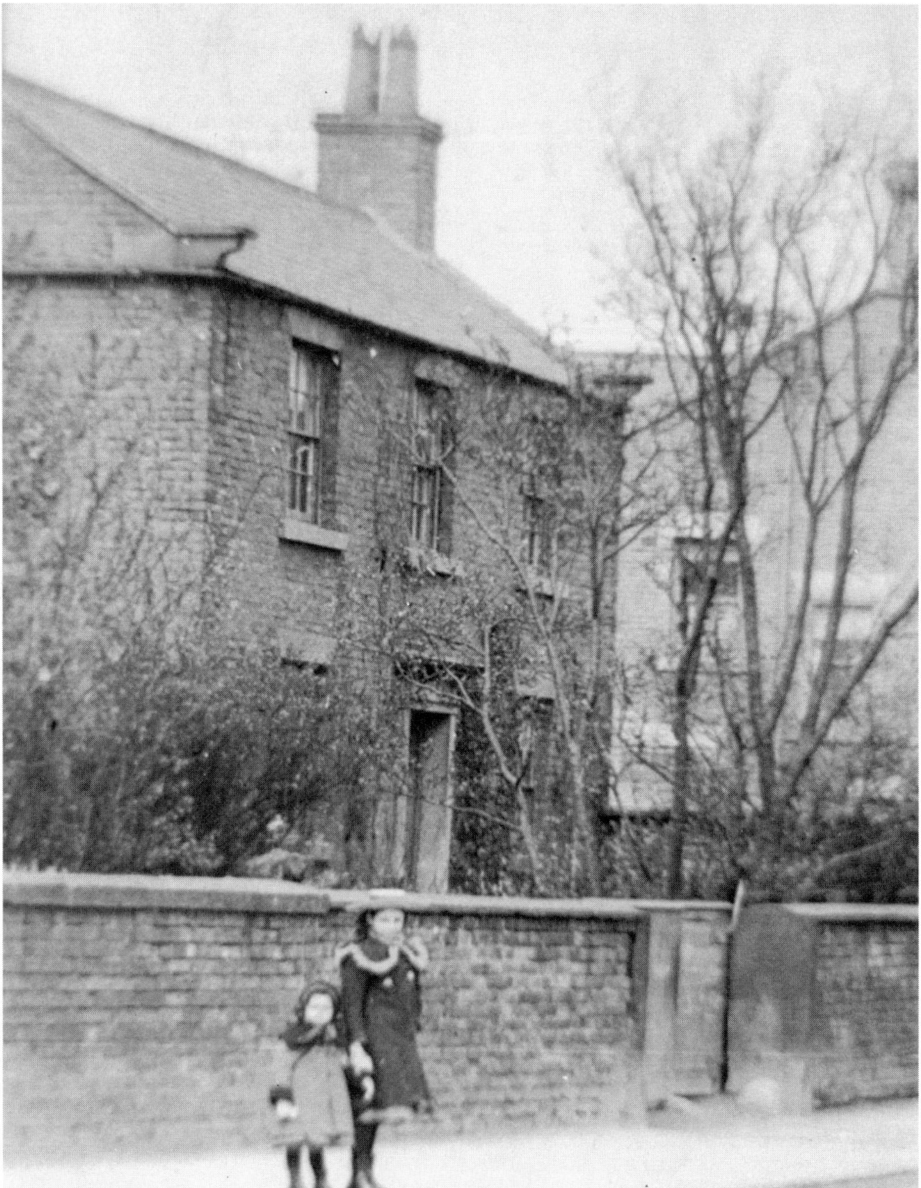

High Street, 1911. This large house, which stood just before the Elm Tree public house, was almost a twin of butcher Marples's house across the street. Belonging to Mrs Fisher, a private secretary and church worker, it was later extended and three mock Tudor frontages were added; it all became the Three Gables. Occupied for many years by Dr James Hutchinson, it was converted into shop premises after his death.

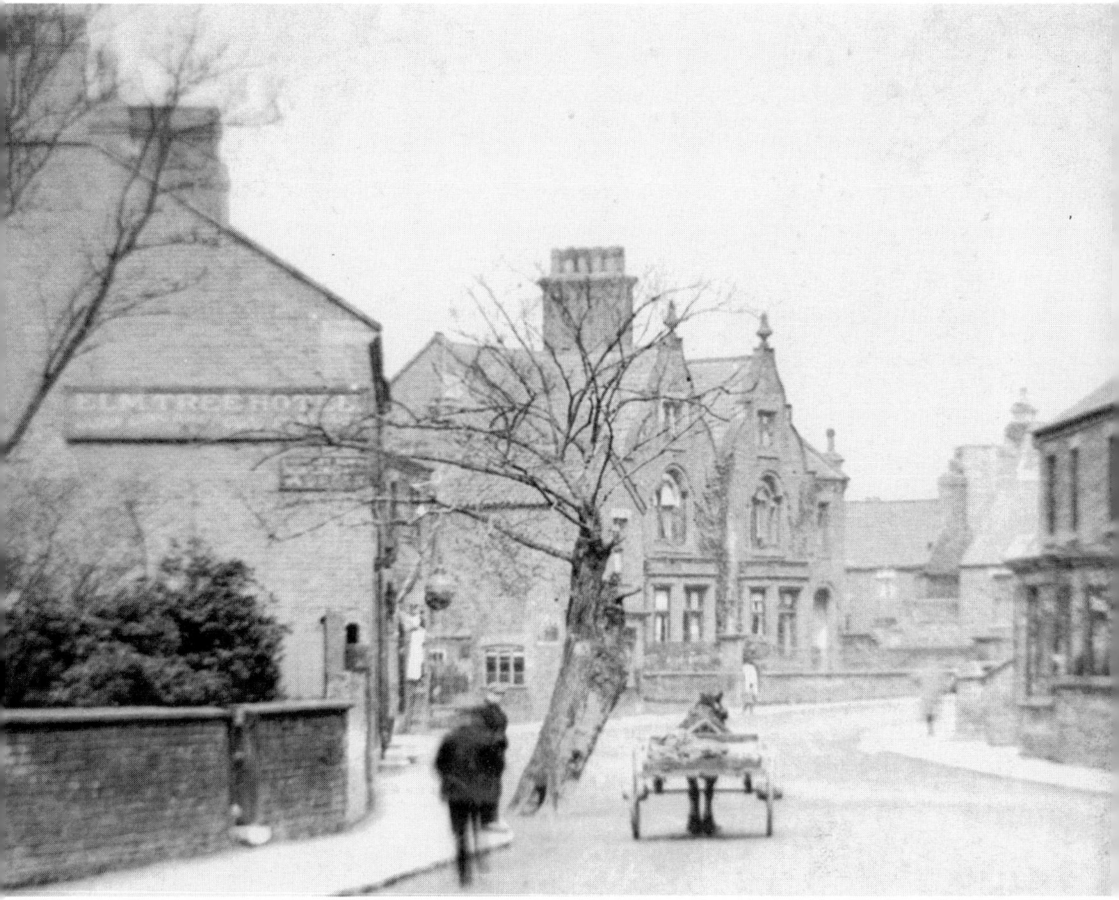

The Elm Tree Hotel, High Street, 1911. Leaning out into the road, the old elm tree that gave the inn its name was so hollow that children used to hide inside it. John Lingard, named as the licensee on the board, had moved here from the Nag's Head on Chesterfield Road in 1900. The carrier's cart passing between the tree and the entrance to Porter Street is heading towards Mrs Middleton's sweet shop (hidden behind the tree). Sir Josiah Court, one of the local doctors, once had to take refuge in the shop from an irate schoolmistress chasing him with her umbrella. Behind this shop was the old armoury where arms for the volunteers were stored. The first of the two large houses was the home of Mr Joseph Martin of Hardy and Martin, the mineral water manufacturers.

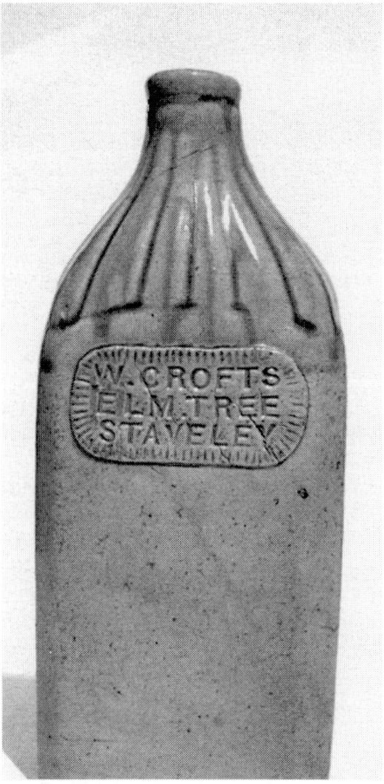

A stoneware slab-seal spirit flask in use between 1860 and the 1880s, unearthed from the rear of the Elm Tree during excavations for Morrison's store. It was probably made by Pearson's Pottery of Chesterfield for William Crofts, who was landlord from 1882 to 1899.

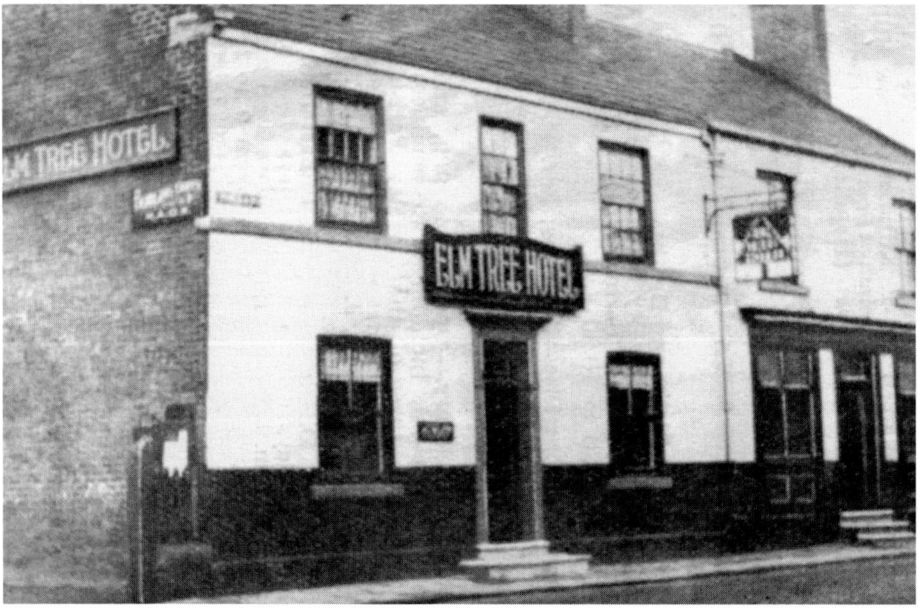

A front view of the Elm Tree Hotel in 1933 when Joseph Baker was the licensee. I have only been able to trace the Elm Tree (as an inn) back to 1881. Before then it may just have been an unlicensed beerhouse.

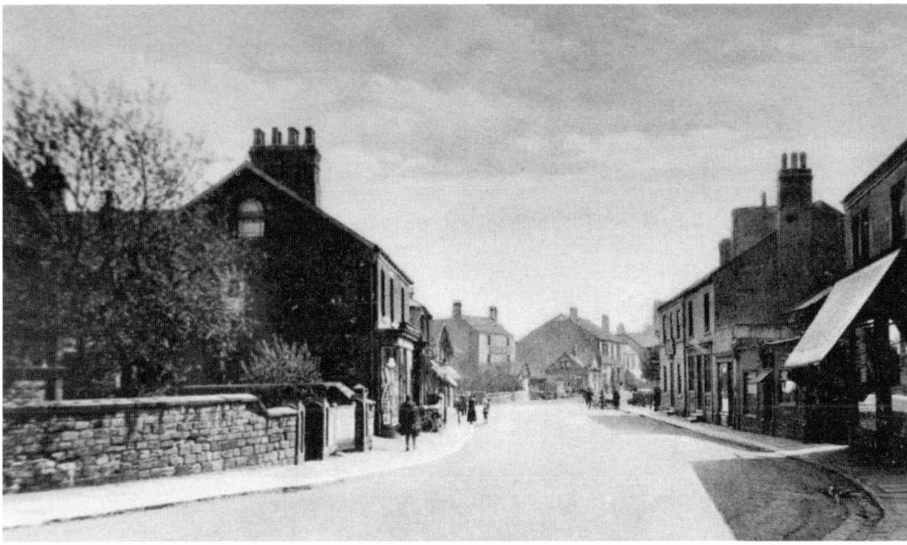

Looking south along High Street towards the Devonshire Arms on the centre left, 1912. The gentleman on the left is just about to pass Singleton's grocery and corn store and is heading for the group at the top of Porter Street. The shop blind is protecting the goods in the window of Hunter's the Teamen, another grocery store.

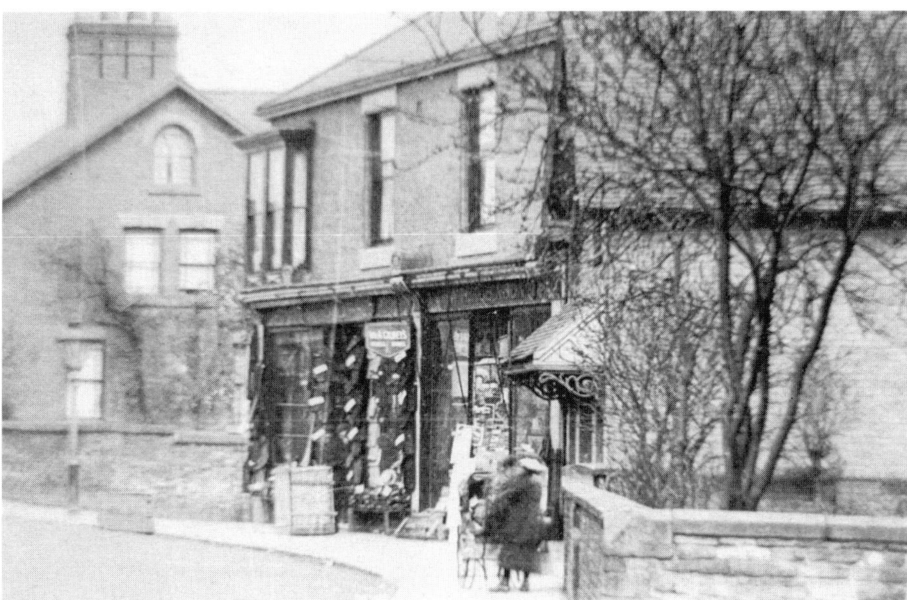

High Street, 1911. Passing the wall around Marples's garden, the lady with the pram has reached their butcher's shop. The wares of Thomas Naylor the tailor and pawnbroker decorate his shop front. Sir Josiah Court's house behind the lamp was a suggested location for the 1820/30s public house the Green Man.

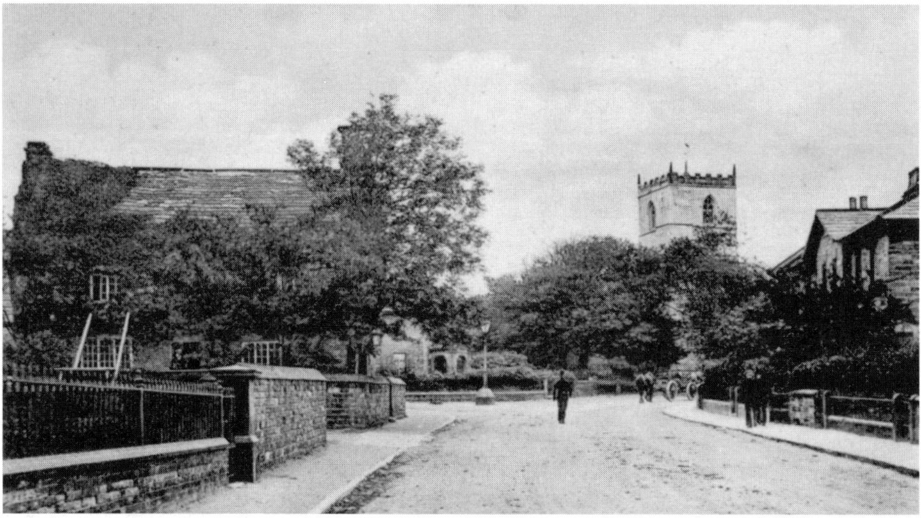

Summer in High Street, 1907. The farm cart propped against the wall is inside the entrance to Stone's farm, which is by the side of the old Chantry House. The farmhouse was later sold to Mr Reed, a well-known local dentist.

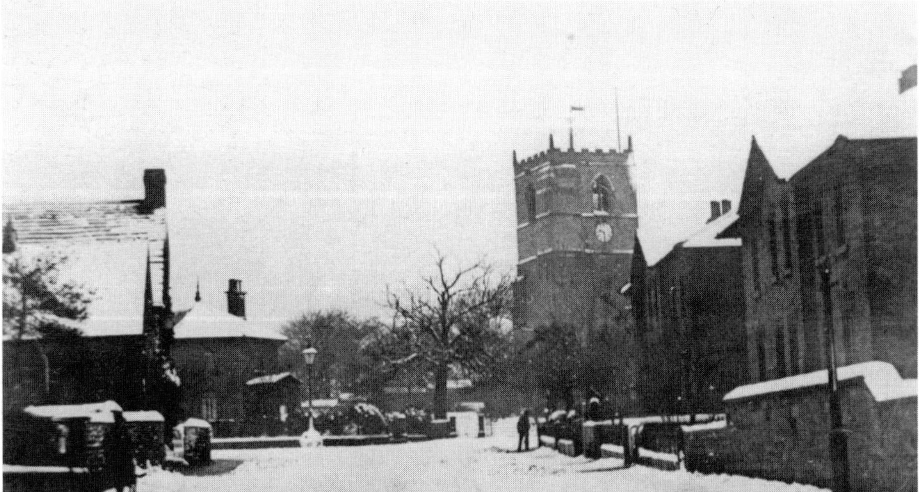

Winter in High Street, 1924, Behind the gas lamp stands the 'round' house of the Church School buildings. The Misses Swanson lived here and taught at the girls' school. Mr Craven, head of the boys' school, lived in the second house on the right.

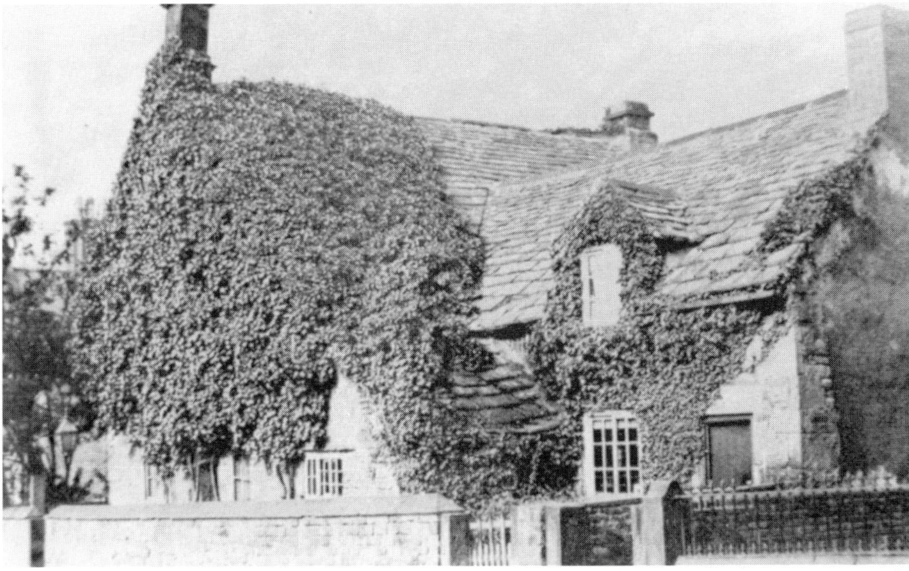

The Chantry House, 1920. Standing a little way from the church the Chantry is thought to be a thirteenth- or fourteenth-century building founded by the Frecheville family. A number of skeletons, thought to be family members, were found during early repairs. Still retaining some of its 3 ft thick walls it has in times past been used as a mechanics' institute, a library and a youth club. After standing derelict it has now been restored.

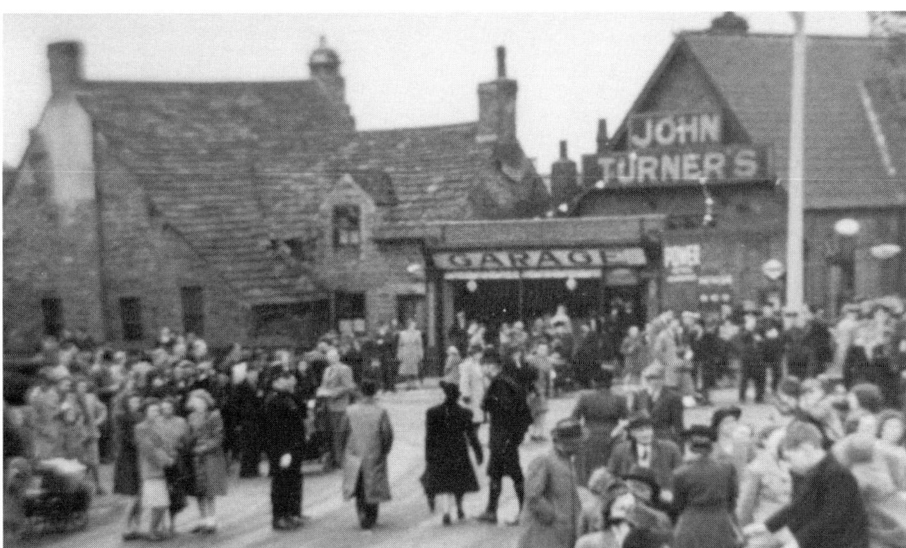

Church Street corner, High Street, 1945. People have gathered to wait for the participants of the Victory Parade to emerge from the church service. John Turner's garage is at the top of Constitution Hill; the frontage has changed its use many times but is now a garage once again.

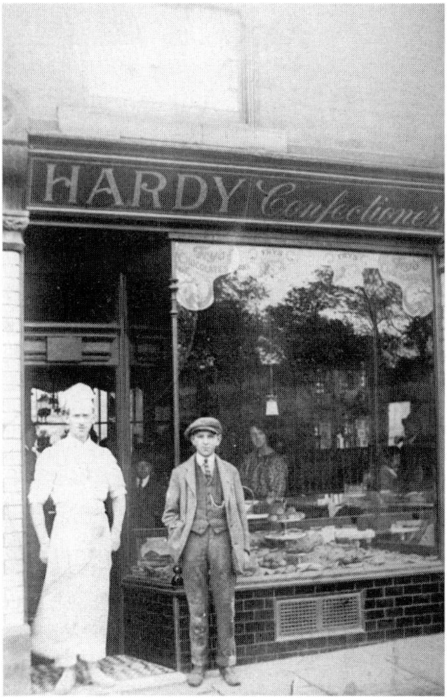

Church Street, 1922. Mr Len Brownlow in suit and cap stands outside William Hardy's confectioners. This is a glimpse of things to come, as Mr Brownlow went on to become a master baker, well known for his pork pies.

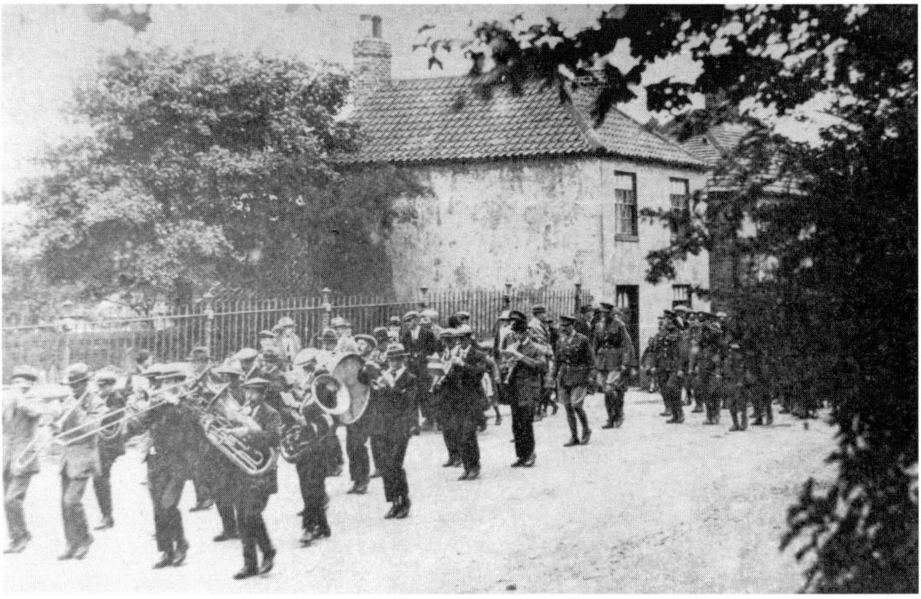

Marching over the top of Duke Street a Remembrance Day Parade prepares to enter the Garden of Remembrance (behind the railings). The white house behind the marchers is now Duke Street Motors.

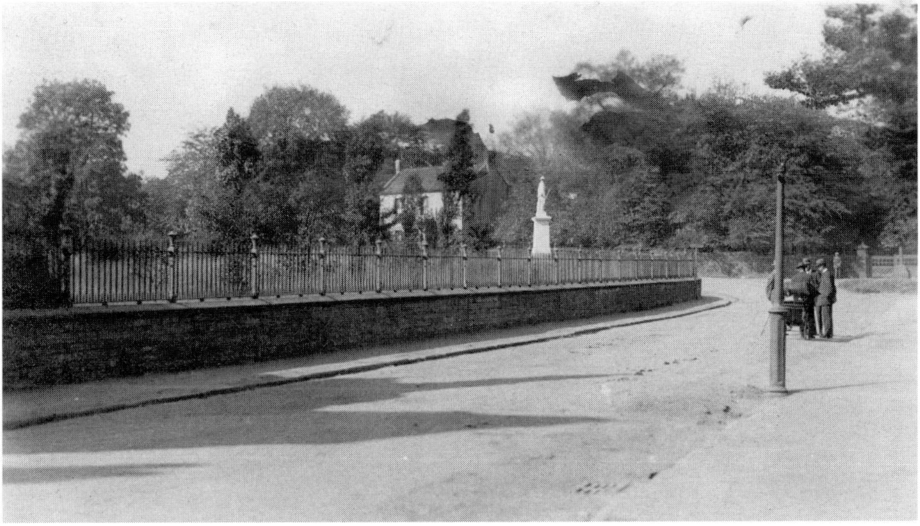

The Garden of Remembrance, 1922. Beyond the memorial is Mrs Mary Berrington's Private School, which stands in the grounds of the rectory (this rectory drive actually had gates!). The gentlemen on the right do not seem too interested in the occupant of the pram.

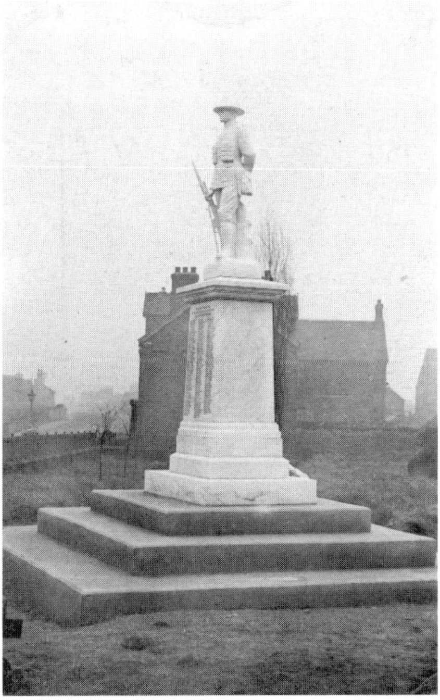

The War Memorial, 1920. The memorial was unveiled by Dr Josiah Court, and erected in front of what was the graveyard until the cemetery opened in 1884. It was later moved further back and gardens were set around it. Some of the old gravestones are still visible at the rear.

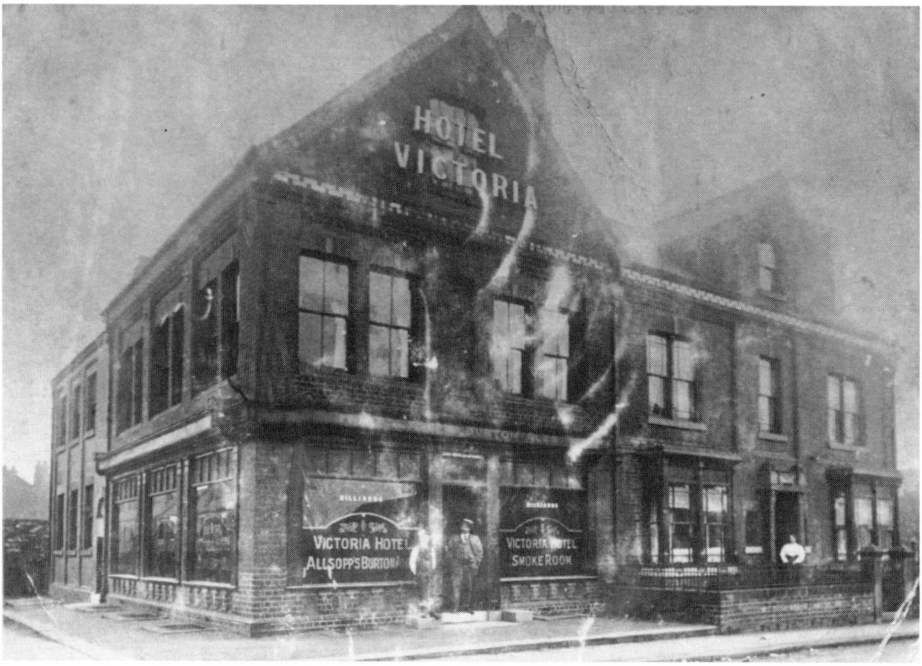

The Victoria Hotel, 1909 – not a very good photograph but still showing what a splendid-looking building it was. The landlady Mrs Agnes Bates is standing by the door to the living quarters. It is still a thriving public house and the interior has recently been modernized.

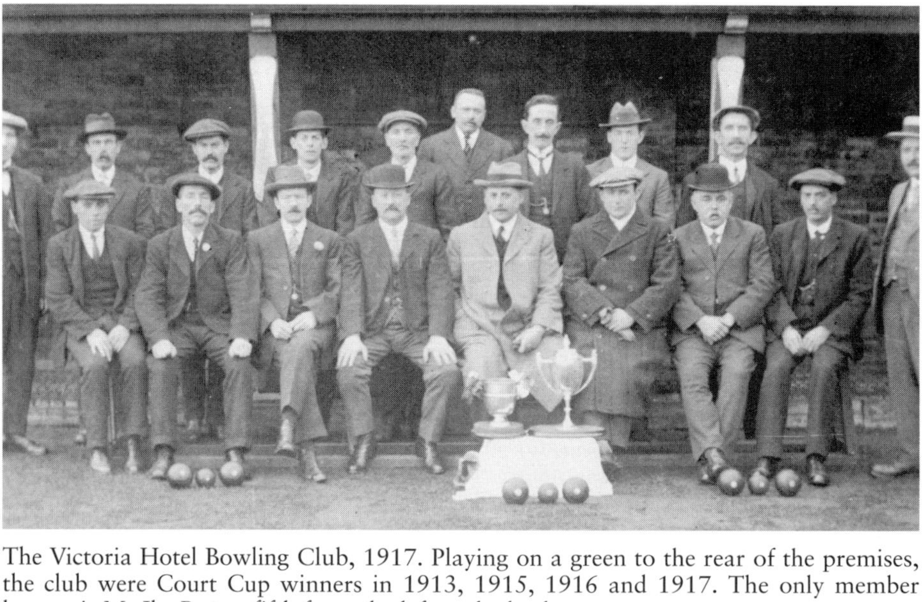

The Victoria Hotel Bowling Club, 1917. Playing on a green to the rear of the premises, the club were Court Cup winners in 1913, 1915, 1916 and 1917. The only member known is Mr Ike Potter, fifth from the left at the back.

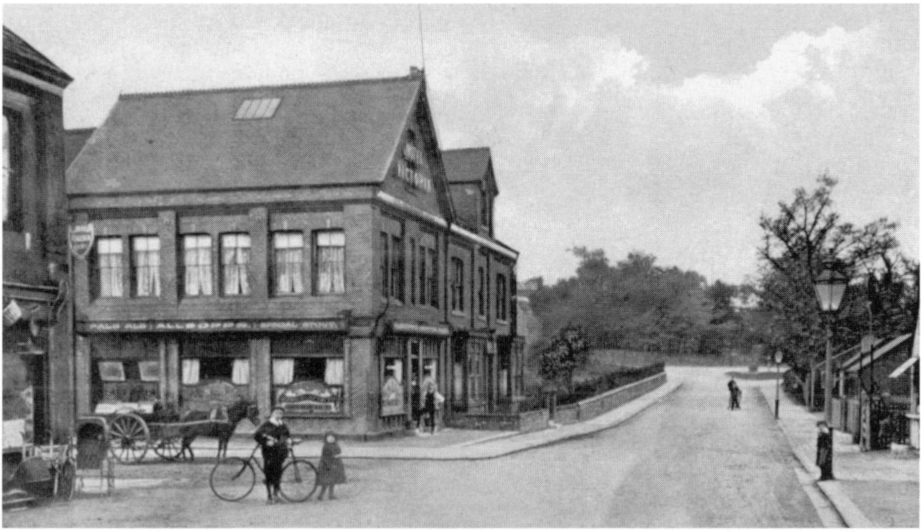

Looking at Lowgates, 1907. Across from the Victoria Hotel the general dealer advertises Raleigh cycles (a possible customer is watching the cameraman). Behind the boy and gas lamp is the entrance to Fletcher's Brush Manufactory, always known as the 'brush shop yard'.

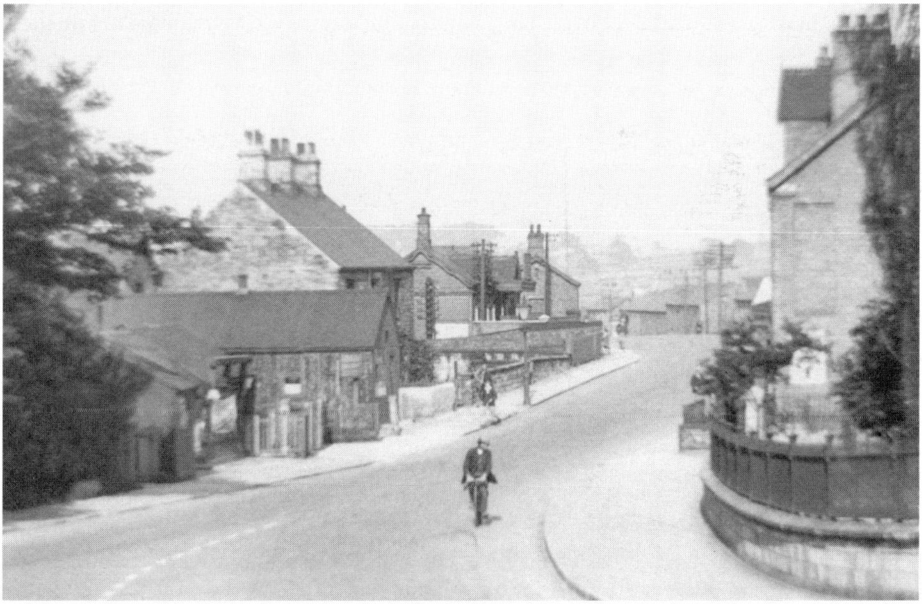

A postcard by Cragg looking eastwards down Lowgates, 1922. The two old wooden shops on the left were Albert Marshall's boot repair business, latterly Warrens, which burnt down in 1969, and the sweet shop run by Rosie Meakin, before Sue Taylor took it over. James's famed fish and chip shop is alongside. There is a driveway to a coal yard between the sweet shop and chip shop.

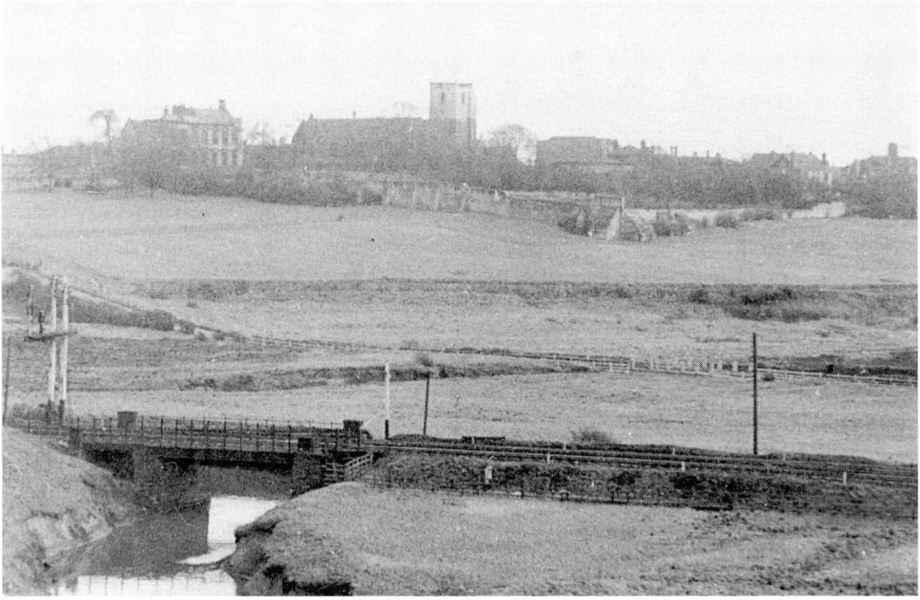

The view from the spoil tip at Hartington, with the LMS rail line from Seymour to Barrow Hill crossing the River Rother, 1950s. Beyond, Hall Lane runs from left to right with the line of the canal above. The church and rectory stand high within their boundary wall.

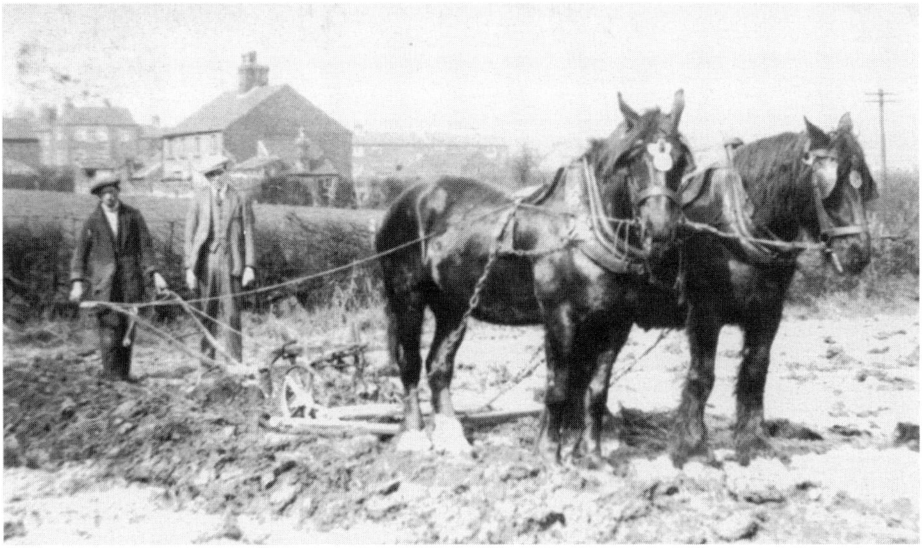

Lowgates, 1928. Tapton and Bess, with handlers Arthur Holmes and Sam ?, at a ploughing match on farmer James Mullins's field. Lilleman's cottage, with its small sweet and grocery business in the front room, hides Renshaw's Row and the Smith's Arms public house.

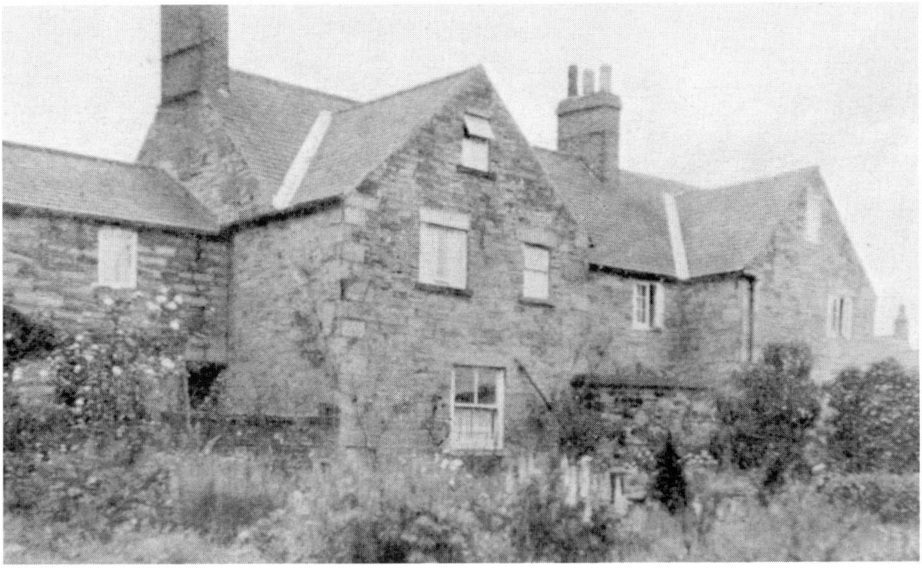

Netherthorpe Old Hall, 1960. In 1543 the Hall was the residence of Robert Sitwell of Eckington, a co-founder of Netherthorpe School. After numerous alterations, but still retaining some of its original shape, it became a farmhouse. It was demolished to make way for housing.

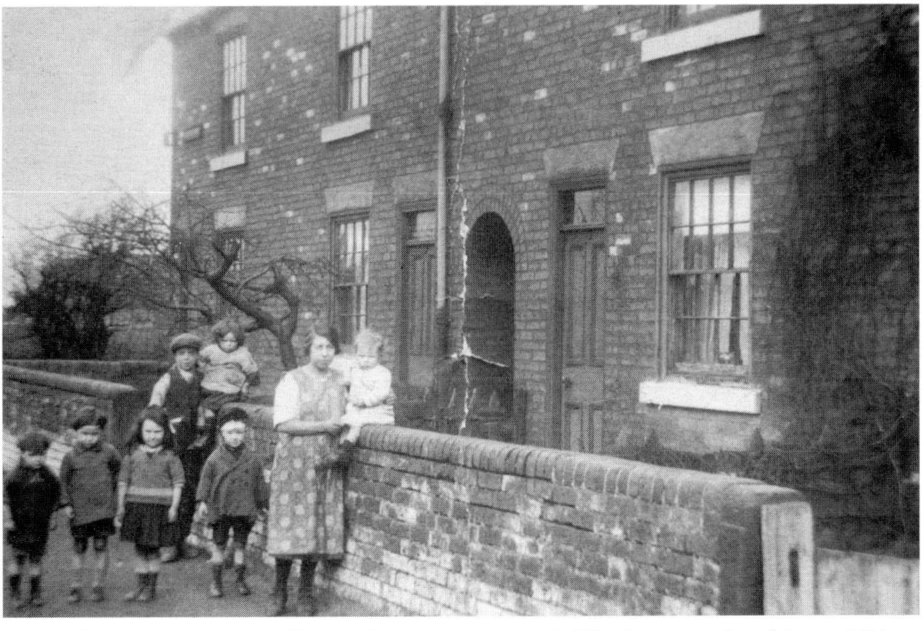

Netherthorpe Row (originally Garfitt's Row), *c.* 1912. The Townsend and Pegg children pose outside their homes. This small row of houses stood on the pathway from Netherthorpe to the Fan road which led over the footbridge of the LMS railway.

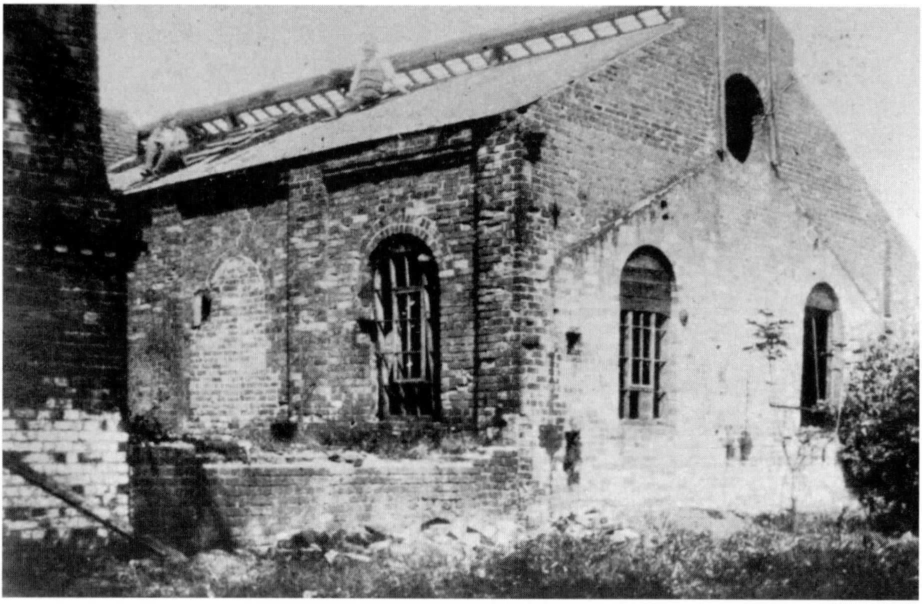

The dismantling of the Spade and Shovel Factory, Norbriggs, 1958. Producing a wide variety of shovels, spades, forks and tools, the works were begun in 1810 by a John Butler; according to Pigot's Directory Thomas Dudley acquired the business in 1835.

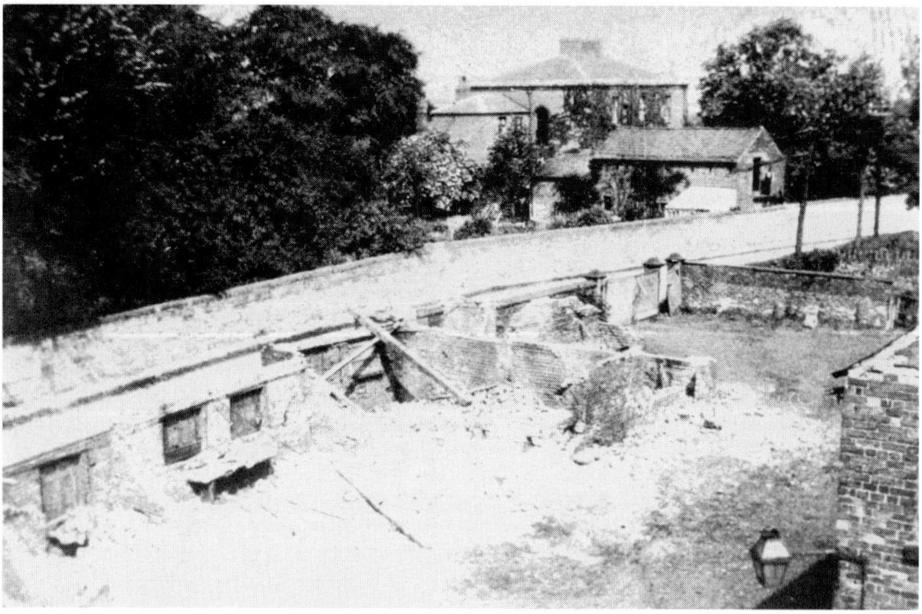

The final outer wall of Dudley's works, 1958. Bordering on Post Lane (now Norbriggs Road) the large house opposite is Norbriggs House, one-time home of relative John Dudley. During the war the factory was used for jam and pickle making.

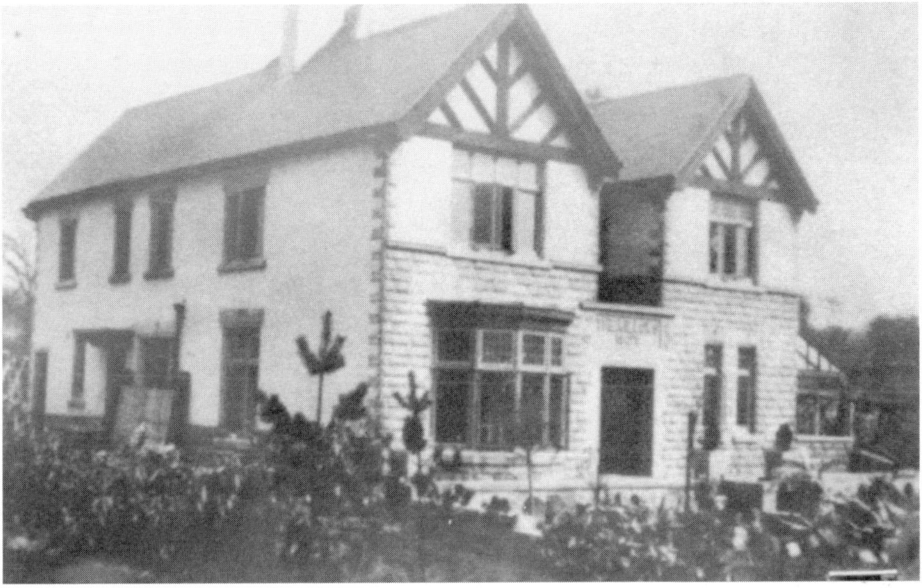

The Willows, 1965. This was built on the site of Dudley's Shovel Factory at Norbriggs for Jim Boldry, who was the owner of the furniture and household goods emporium at Lowgates. The house has since been replaced by a nursing home.

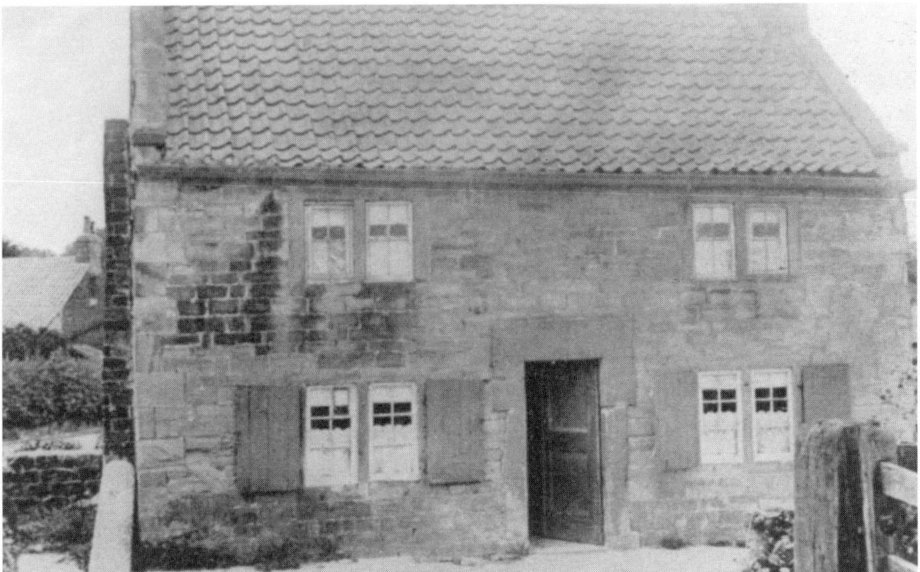

The Toll House, 1880. Guardian of the road into Staveley, the house stood on the corner of Post Lane at Norbriggs and collected tolls until 1883. For those in the know, a short cut passed from the main road behind Norbriggs house, so avoiding the toll. The house was demolished in 1906.

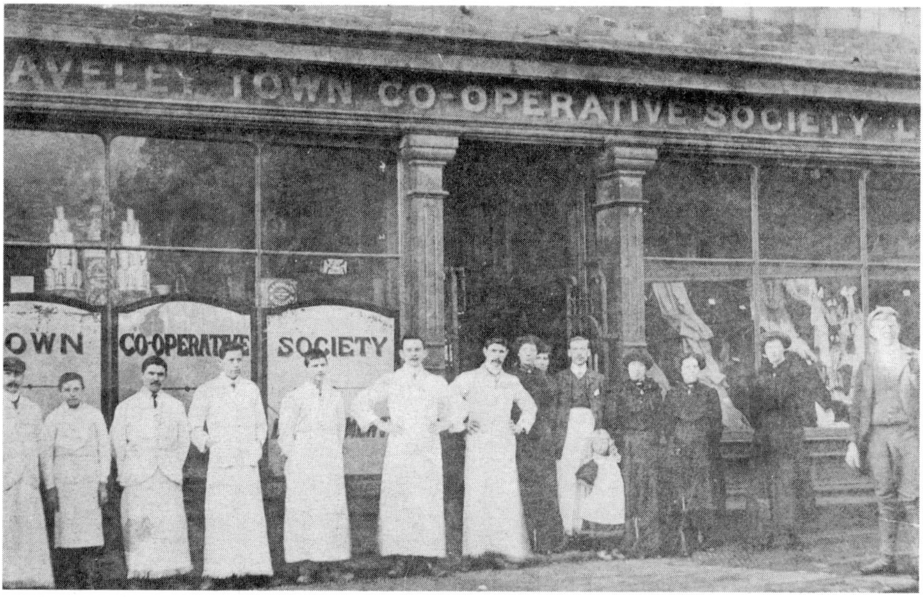

Staveley Town Co-operative Society, Duke Street, erected in 1894. In 1895 it went under the unwieldy name of Staveley Free Labour and Industrial Provident Co-operative Society. In 1862 the first co-op in Staveley was opened at Speedwell Terrace under manager Richard Martin.

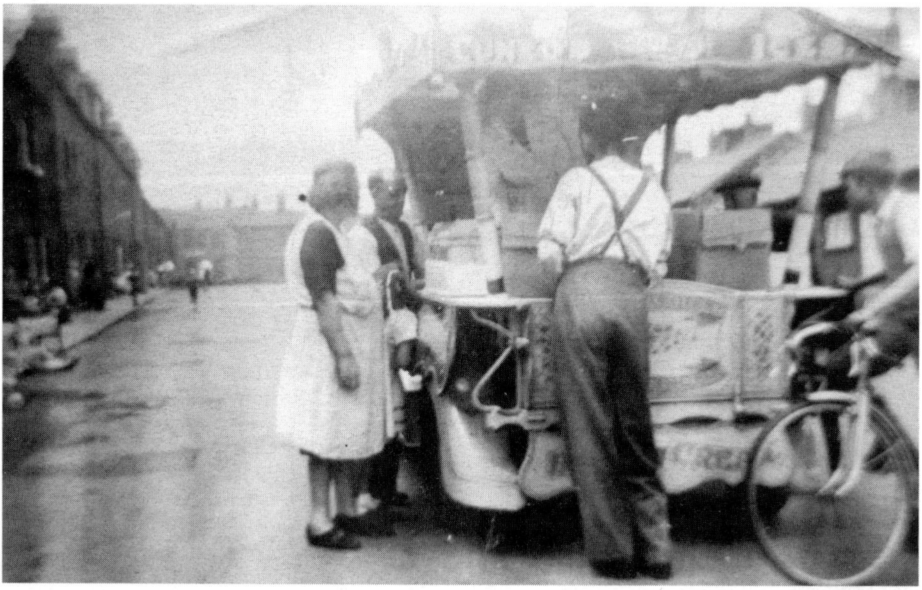

Speedwell Terrace, 1948. Cuneo's beautifully decorated ice-cream van was always welcomed by both adults and children. Here Tommy Hunt and Lily Schofield await their turn. Standing on the middle row of the terraces, the Drill Hall can be seen beyond the houses.

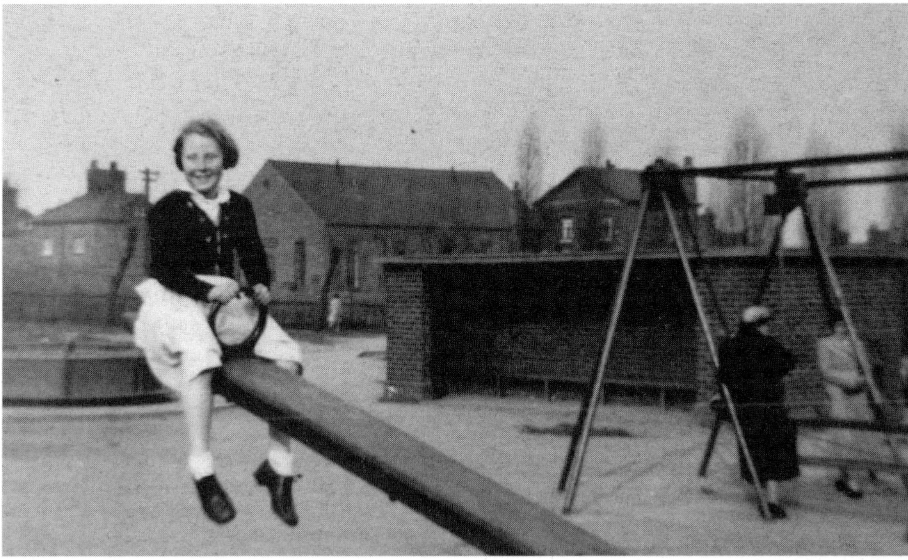

King George's field in the 1950s, with swings, slides, see-saws and so forth for the children, while bowling greens and tennis courts were for the adults. The Speedwell Mission at the top of the terraces is the building over the Inkersall Road. Do you remember going there to be immunized or to pick up the free orange juice for baby?

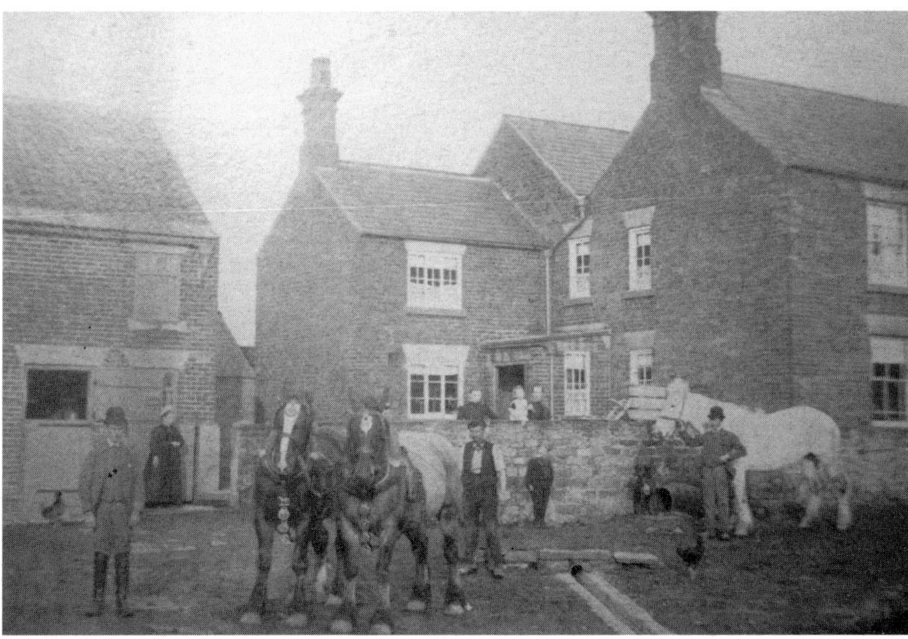

Bennett's Farm at Inkersall, 1892. With the horses decked in their brasses, members of the family and workforce pose for the camera after a ploughing match.

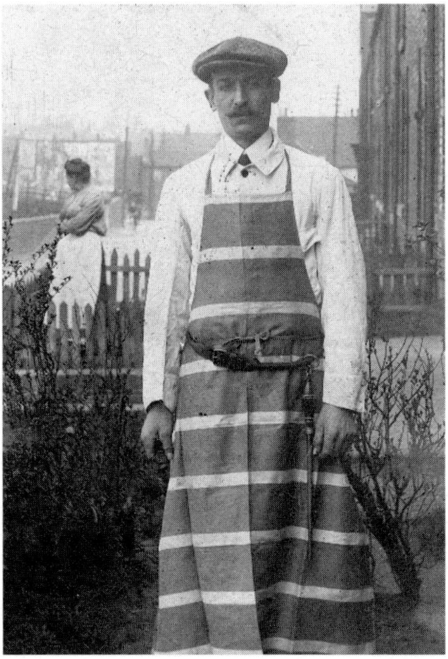

John George Kerry ready for business. The official pig killer from Prospect Place, Inkersall Road, has his steel knife-sharpener hanging from his belt. The neighbourhood boys always gathered at slaughtertime, eagerly waiting for the pig's bladder with which to play football.

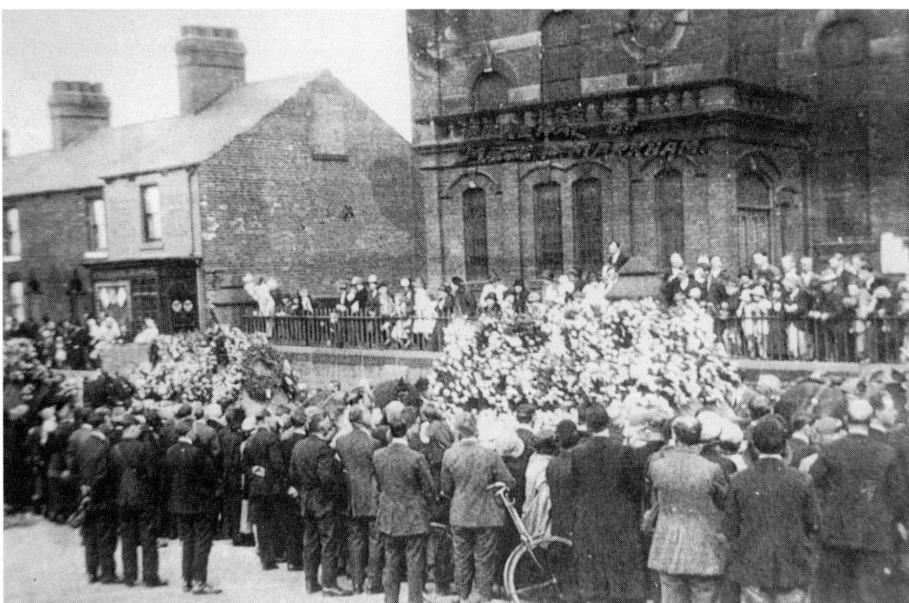

Inkersall Road, 1926. C.P. Markham's funeral passes the Zion chapel en route to the cemetery, a few yards further along the road. Interred in Staveley at his request, Mr Markham wished to be buried so that the wind might blow the smoke from his Devonshire Works over his grave.

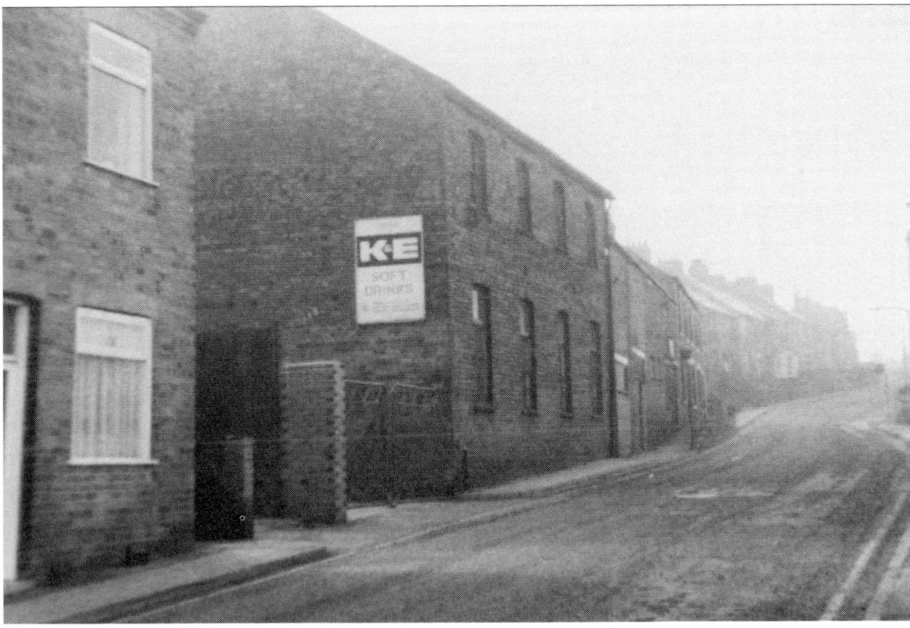

Kendall and Elliott's Soft Drinks Factory, 1960. Brothers Charles, Samuel and Jim Kendall started the business at Mill Green during the 1896 coal strike and built the Jubilee Works shown above in the early 1900s. The name changed in 1921 when Mr Helmer Elliott bought the business. It was closed in the 1970s.

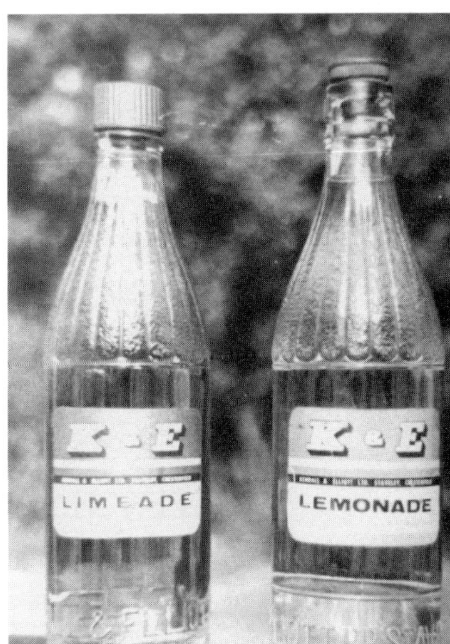

Limeade and Lemonade, two products of the Kendall and Elliott factory, 1960. The firm also bottled port and sherry and some British wines. Pickles were produced in the winter and the workers mended cases in order to keep themselves in work. The Kendall Brothers were also proprietors of the Central and Empire cinemas.

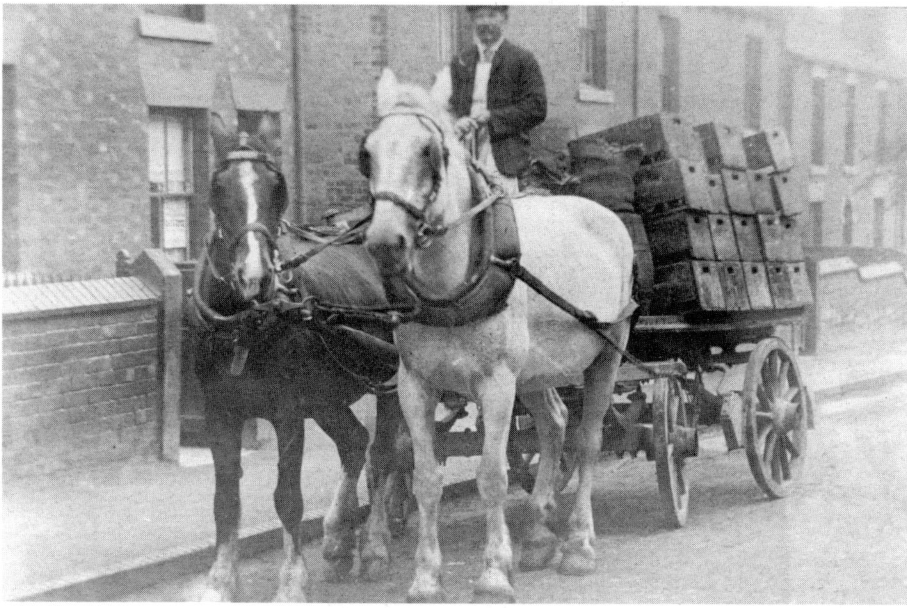

Hardy and Martin's delivery man Mr Albert Hickton, Brimington, 1920. The Mineral Water Factory, which was opened on Devonshire Street in the early 1900s by cousins Joseph Martin and Gerald Hardy, was also the first in the area to bottle milk.

HARDY & MARTIN'S

HIGH-CLASS MINERAL WATERS,
UNSURPASSED FOR QUALITY.

SODA WATER IN SYPHONS.
Also in Screw and Ball-stoppered Bottles.

HOP BITTERS BREWED FROM CHOICE HOPS.

NON-ALCOHOLIC FRUIT WINES.

VINEGAR AND PICKLE MANUFACTURERS.

WORKS :

STAVELEY, near Chesterfield, and
KIRKBY-IN-ASHFIELD, Notts.

Prompt Attention given to Delivery.

An advertisement for Hardy and Martin's mineral waters, 1921. The manufacture of vinegar and pickles were winter occupations along with the whitewashing and repair of shelves. The firm regularly ran transport into Chesterfield and the Hardy family were also local farmers and butchers.

SECTION TWO

Church and Chapel

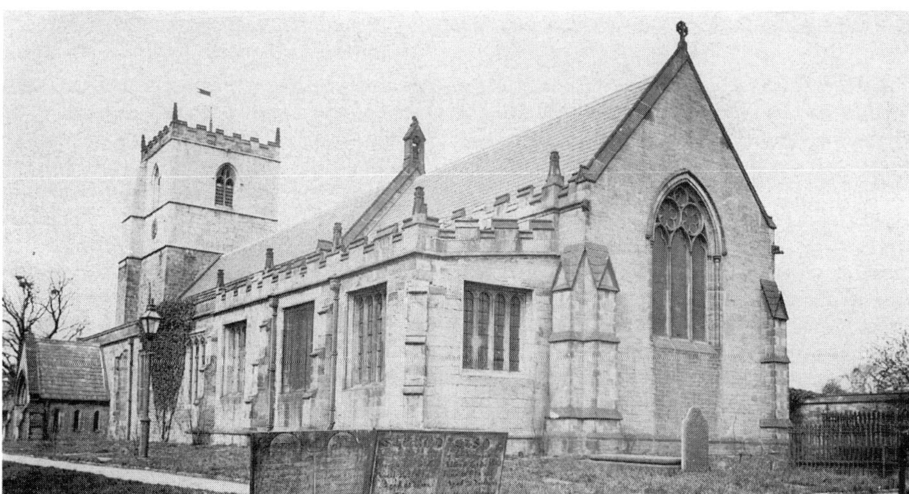

The Parish Church of St John the Baptist, 1904. This church of Norman origin is the centre of worship for the Staveley community, with mission churches serving the outlying areas. The castellated tower, erected in stages from 1200 to 1690, contains eight bells. A small oak door that survives in the south wall is dated 1696. Some gravestones can be found by the perimeter wall.

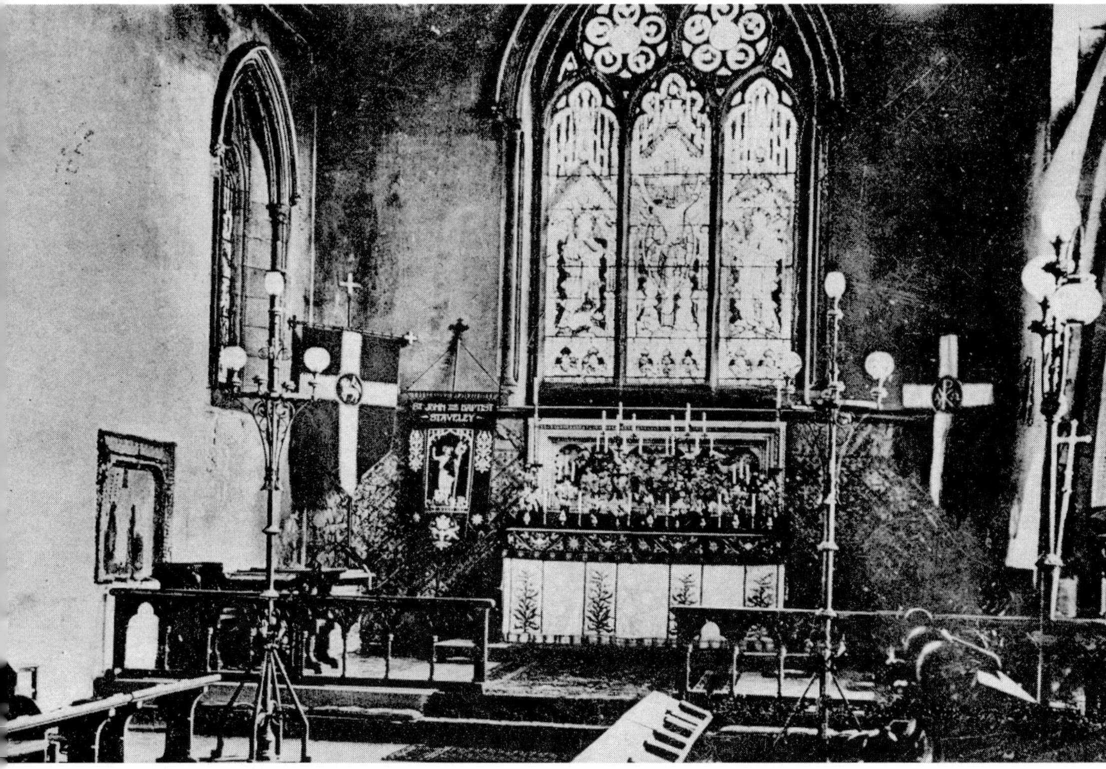

The chancel, 1918. The church has a central nave with adjoining north and south aisles. The north aisle leads to St Michael's altar, the south aisle to the altar of Our Lady. Beyond the Lady altar is the vestry and the Frecheville Chapel. Situated in front of St Michael's Chapel is the miners' shrine where a figure of St Michael, patron saint of those who work in dangerous places, stands above a miner's lamp and a piece of Ireland Colliery coal. In the wall of this chapel is a carved medieval Easter Sepulchre, a treasured possession in which the Blessed Sacrament was kept from Maundy Thursday until Easter Day. This photograph shows the chancel with the High Altar, the church banners, which were carried in all church processions, and to the left, set on the wall, a brass plate showing Sir Peter Frecheville with his eight sons faced by his wife Maud and seven daughters. The church contains many monuments to the Frecheville family including two large marble tombs in the Frecheville Chapel. The church font is also thought to be of Norman origin, dating from around 1175.

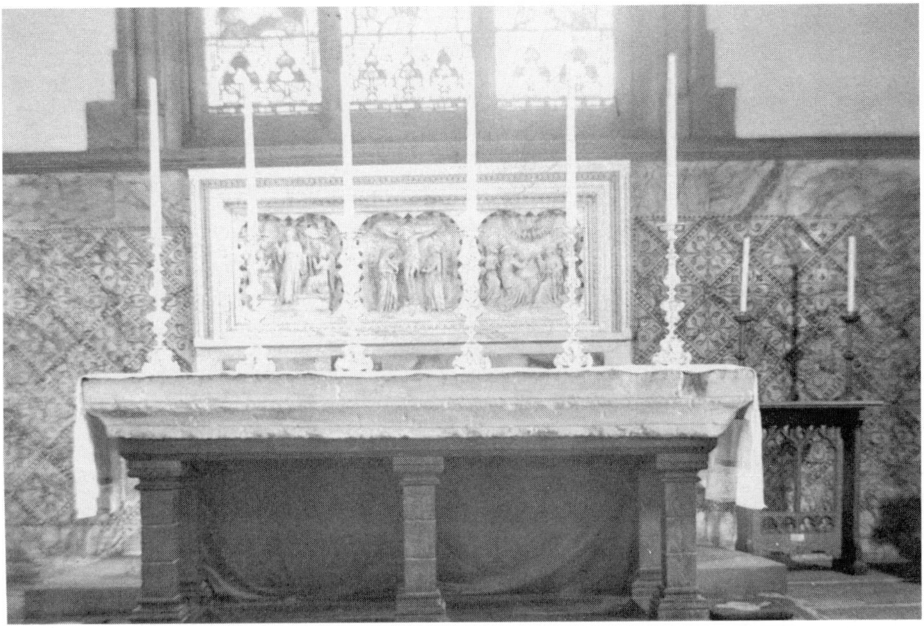

The High Altar, 1940. The great altar stone dates from the fourteenth century and is one of the largest intact altar stones in England. The stone has five consecration crosses carved into it, one at each corner and one in the centre representing Our Lord's wounds.

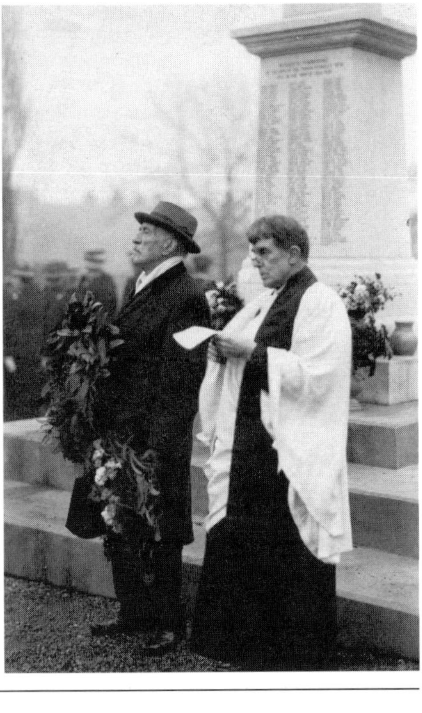

Remembrance Day Service, 1924. Standing by the War Memorial are Sir Josiah Court, prominent citizen and doctor, and Canon Charles Hurlock Molineux, Rector of Staveley 1888–1927. A lych-gate was erected to the memory of Sir Josiah after his death in 1938. Canon Molineux had a window dedicated to him by his friends set in the Frecheville Chapel.

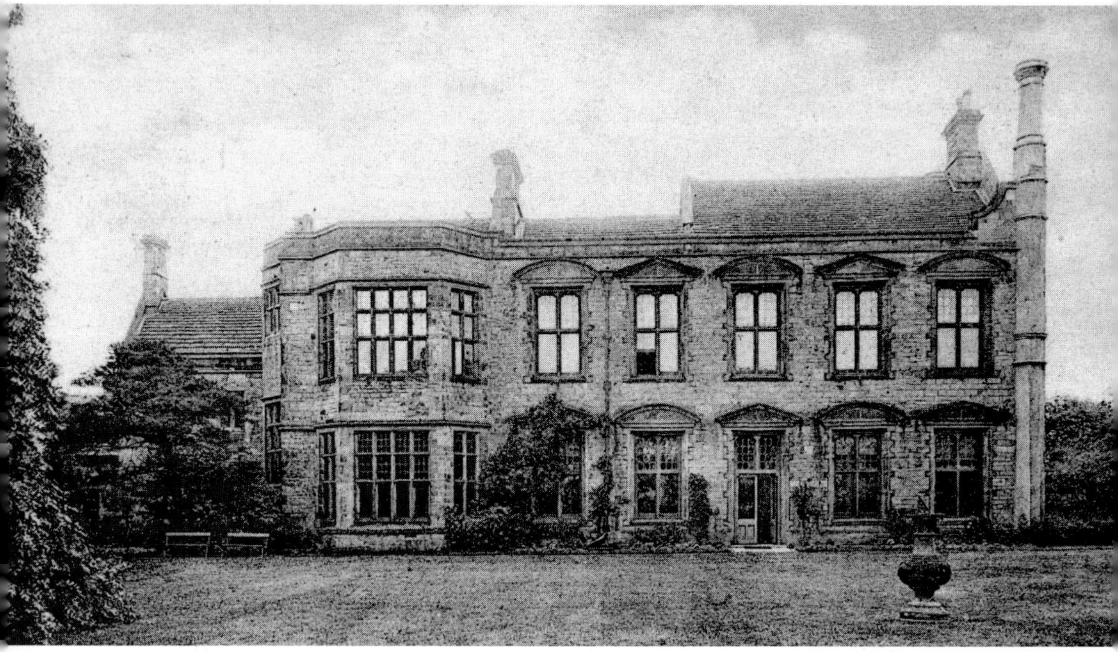

A rear view of Staveley Hall, 1906. The Hall was built in 1604 by Peter Frecheville on the site of a previous house, which could possibly have been the manor house of Ascuit Musard, Lord of the Manor after the Norman Conquest. In 1644 the Hall was garrisoned against the Parliamentary troops by John Frecheville (son of Peter), a staunch Royalist, but surrendered to Major General Crawford, who had marched down to Staveley after taking nearby Bolsover Castle. John was later made a peer for his loyalty to the Crown. In 1681 the house was sold to the Duke of Devonshire. Plans to demolish the Hall in 1750 were halted by the Reverend James Gisbourne, who chose to live there after its restoration in the 1770s. It was used as the rectory by successive rectors and curates until a smaller, more manageable, residence was built in the rectory grounds. The Hall was then taken over by the Staveley Council for use as offices. The outbuildings and stables have since been extensively renovated and sports and leisure facilities provided in the grounds.

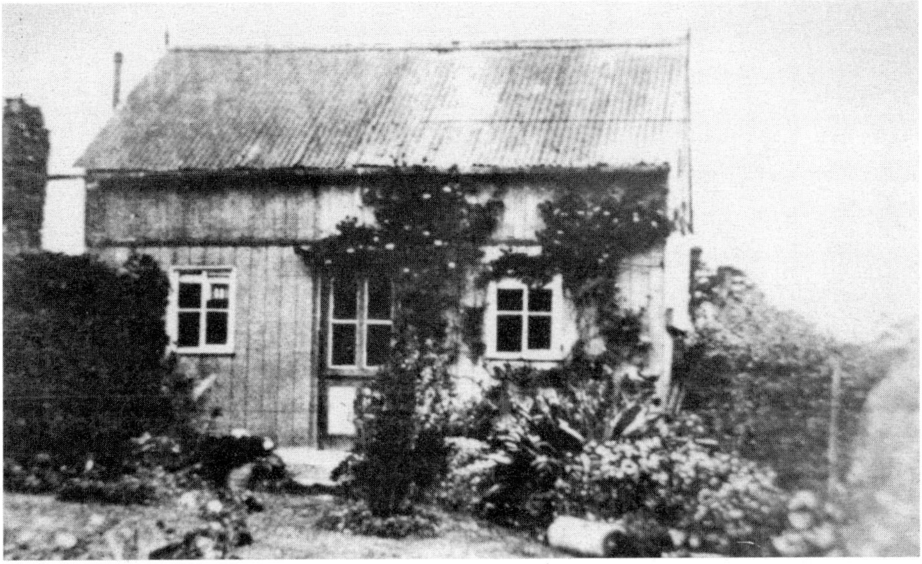

The Chapel in the Field, Inkersall, 1863. The beginning of Methodism in Inkersall took place in a farmhouse kitchen owned by a Mr Rodgers. When the kitchen became too small this wooden outbuilding, adjoining the home of a Mr and Mrs Woodhead, provided an alternative meeting place.

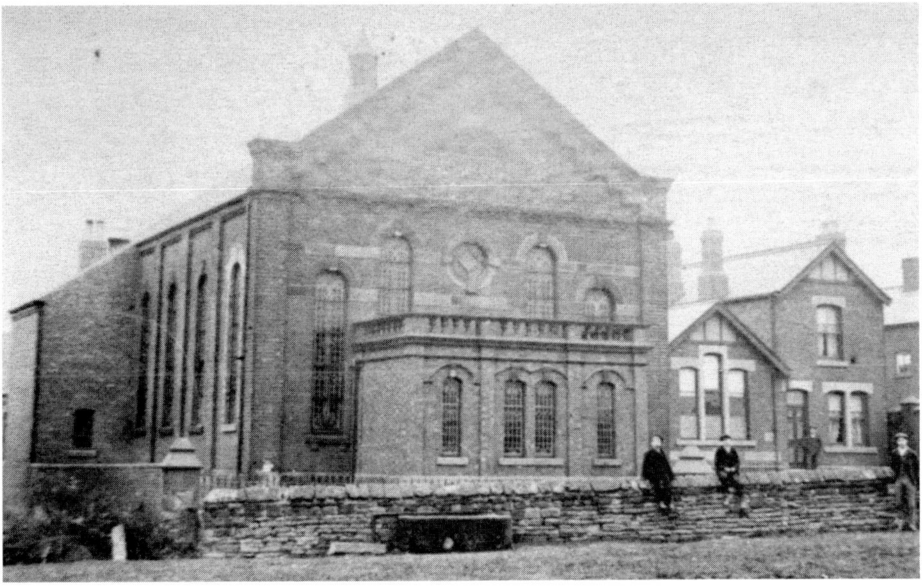

The Zion chapel, Inkersall Road, 1912. The original chapel was erected here in 1873, but was destroyed by fire in 1904. Rebuilt and opened in 1908, it was finally closed in 1969 and has not been replaced. The boys are sat on the wall surrounding the Crown field, one time venue for the Staveley Feast.

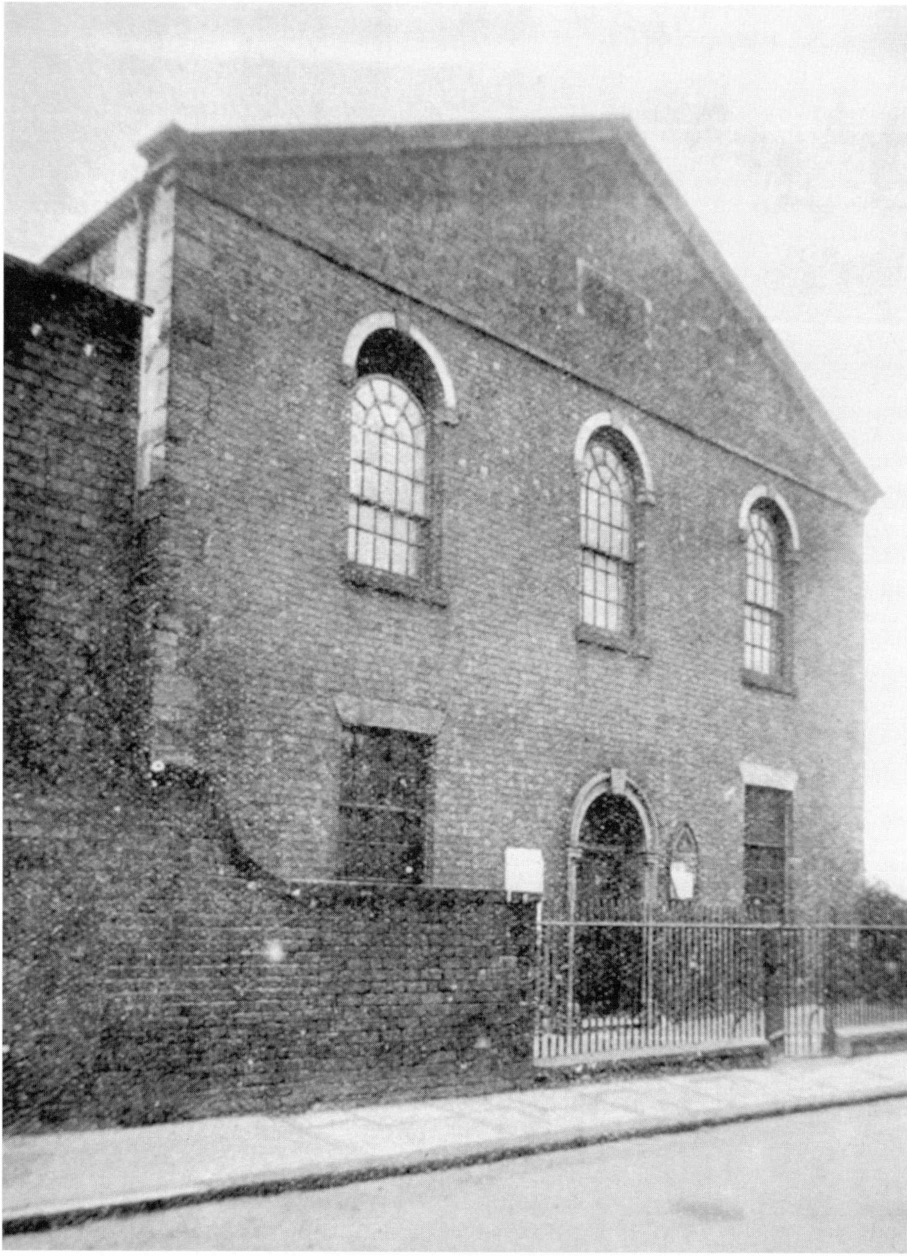

New Street Methodist chapel, 1849. The first chapel was opened in 1827 and so began the Sunday schools in Staveley. This much larger chapel was added in 1849. After moving to a new location on Chesterfield Road corner the small chapel was used for a time by the Salvation Army. The larger building became the Kendall Brothers' Central Cinema and later Joe Davis's Billard Hall.

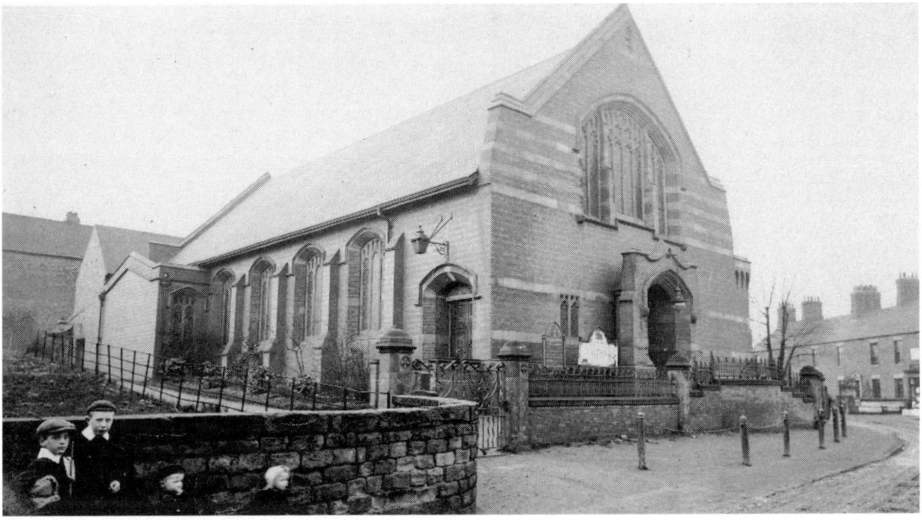

Wesleyan chapel, 1905. This was the new church, built at a cost of £4,400, which replaced the chapel in New Street. At the laying of the foundation stone a bottle containing coins and service records was placed underneath. It was removed to the vestry after the ceremony for safe keeping, from where it was stolen that night.

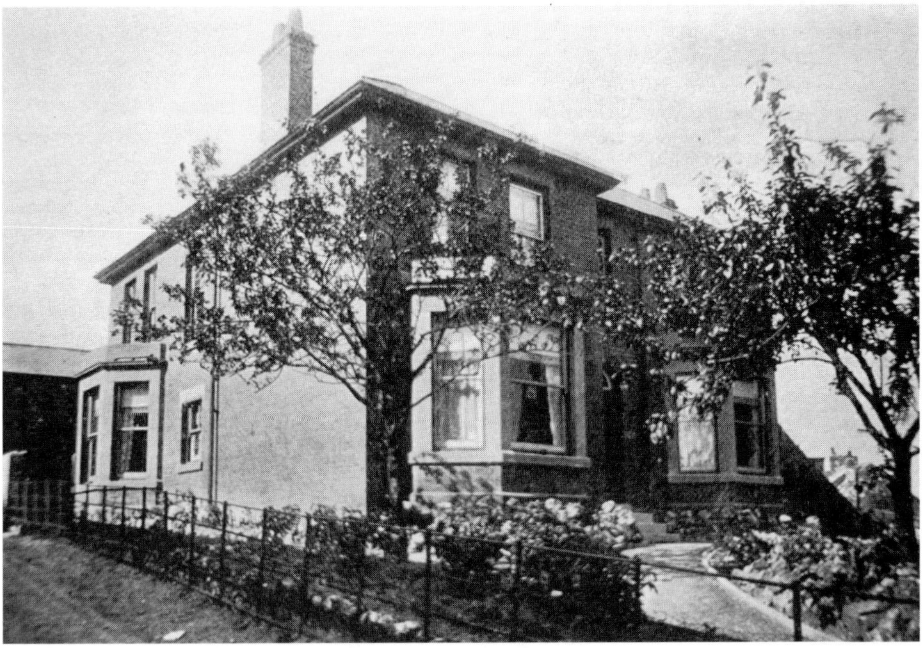

The Manse, 1908. The Chesterfield Methodist Circuit built this magnificent manse for the Staveley minister beside the new church. A schoolroom was provided to the left of the church at a later date. Sycamore House, an old farmhouse, stood at Ivy Dene to the rear of the Manse.

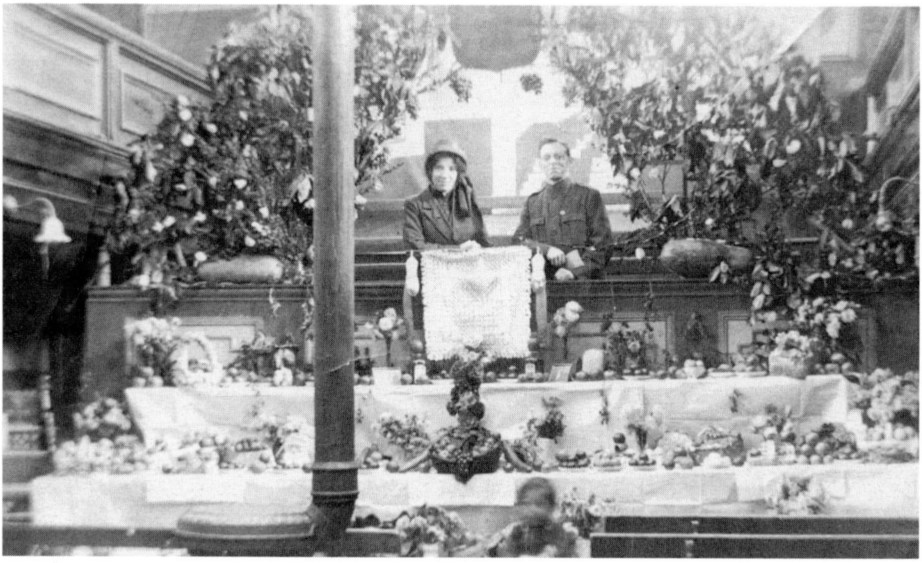

Salvation Army, 1924. This beautifully dressed display is for the Harvest Festival in the old Salvation Army Hall in New Street, which comes complete with central heating – a large iron stove in the centre of the room.

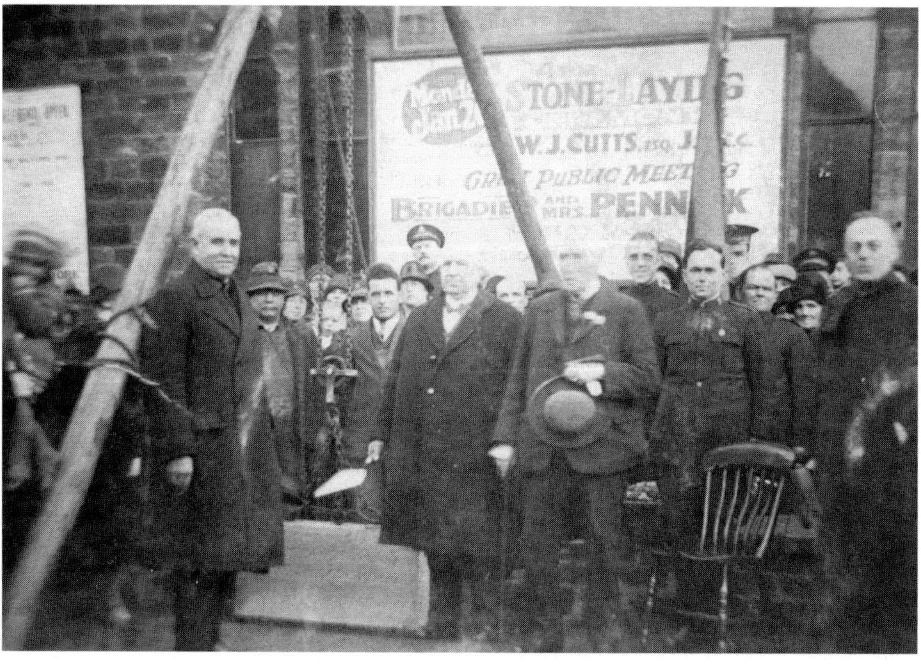

The stone-laying ceremony at the Salvation Army Hall, High Street, 1930. Mr W.J. Cutts, JP, wields the trowel, with Sir Josiah Court and Brigadier Pennick standing by, to commemorate the occasion of the Salvationists taking over the former girls' school building.

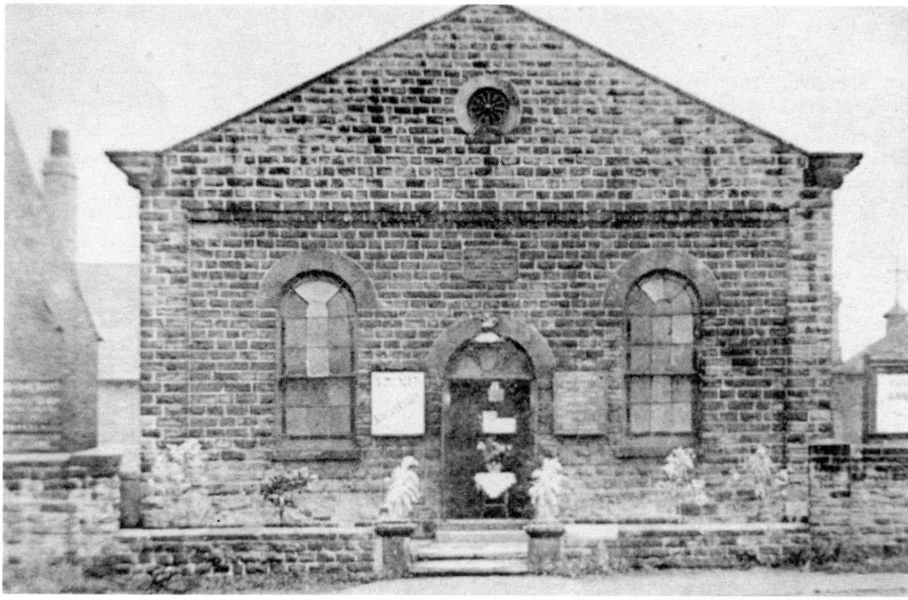

Lowgates Free Church, established 1874. The first services for this new chapel were held in 1870 in a clubroom of the Speedwell Inn, Lowgates, thanks to the kindly assistance of landlady Mrs Marples. A site was then purchased from the Duke of Devonshire for a nominal 10*s* and the chapel was built with stone from the Woodthorpe Quarry.

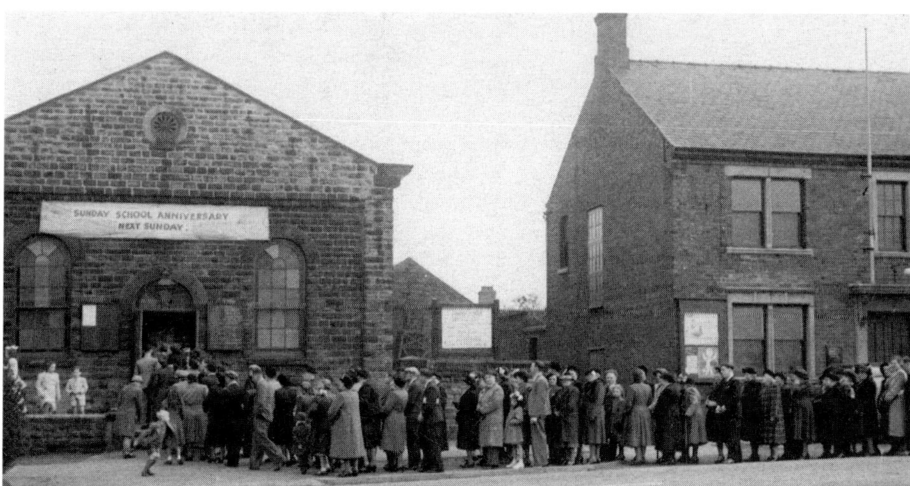

Waiting for the 75th Chapel Anniversary, 1949. On the Sunday morning of the anniversary adults and children, dressed in their finest clothes which were often bought for the occasion, walked around the streets stopping for hymns and prayers at various locations. There was always great excitement as the children were arranged on tiered platforms for the afternoon and evening services.

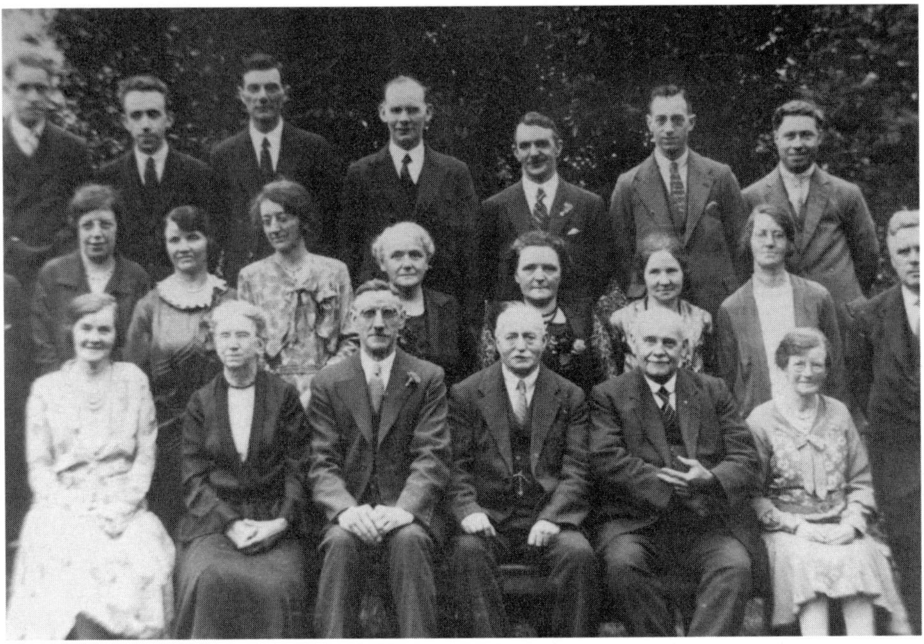

Some of the ladies and gentlemen, photographed in 1930, who have served Lowgates Chapel over the years. Back row, left to right: John Taylor, F. Bacon, Elmer Scott, J.H. Elliott, -?-, ? Stephens, M. Berresford. Middle row: W. Weatherall, Cis Purdy, L. Bentley, M.F. Bacon, Mrs Barnard, Mrs Bacon, Mrs Woodhead, W. Ward. Front row: Mrs Ward, Mrs Purdy, Mr Barnard, Mr Hodson Sen., George Elliott and Miss Brodie.

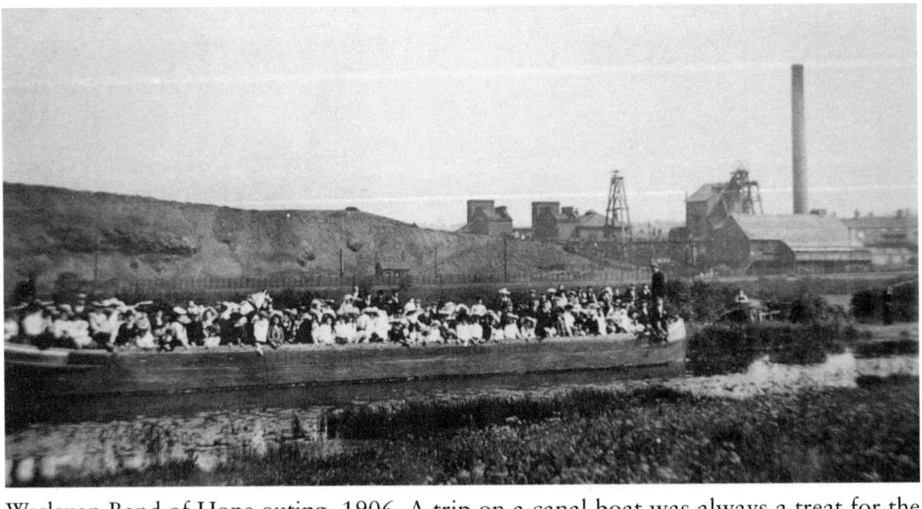

Wesleyan Band of Hope outing, 1906. A trip on a canal boat was always a treat for the Sunday school members. After setting off from Wharf Lane basin by barge, a popular destination was Renishaw Park.

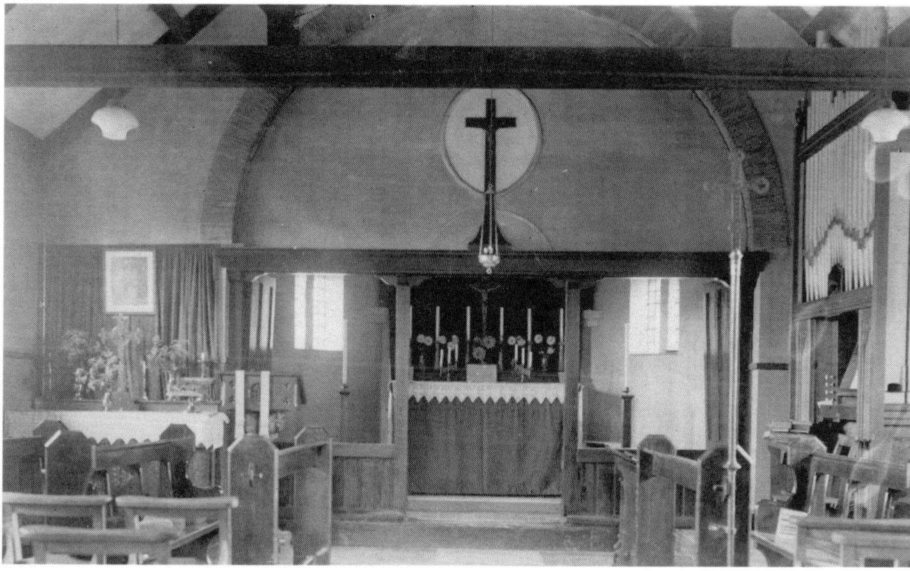

The interior of St Paul's Mission Church, 1940. This small church at Mastin Moor was one of the sister churches of the Staveley ministry along with St Alban's, Poolsbrook, St Peter's, Woodthorpe, St Columba's Hall, Inkersall, and St John's, Handley.

St Paul's Church, 1921. This article from the *Staveley Church Magazine* gives a brief account of the Whit Monday treat. All the church Sunday schools celebrated in this way. During the war years each child would contribute something edible towards the tea.

ST. PAUL'S, MASTIN MOOR.

On Whit Monday, the usual Sunday School Treat took place, when upwards of 120 Scholars, Teachers and Friends sat down to tea. This included an invitation to any scholars who did not attend any Sunday School.

After tea, the company adjourned to a field in Happy Valley, kindly lent by Mr. Gregory.

Games, Races, etc., were indulged in. The arrangements for the tea were in the hands of Mr. J. Whitworth (School Secretary), assisted by a willing band of workers to whom our best thanks are due. After giving three hearty cheers to Mr. Gregory for his kindness in lending the field, a most enjoyable day was brought to a close by the singing of the Doxology.

OFFERTORIES.

	£	s.	d.		Com.
Brought Forward	4	9	9	...	—
April 24.—	1	4	7	...	26
May 1.—	0	18	9	...	—
,, 8.—	0	17	2	...	—
,, 15.—	1	1	0	...	—
	£8	11	3		26

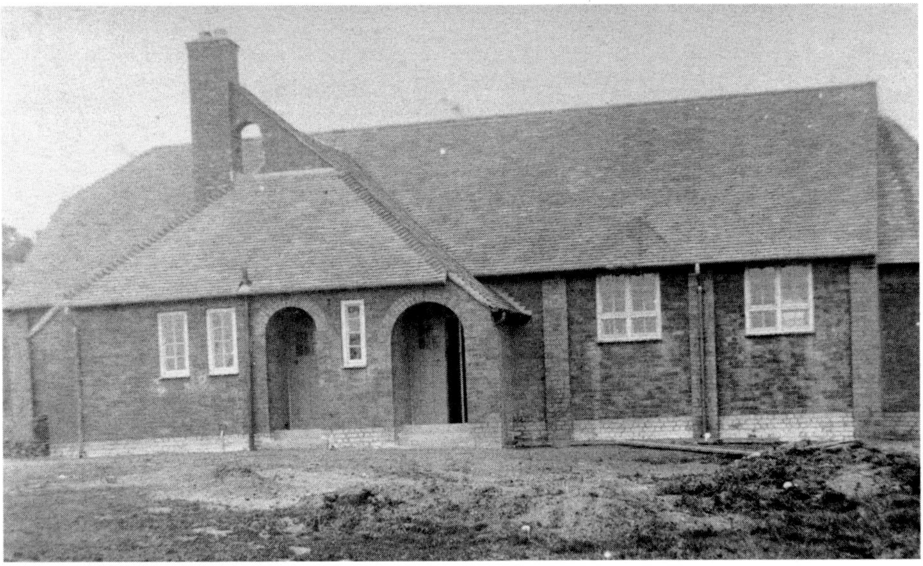

Mastin Moor Mission Church, date unknown. This building still stands in the middle of Mastin Moor hill but has now been converted into bungalows. The Primitive Methodists also had a place of worship a few yards further up the road.

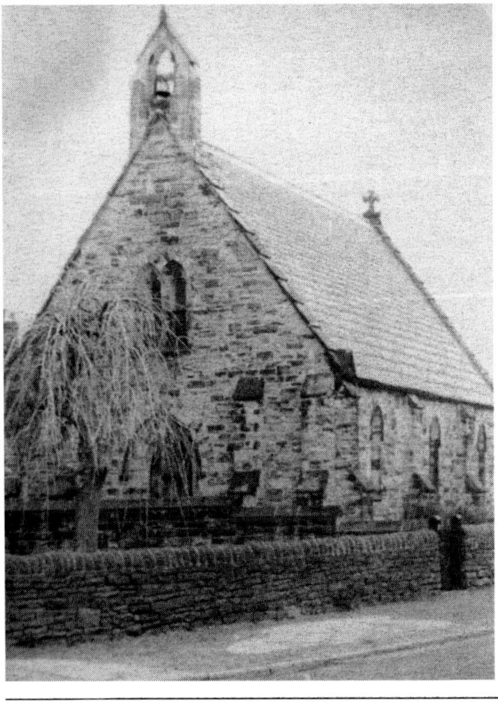

St Peter's Church, Woodthorpe, 1950. Built in 1849 by the Duke of Devonshire on the site of a former Chapel of Ease, the church is no longer used as a place of worship. Standing opposite were the almshouses, supplied for eight poor men and women of the parish, on the end of which stood the bell that is now mounted on the church roof.

SECTION THREE

By Canal and River

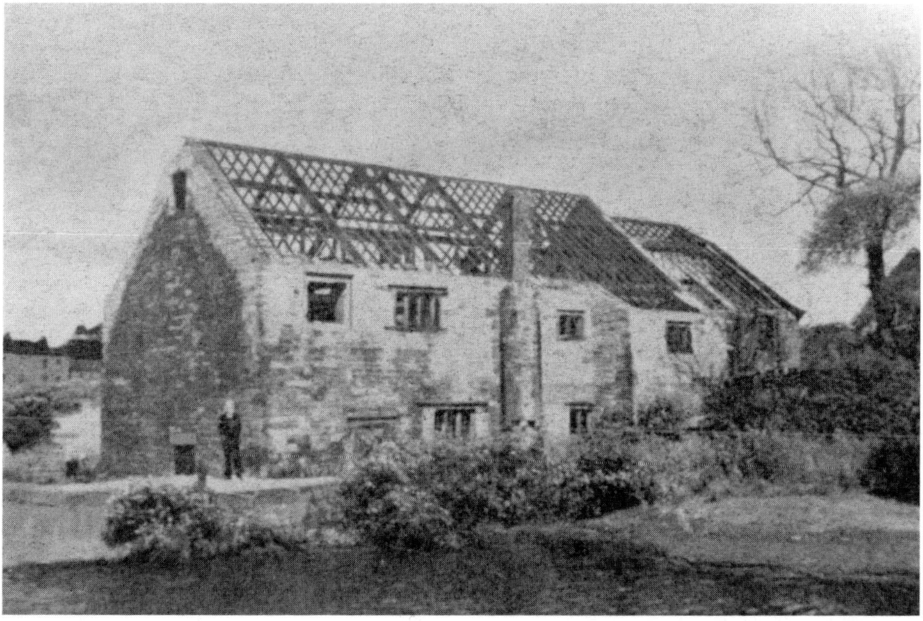

The old corn mill, Staveley, *c.* 1930. The water-mill, situated between the River Rother and the canal, was one of the features of Staveley mentioned in the Domesday Book. Built of stone with a wheel at either end, the mill was used by the farmers of Staveley and all the surrounding districts, who brought not only corn to be milled but all the local gossip and news. The mill fell into disuse after 1916.

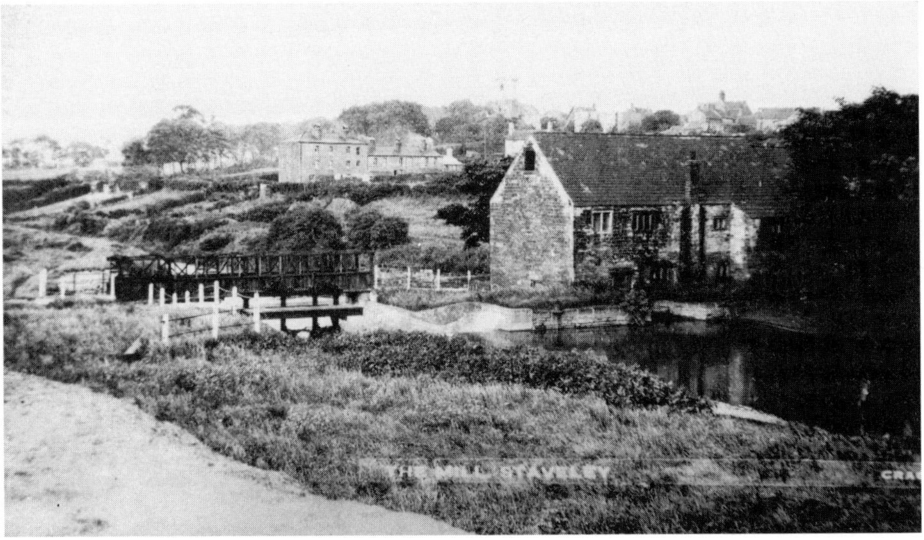

A lovely view of the mill photographed by Cragg, probably late 1920s. This shows how the mill would have looked during its working life. However, the buildings soon deteriorated until all trace disappeared. This is a pity, as today it would almost certainly be classified as a listed building.

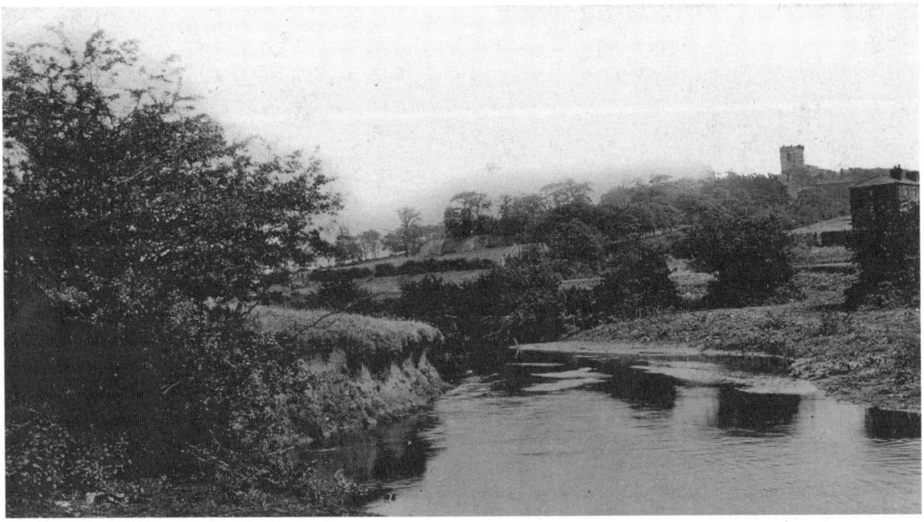

The River Rother from the bridge by the weir at the side of the mill, looking towards the church, 1918. The house just visible on the right is at the bottom of the millhouses, showing the close proximity of the canal to the river.

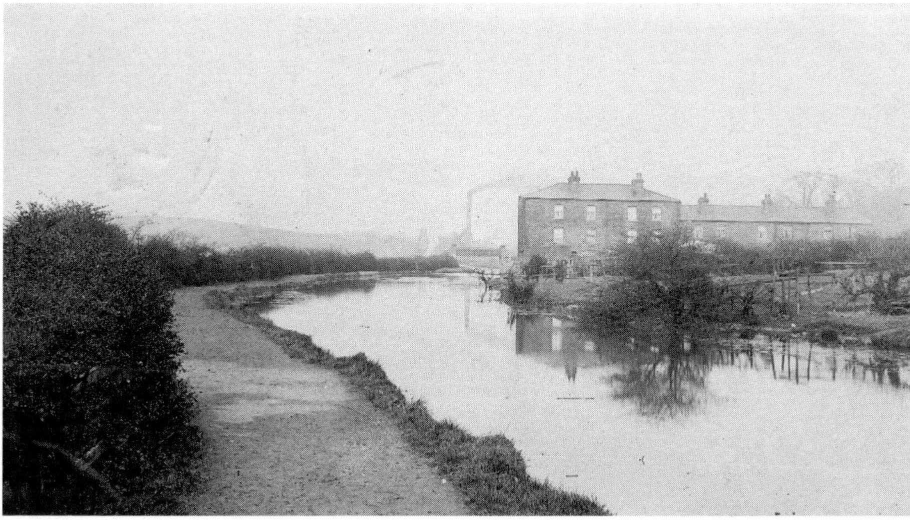

This 1908 postcard by Crowther Cox of Rotherham shows the canal flowing past the millhouses. The bridge at the bottom of Constitution Hill is just visible, with Hartington Colliery chimney smoking at the rear.

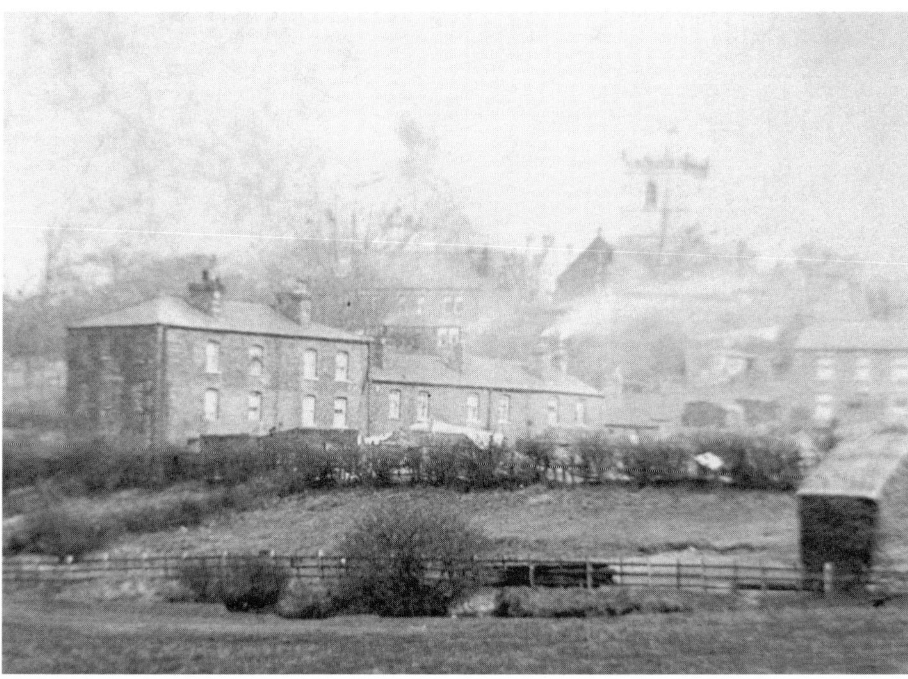

A closer look at the millhouses built for the workers at Staveley Mill, 1902. The row was reached down a narrow roadway off High Street. The houses near the church are Hampton Villas at the top of Constitution Hill.

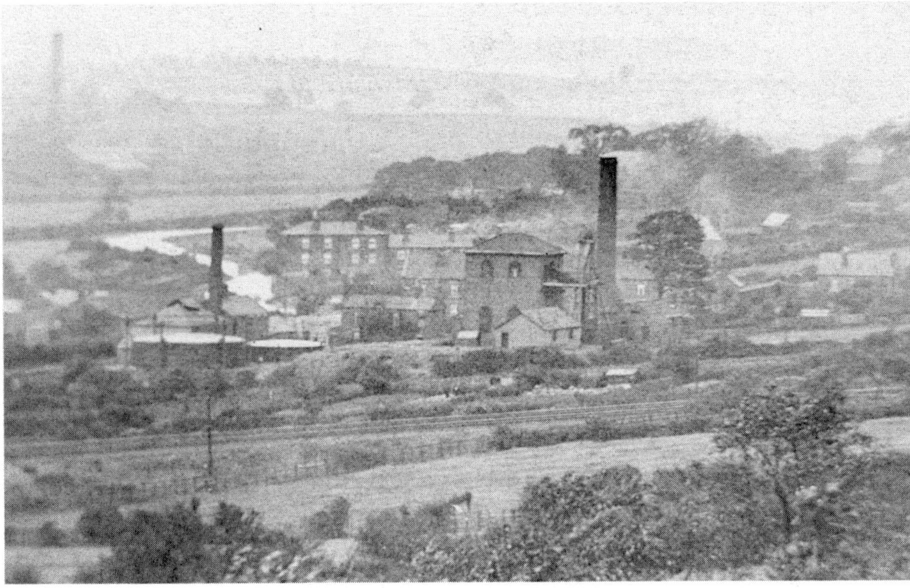

A panoramic photograph of the Mill Green area, 1902. The gasworks on the left was built beside the canal at a cost of £1,800. Gas was introduced for lighting in Staveley in 1861. The building in the centre is the pump-house.

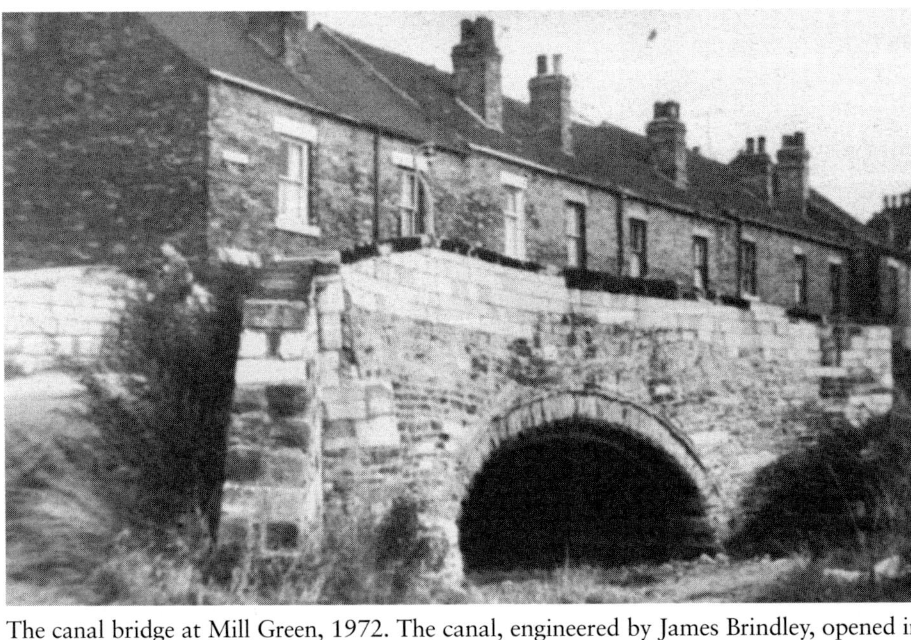

The canal bridge at Mill Green, 1972. The canal, engineered by James Brindley, opened in 1777. In this picture the canal had been filled in owing to mining subsidence. In the wall of the end house was a bricked-up door, which had been used when boats plied the canal.

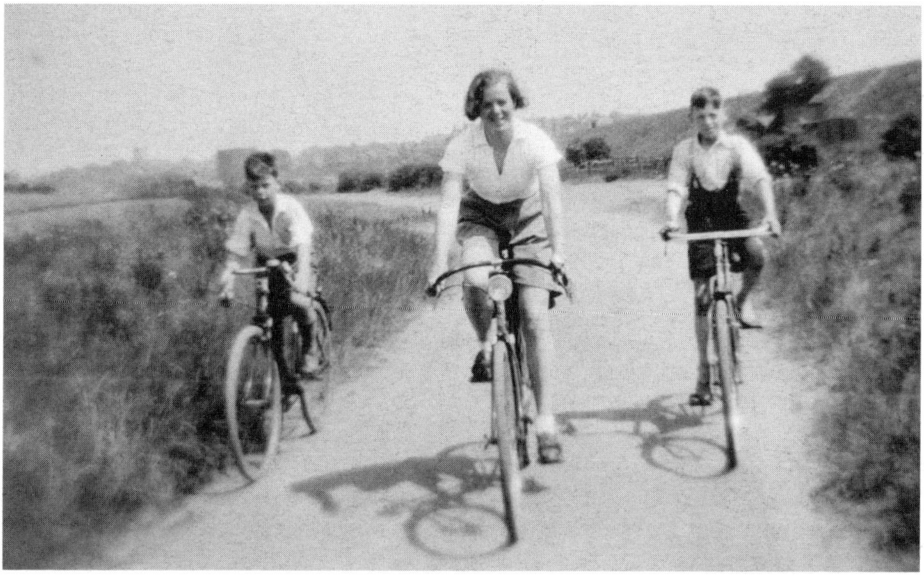

The canal towpath, 1950s. Three cyclists enjoy a ride in the sun from Mill Green to Hollingwood. The canal was one of the main means of transport for the industries around Staveley, besides providing pleasant surroundings for fishing, walking and boat trips.

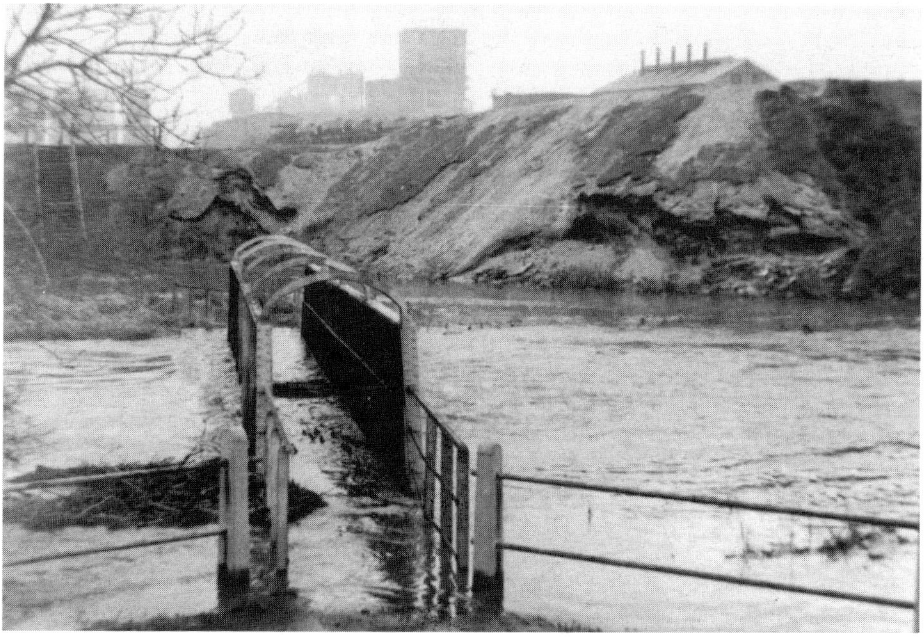

The River Rother in flood, 1932. This bridge over the river carried the footpath from Staveley to Barrow Hill. Situated as it was in the hollow between the canal and the Staveley Works boundary embankment the bridge was always prone to flooding.

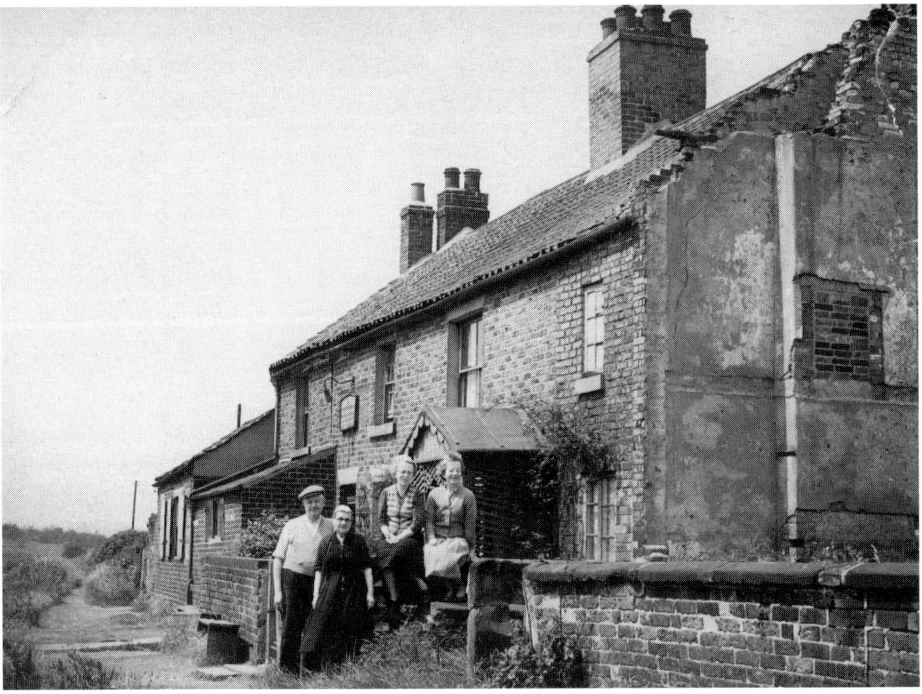

The Wright family at the Canal Tavern, 1936. The tavern finally closed its doors in April 1963 after reportedly serving beer from this site for 300 years. Once a thriving establishment, with the canal travellers and the workers from the nearby ironworks, it could stable four horses and had its own shooting gallery.

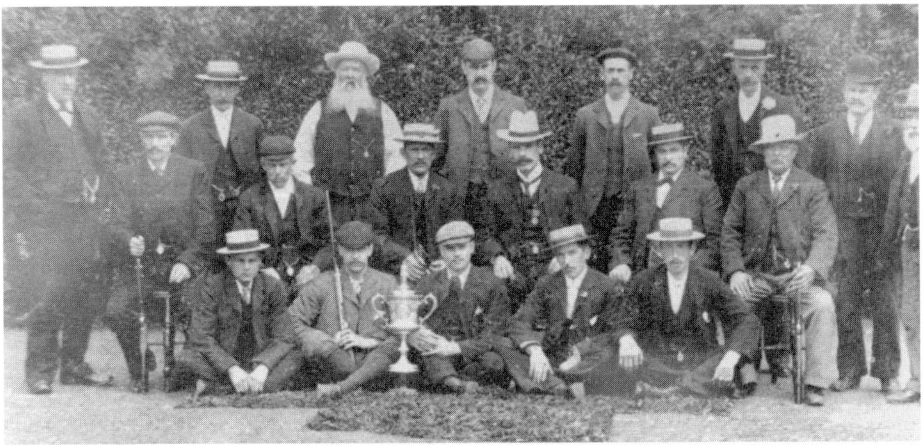

Crack shots of 1904, the Canal Tavern's shooting stars. Standing, left to right: G. Pettifer, A. Williamson Jun., A. Williamson Sen., E. Tulley, W. Nicholls, R. Wright, -?-, Silas Carr. Seated, middle row: T. Arnold, R. Pettifer, T. Allen, E. White, J. Fletcher, W. Hoyland. Front row: O. Brooks, F. Tulley, -?-, M. Williamson, W. Thompson.

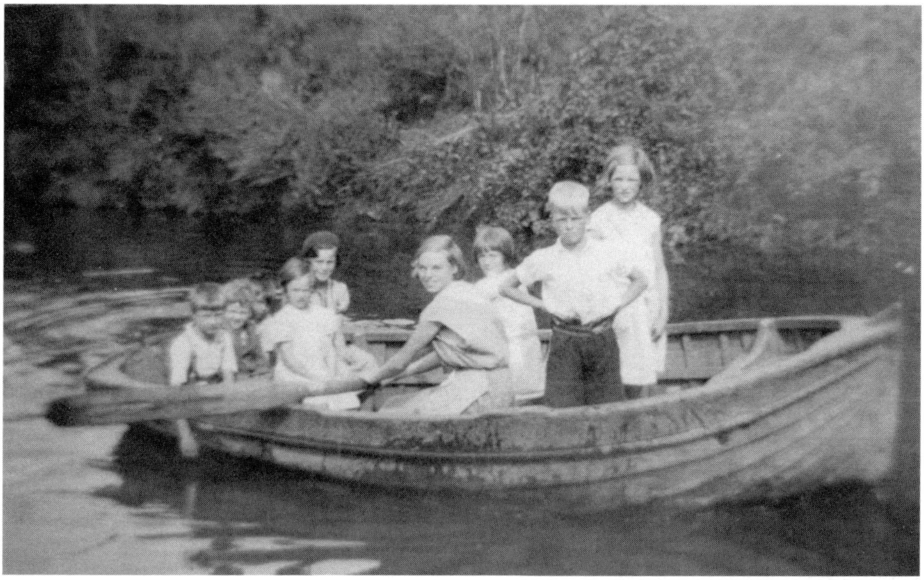

Rowing on the river, date unknown. Canal Row was sandwiched between the canal and the River Rother, giving these children the chance to enjoy their boat. Vera, Albert, and Ida Brooks were joined by Joyce Thompson, Kitty Wright, Margaret and Gerald Walsh and one other whose name is not known.

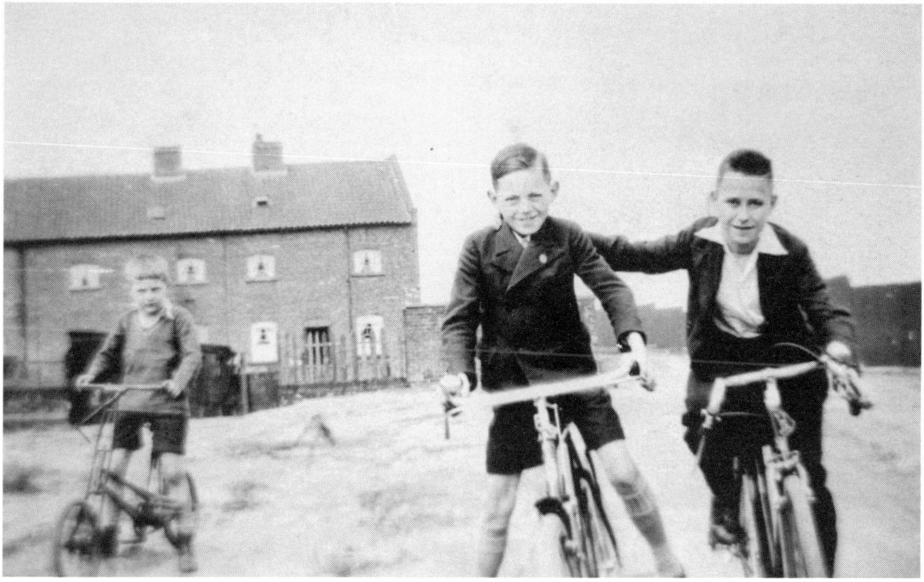

The canal towpath, 1940s. The boys pose for the camera before setting off on their ride. The house in the background was 9 Canal Row, now demolished. Standing beside the Canal Tavern, Canal Row was known locally as 'Frog Row'; one of the houses there also sold fish and chips.

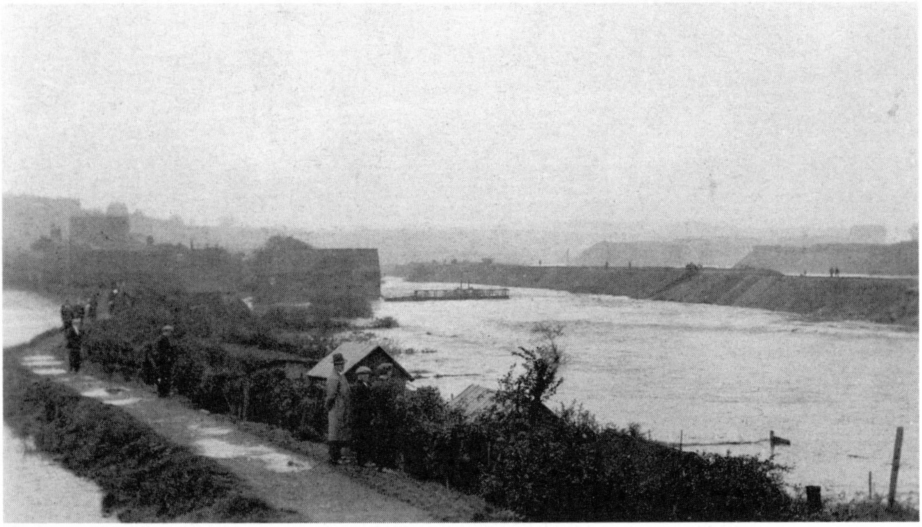

Mr Cragg is once again on the scene to capture the Staveley floods of 1932; the spectators are standing on the canal path. Even though this was a regular occurrence the floods were nevertheless an impressive sight.

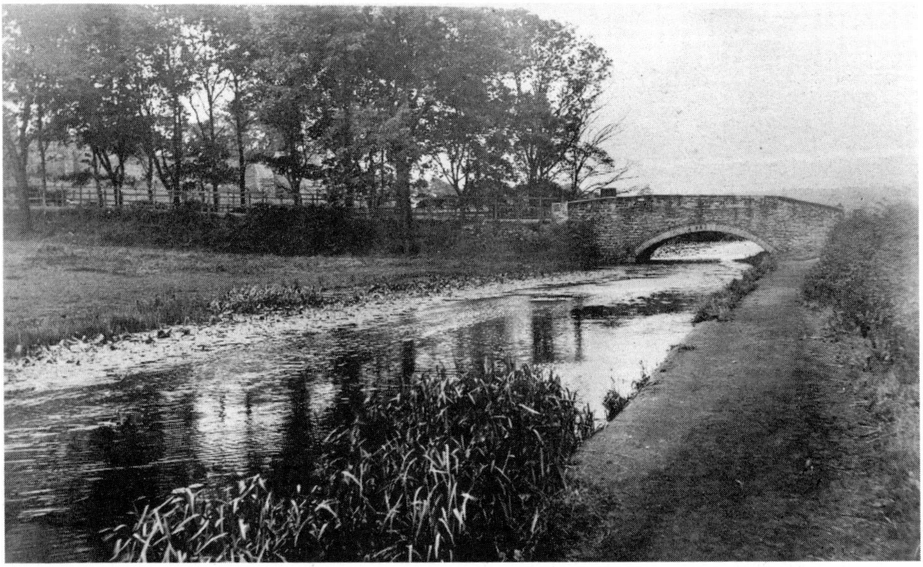

The canal at Hall Lane, 1926. A tranquil scene along the canal, which was always a favourite walk for Sunday strollers. The bridge has been renovated and the local Canal Society is trying to revitalize the canal for leisure use. The rectory boundary wall can just be seen through the trees.

SECTION FOUR

At School

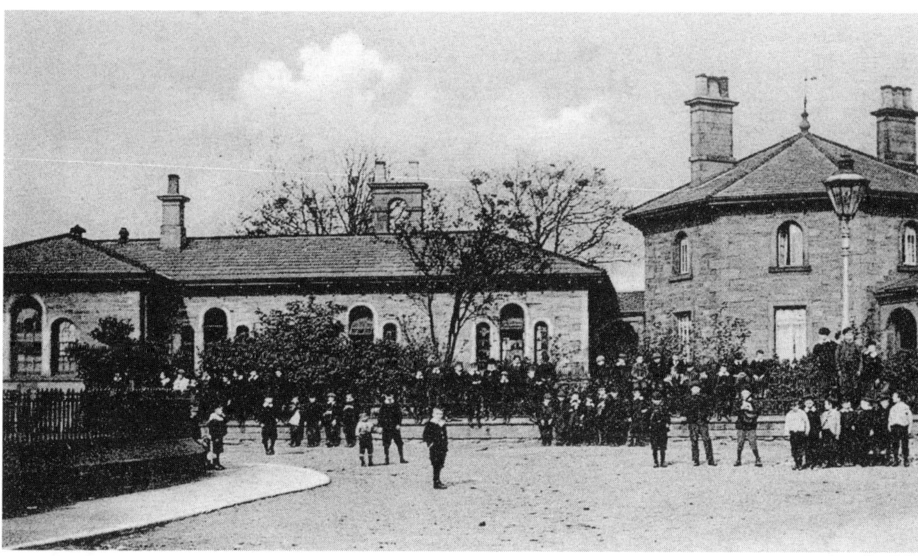

The Schoolhouse, Staveley, 1906. The Public Elementary School was erected in 1844 and enlarged in 1870. It was built as two sides of a square, with an octagonal house at the right angle providing a residence for the master or mistress. Supposedly built to accommodate 350 boys and 230 girls, plus 100 infants, it must have been very overcrowded. By 1906 it was used solely as a boys' school under headmaster John William Stones.

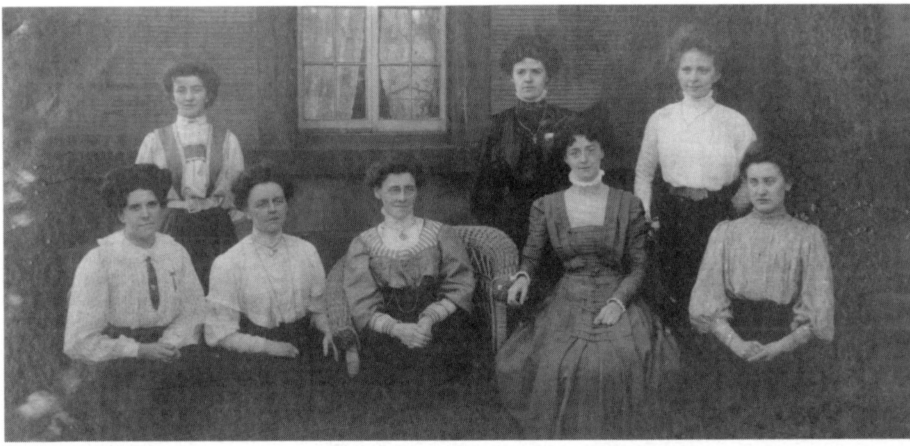

The elegant ladies of the girls' school, 1908. Standing, left to right: Ethel Farmer, Kitty Shaw. Ethel Kenyon. Seated: -?-, Lily Swanson (deputy headmistress), Annie Swanson (headmistress), -?-, Nellie Duffield. The policy at that time stipulated that ladies who married would be required to leave.

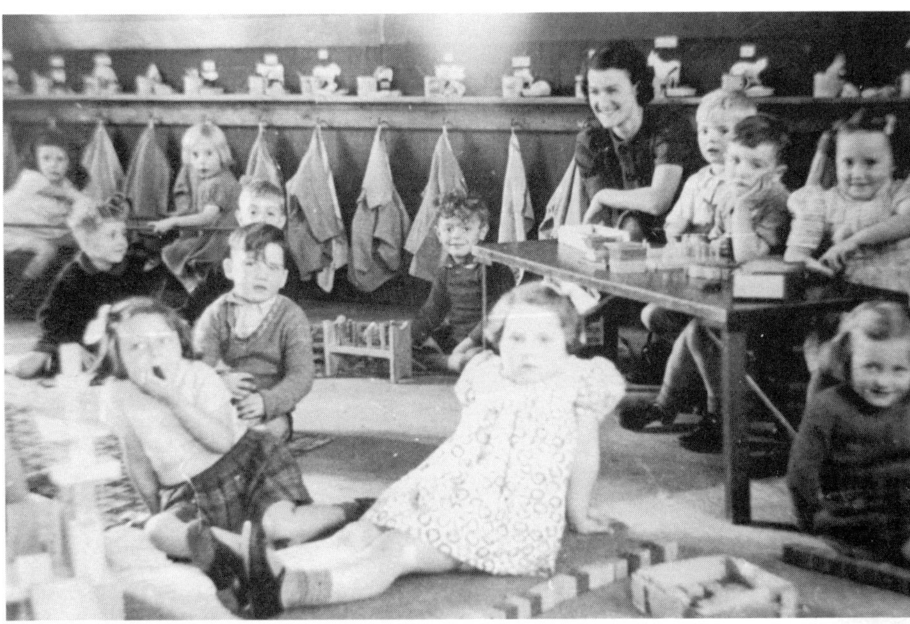

Miss Tompkins's class at the Church School, 1943. With 'Miss' are Ruth Wall, Maureen Jervis, Billy Harris, John Brooks, Anne Mellors, Brian Fenton, Stuart Wall, Harry Carpenter, Hazel Weeks, Esme Barker (centre) and June Stephenson.

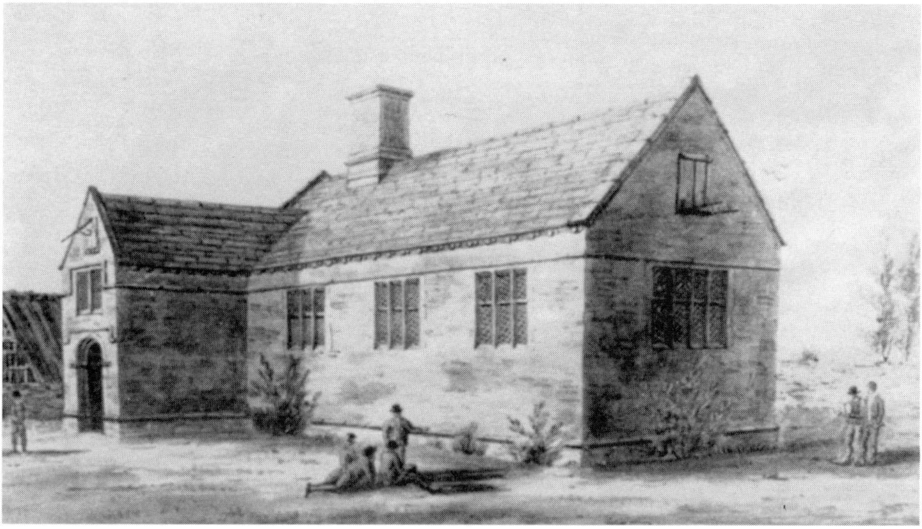

A watercolour print of the old school at Netherthorpe, 1812. This was a free Grammar School, founded in Elizabethan times by Margaret Frecheville, Francis De Rodes and Robert Sitwell, for the use of the parish and surrounding district. Latin was taught free of charge, but additional subjects had to be paid for, a custom which continued until almost 1900.

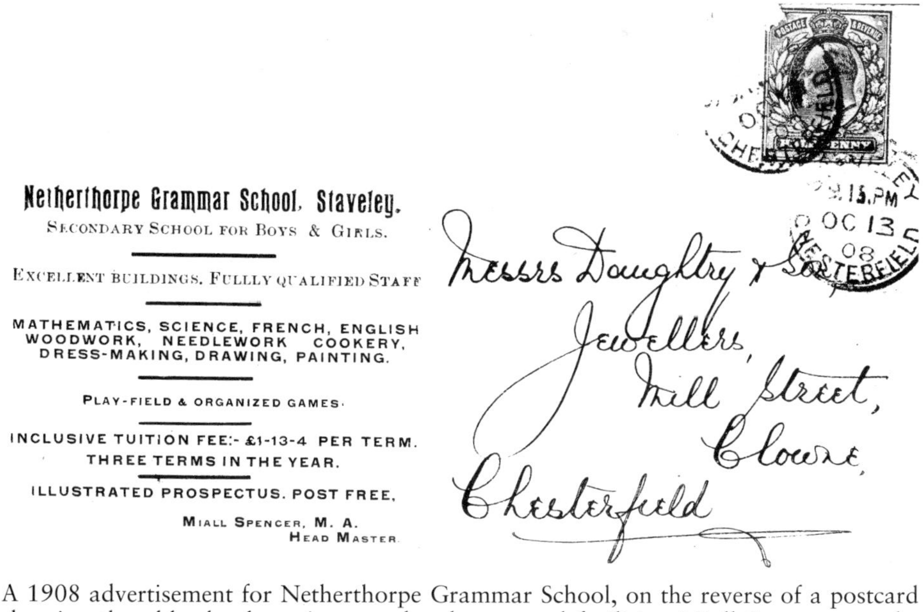

A 1908 advertisement for Netherthorpe Grammar School, on the reverse of a postcard showing the old school, setting out the charges and facilities. Miall Spencer was the headmaster from 1899 until his eyesight failed completely in 1912 and he resigned.

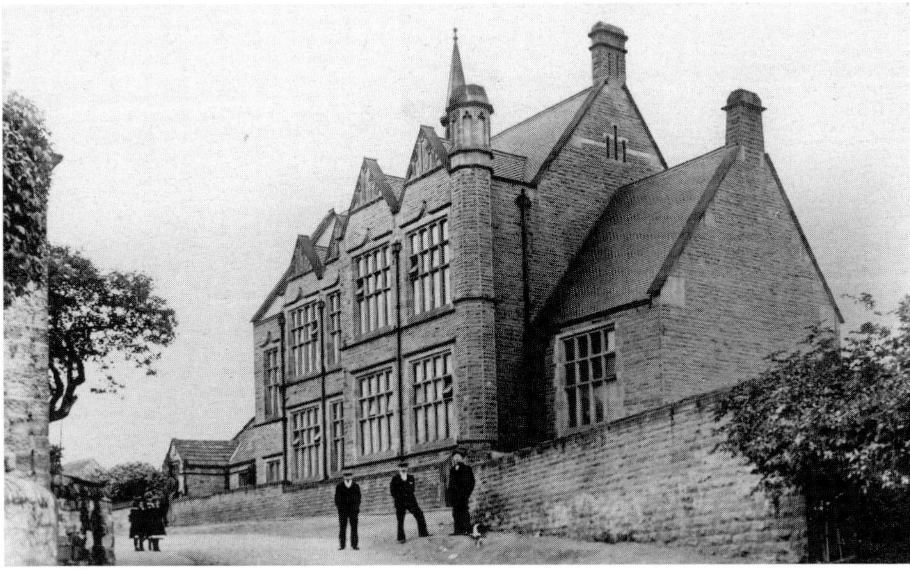

Netherthorpe Top School, 1922. This science block was erected in 1900 and provided physics and chemistry laboratories, cookery and woodwork rooms and much-needed extra space for the increasing numbers of scholars.

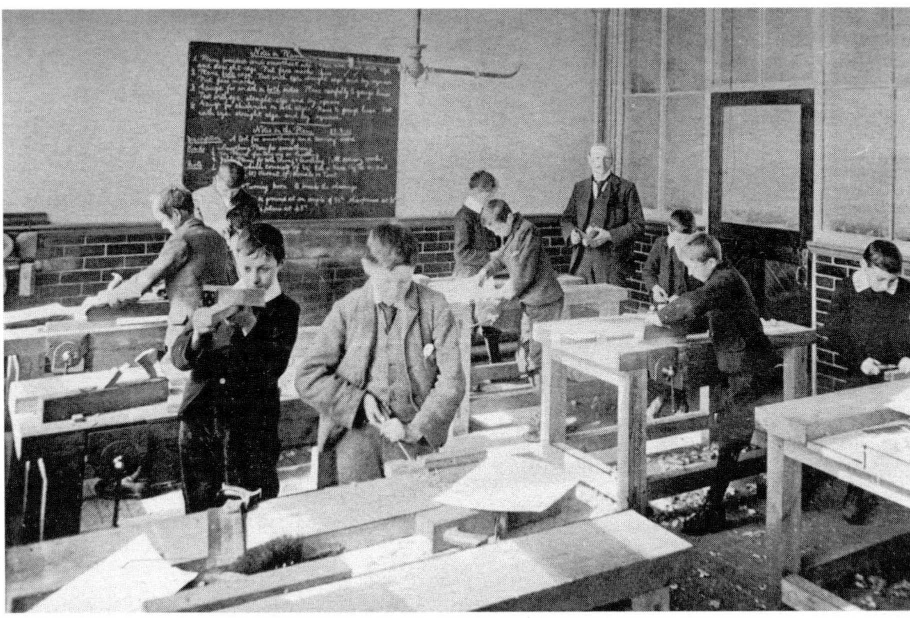

Boys working in the well-equipped woodwork room of the Top School not long after its opening in 1900. With classes through from eleven to eighteen year olds, pupils were eventually bussed in from up to 5 miles away. The school survives today under Grant Maintained status.

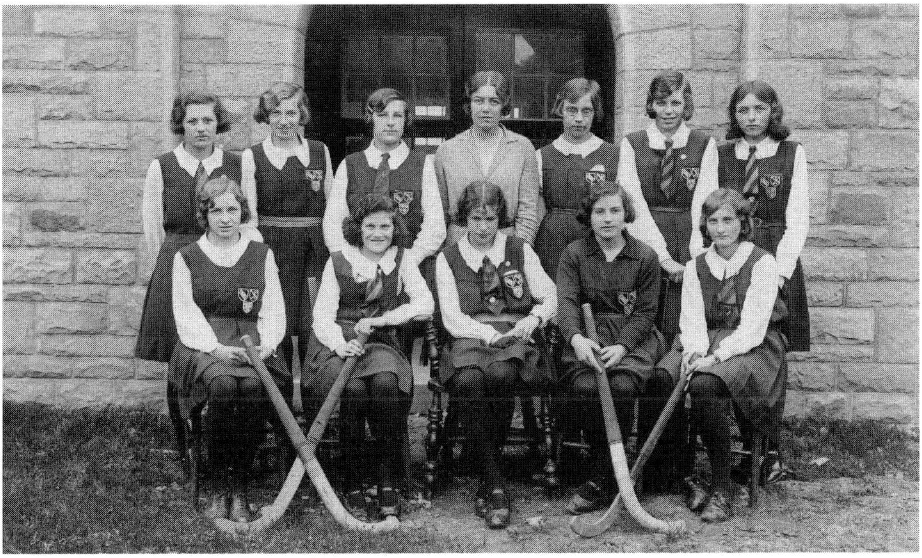

The 1931 Netherthorpe Girls' Hockey Team. Standing, left to right: Jessie Johns, Mary Bacon, Doris Barsby, Miss Merrishaw, Lottie Yeates, Bessie Lund, Myrtle Gibson. Seated: Isobel Twigg, Winnie Haywood, Margaret Jackman, Dorothy Bright, Dora Noden. Girls were only admitted to Netherthorpe School from 1899 onwards.

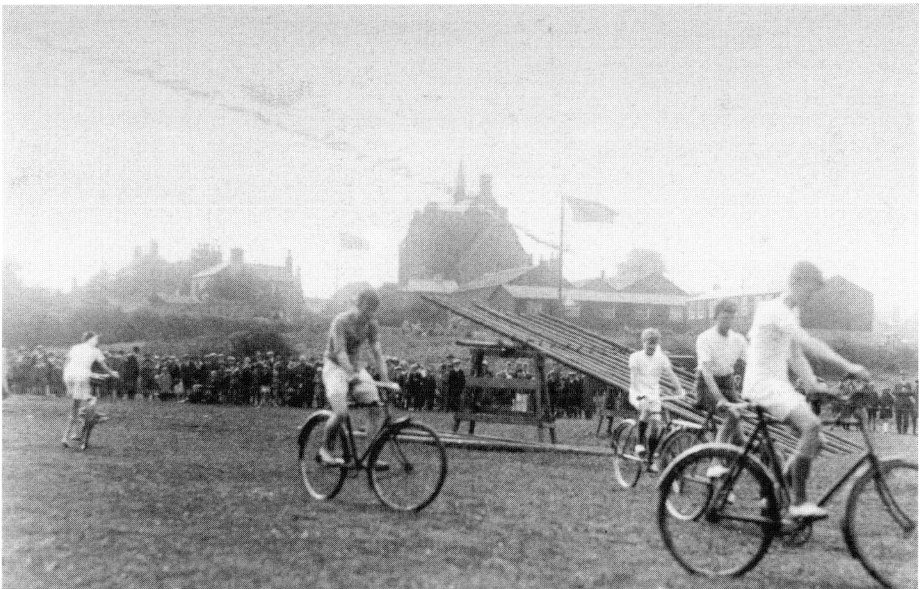

The Grammar School sports day, 1925. The science block on the skyline and the wooden classrooms of the Lower School provide the backdrop for these precarious-looking cyclists. This field was reached by a private wooden bridge over the River Doe Lea.

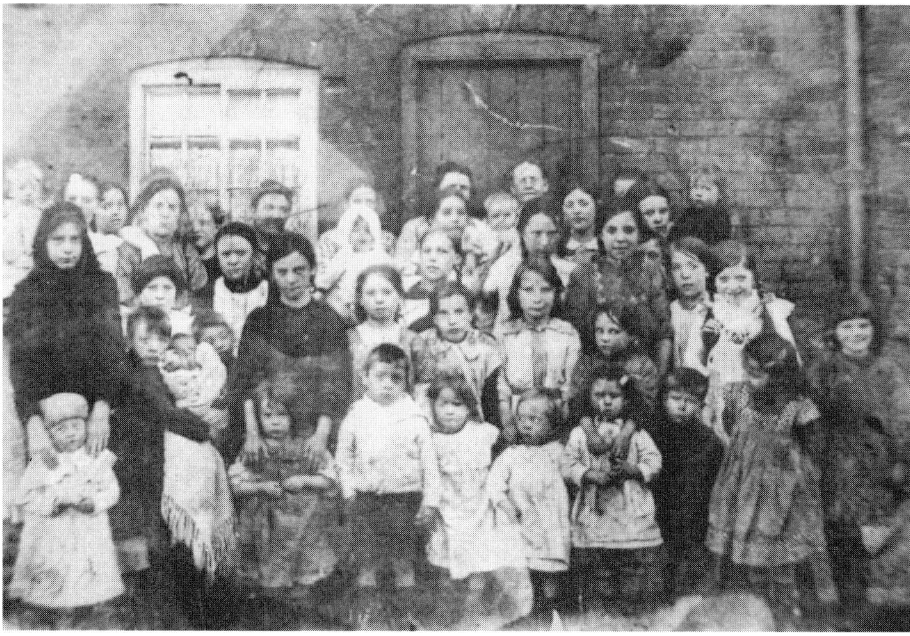

Speedwell schoolchildren in front of one of the houses on Speedwell Terrace, 1914. During these early years the old school logbooks contained many references to deaths from diptheria and whooping cough among the children.

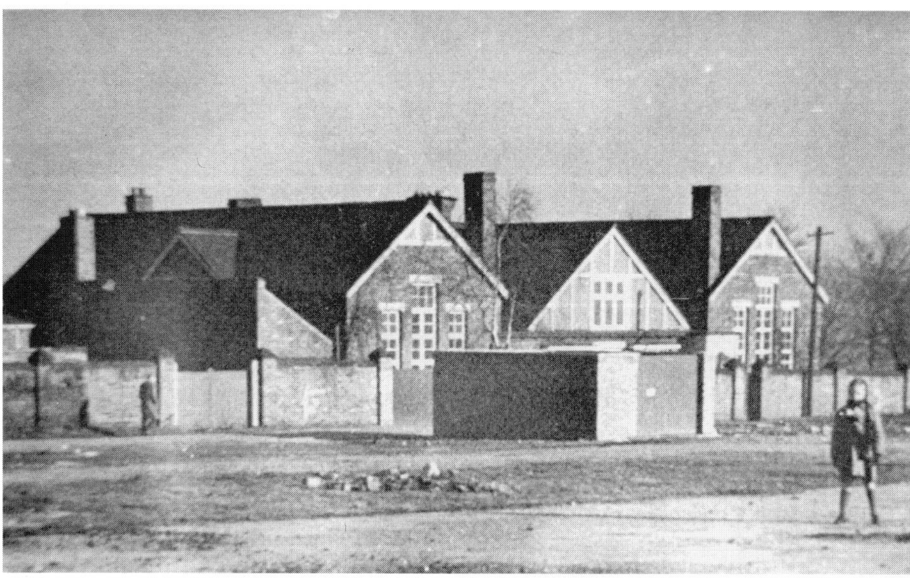

Speedwell Infants School, 1960s. It stands on its own as the houses of the terraces have been demolished. The school burnt down in January 1969 and a new one was built in the open-plan style, adjacent to Middlecroft School.

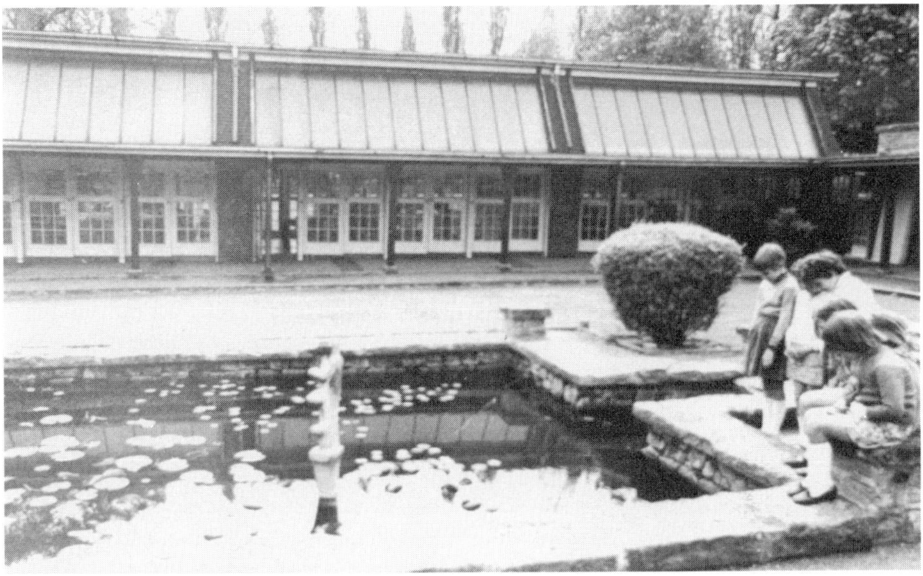

The Junior School quadrangle pond at Middlecroft School, 1965. This photograph was taken just before the buildings succumbed to mining subsidence and had to be demolished. The school was rebuilt on the same site in the open-plan style and re-opened in 1973.

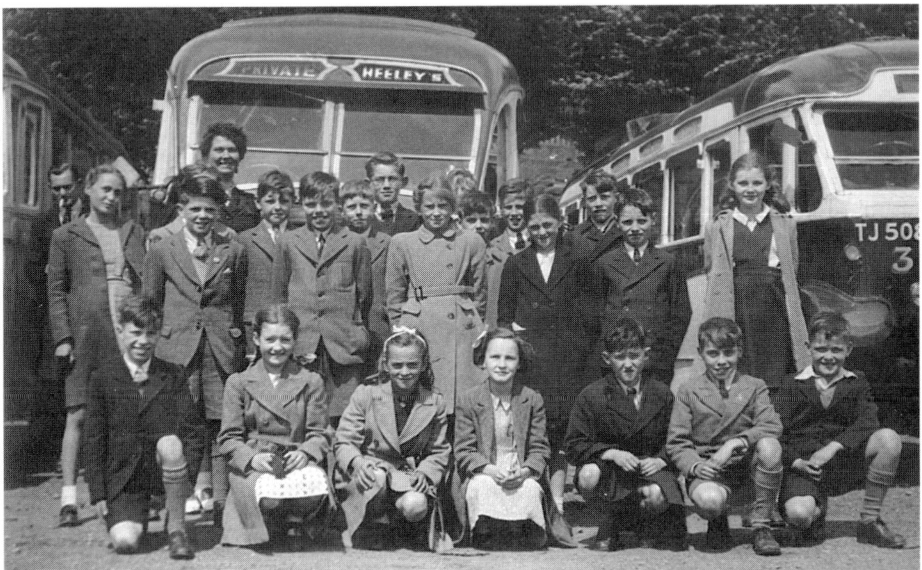

Middlecroft School, 1947. Children pose for the camera before setting out on a school excursion. Standing, left to right: Jean Miller, Phil Swift, Gerald Onions, -?-, Arthur Griffiths, Brian Wilde, -?-, -?-, -?-, Gloria Knight, Trevor Brighton, Edwin Fairs, -?-. Kneeling: Stuart Hunt, -?-, Enid Baker, Barbara Fuller, Brian Turner, -?-, -?-. The teacher's name is not known.

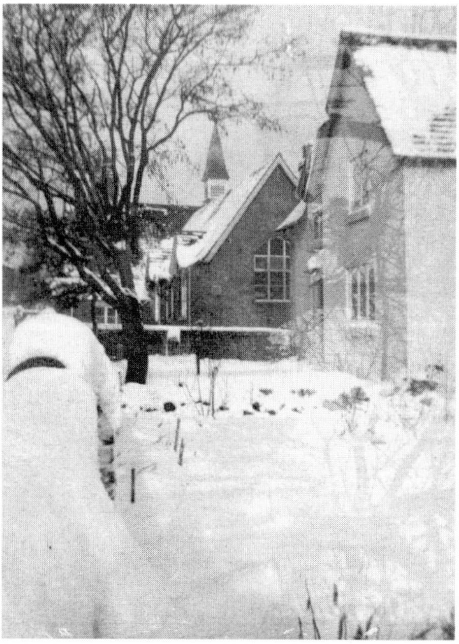

A winter's day at Woodthorpe School and schoolhouse, 1960. The school on the Seymour Road was provided by the 7th Duke of Devonshire in 1861/62 to accommodate 258 children. Woodthorpe was only a small village but the mine sunk at Seymour in 1860 brought in more workers and children.

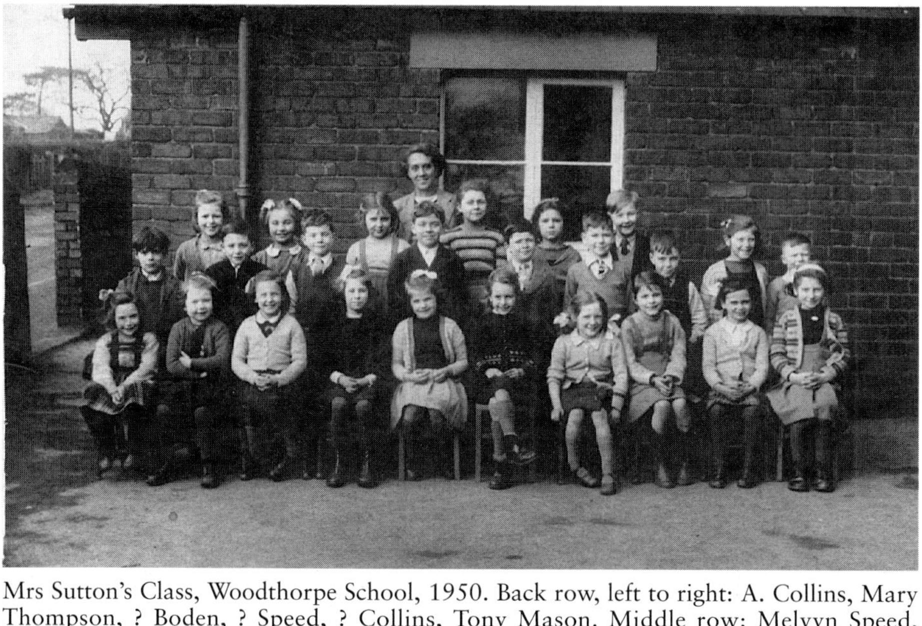

Mrs Sutton's Class, Woodthorpe School, 1950. Back row, left to right: A. Collins, Mary Thompson, ? Boden, ? Speed, ? Collins, Tony Mason. Middle row: Melvyn Speed, Adrian Cauldwell, Raymond Taylor, Graham Hinchcliffe, Melvyn Evans, Tony Daffin, Alan Walker, Gillian Stuart, Ralph Needham. Front row: Anthea Billings, Maureen Barley, Janet Mosley, Hilary Brooks, June Dyble, Ruth Brailsford, Susan Blunt, Maureen Speed, Kathleen Roach, Hazel Jones.

SECTION FIVE

The Railways

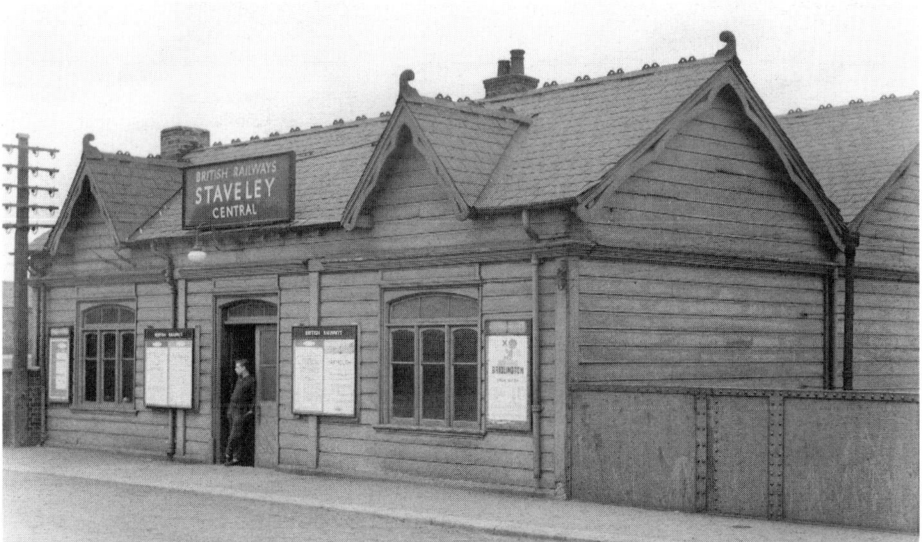

Staveley Central station, 1952. A line from Beighton to Staveley was opened in 1892 by the Manchester, Sheffield and Lincolnshire Railway. By 1950 the passenger traffic was beginning to dwindle and the station finally closed in 1963, although it did run one or two special excursions during the following year. Today the station has completely disappeared.

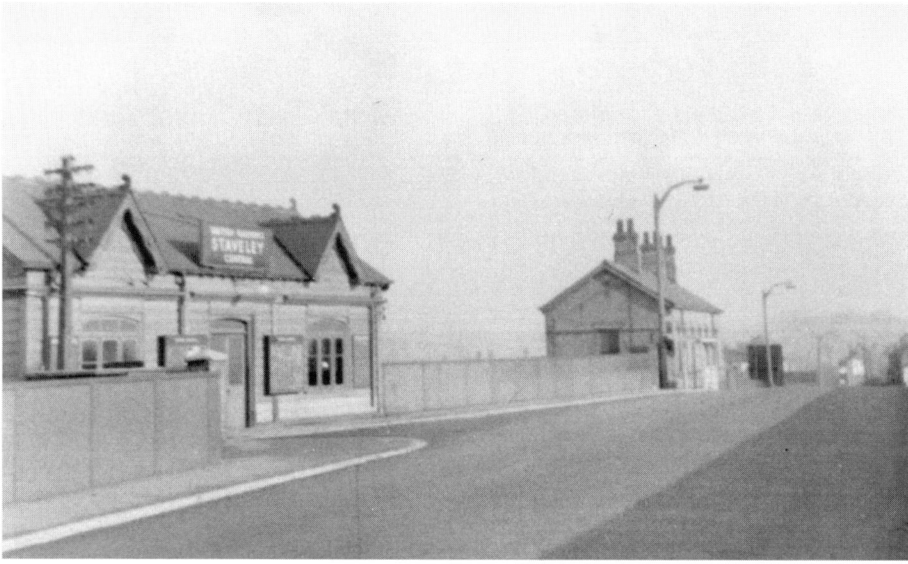

The station bridge, 1952. Another view of the station frontage showing the curve (left) where the goods ramp ran down to the platforms. The house just over the hill, purchased when the bridge was built, became the locomotive shedmaster's residence.

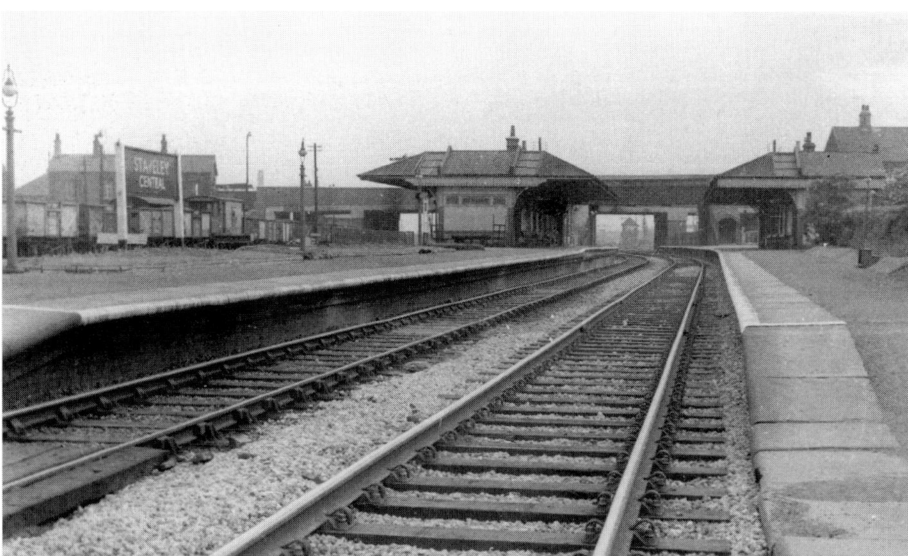

Staveley Central, 1955. Looking towards the road bridge these were the two main platforms. The covered entrance off the right-hand platform led up to the walkway over the lines and into the station, which was hidden behind the waiting rooms on the left.

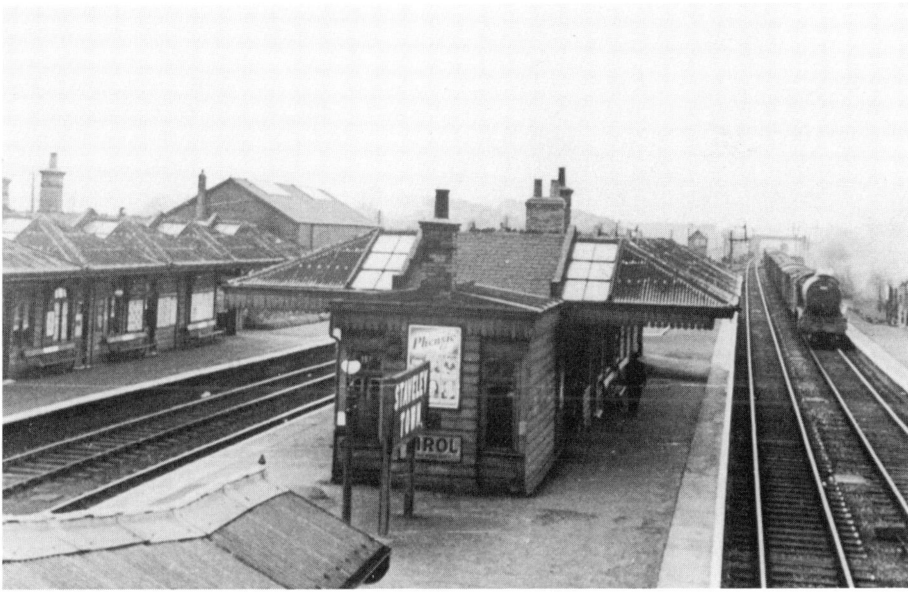

Staveley Town station, 1940. The station was renamed Staveley Central in 1950. The people who used the station will perhaps remember the seemingly endless baskets of pigeons, either waiting to be released or to be transported to another station for release by the race stewards.

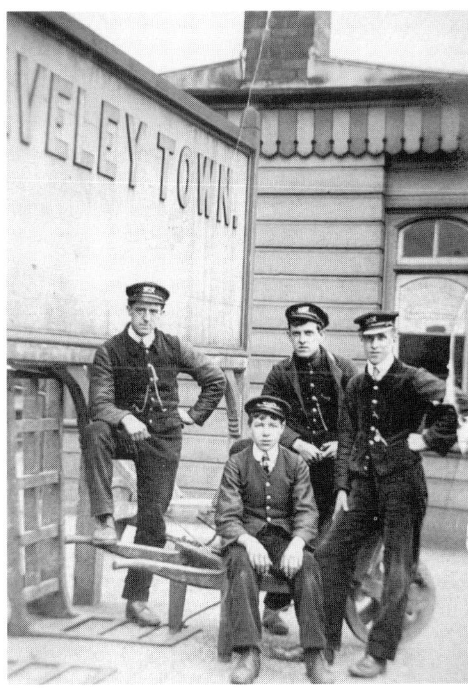

Staveley Town staff, 1910. Mr Walter Swallow (seated) and three colleagues take a break. Staveley was a very busy station, with both passenger and freight traffic, until an expanding bus service provided an alternative means of public transport and the freight took to the road.

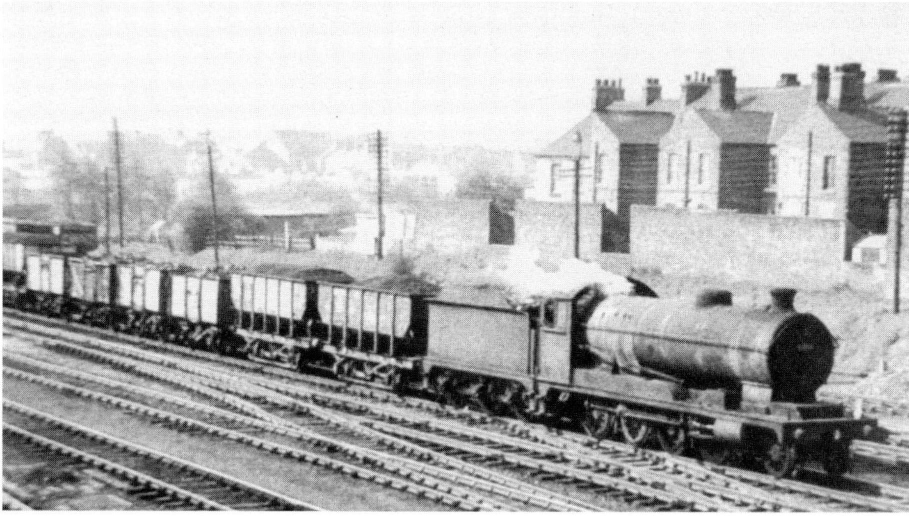

A freight train coming off the loop, 1950. The coal wagons passing the backs of the houses of Wateringbury Grove are just about to enter the station. They are probably en route to the extensive goods yards at Lowgates, where the engines worked day and night shunting goods and wagons.

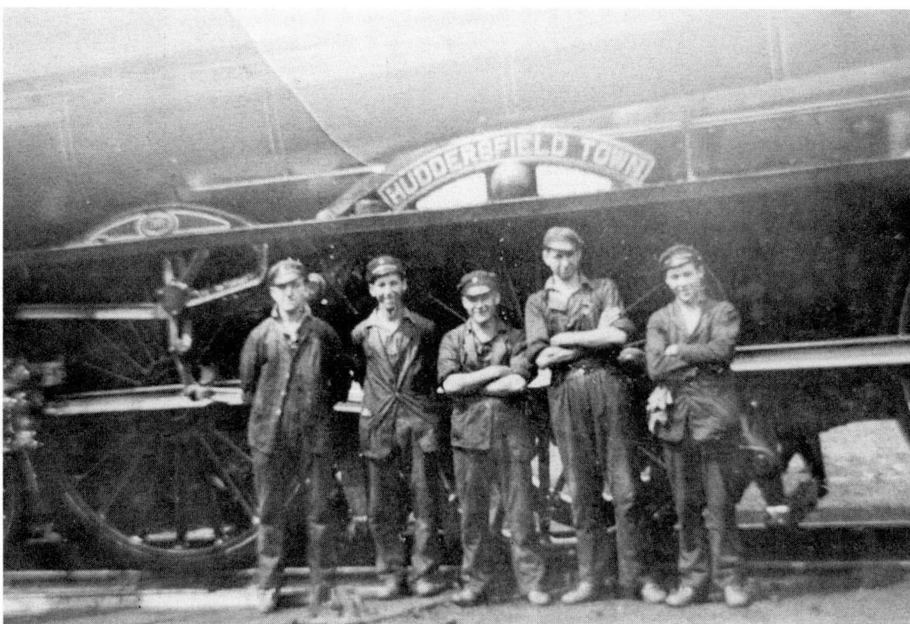

Outside the engine sheds, 1940s. The railway workers posing by the engine *Huddersfield Town* are, left to right: Sid Rimmington, Joe Fletcher, Juddy Scofield, Jack Mosley, unknown. For the train-spotters, many named engines ran through Staveley, the *Flying Scotsman* being a frequent engine on the 10.00 p.m. Master Cutler train.

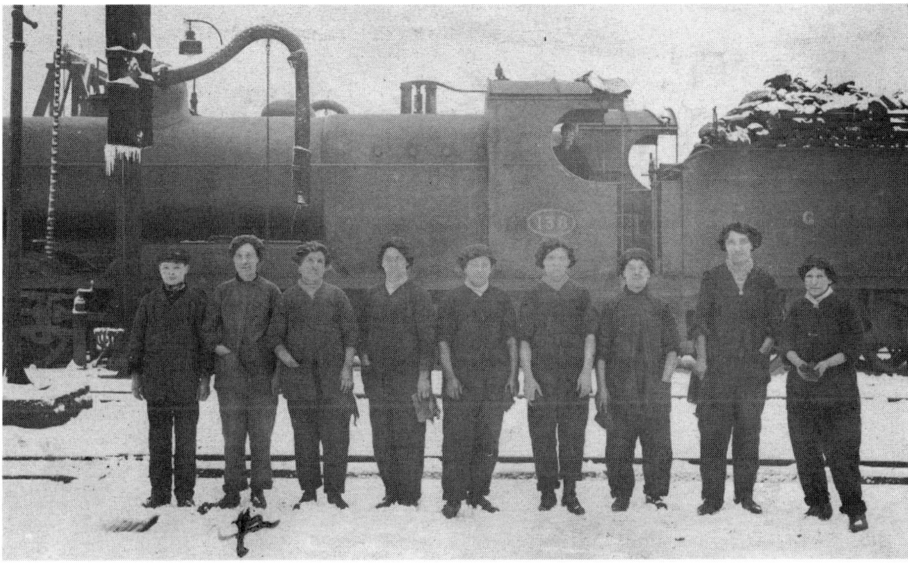

Staveley engine sheds in snowy April, 1916. During the war years the ladies took over the cleaning and maintenance of the engines. Among those taking a breather are ? Uttley, Sally Townsend, ? Goodwin and ? Carpenter.

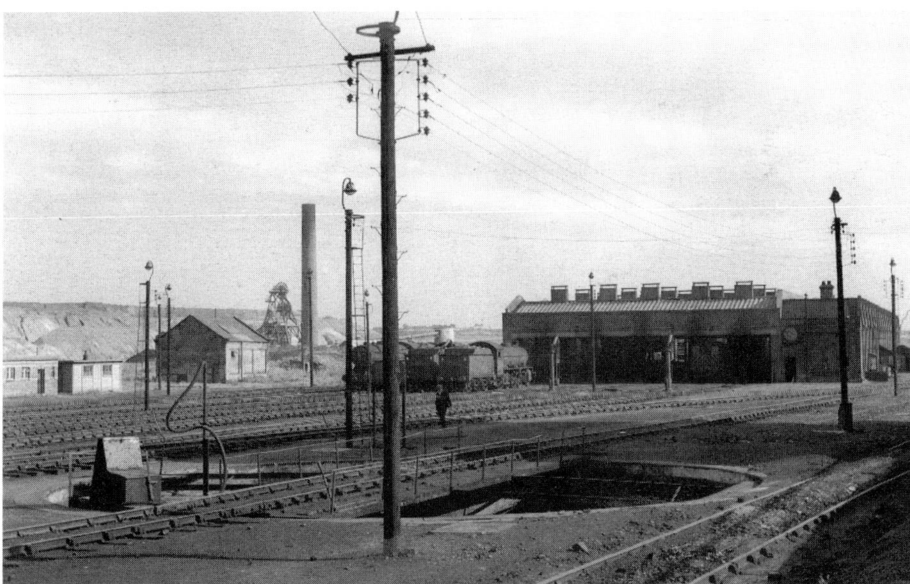

Staveley sheds and roundhouse, 1964. Staveley was a large depot with twelve tracks in the sheds and, with the outside ones, had standage for eighty engines. Ireland Colliery, seen at the rear, had a single track running down to it with an incline so steep a locomotive could only pull out twelve loaded wagons at a time.

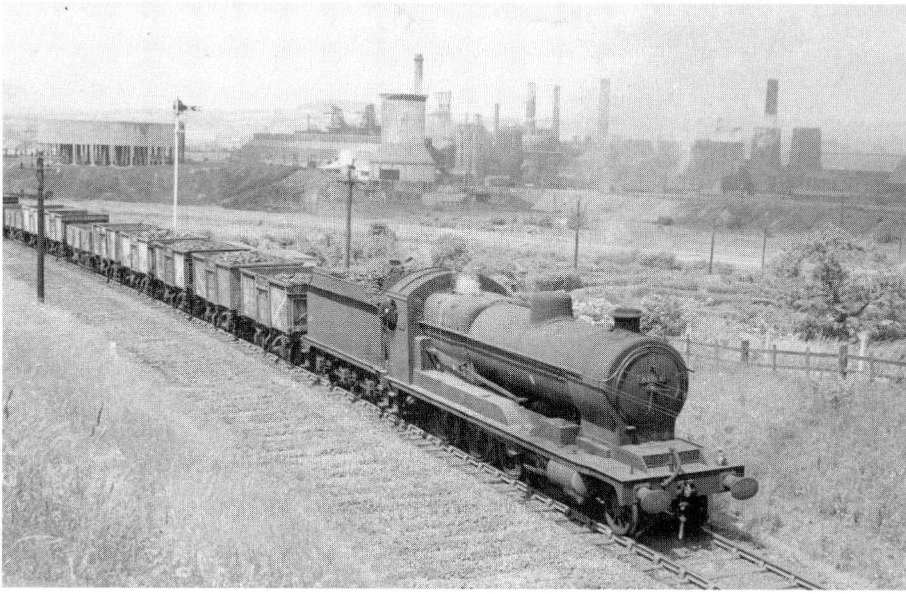

Engine 63913 on the loop, 1963. This branch line to Chesterfield opened in 1892. One track has already been removed and the other one was taken up in 1964. The allotments separate the railway from the canal, with the Devonshire Works dominating the background.

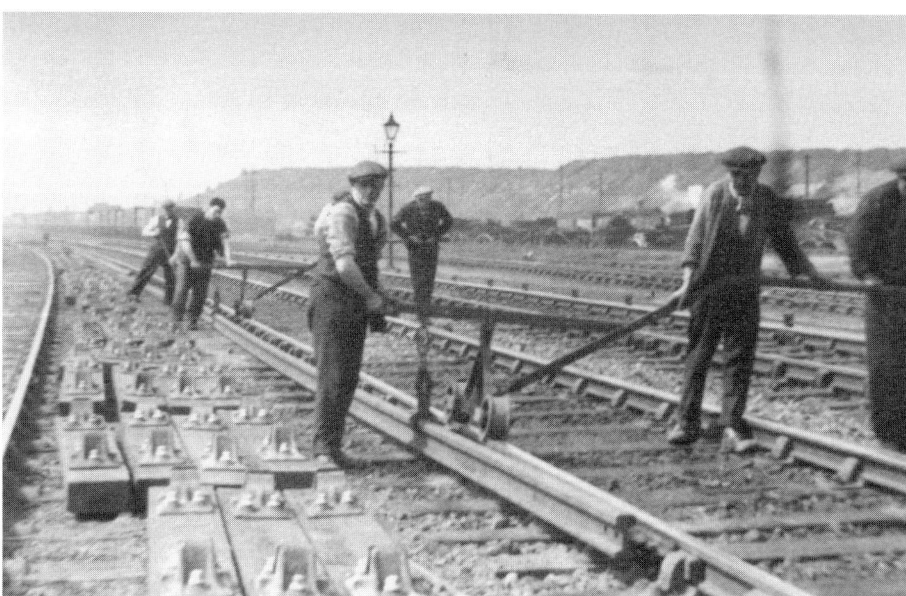

William Bradley (front, left) platelaying near Staveley Works station, 1935.

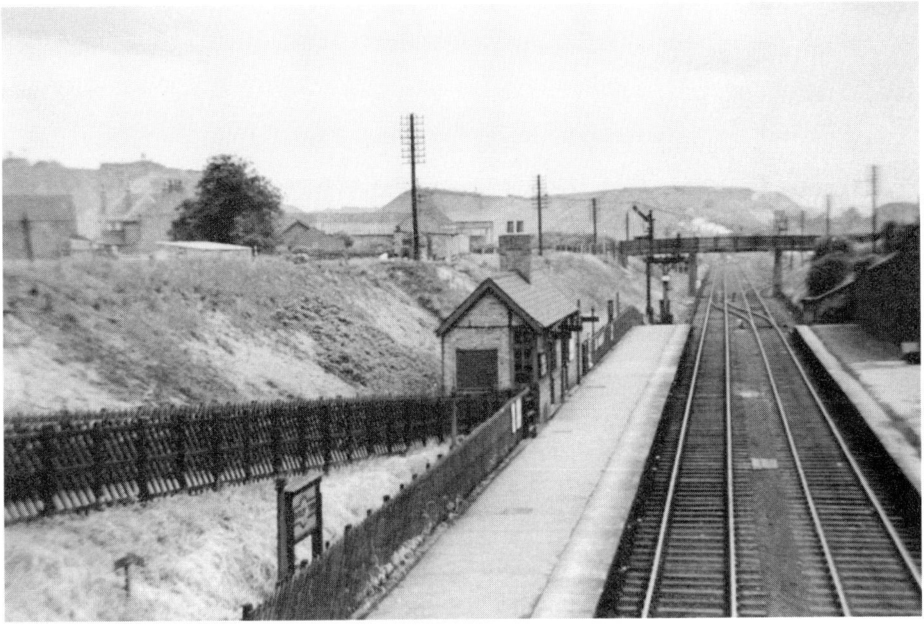

London Midland and Scottish railway station, Fan Road, 1950. When it opened in 1888, this was originally called Netherthorpe station. Looking down the line to Ireland Colliery one can see the footbridge which connects Fan Road to Netherthorpe on the left.

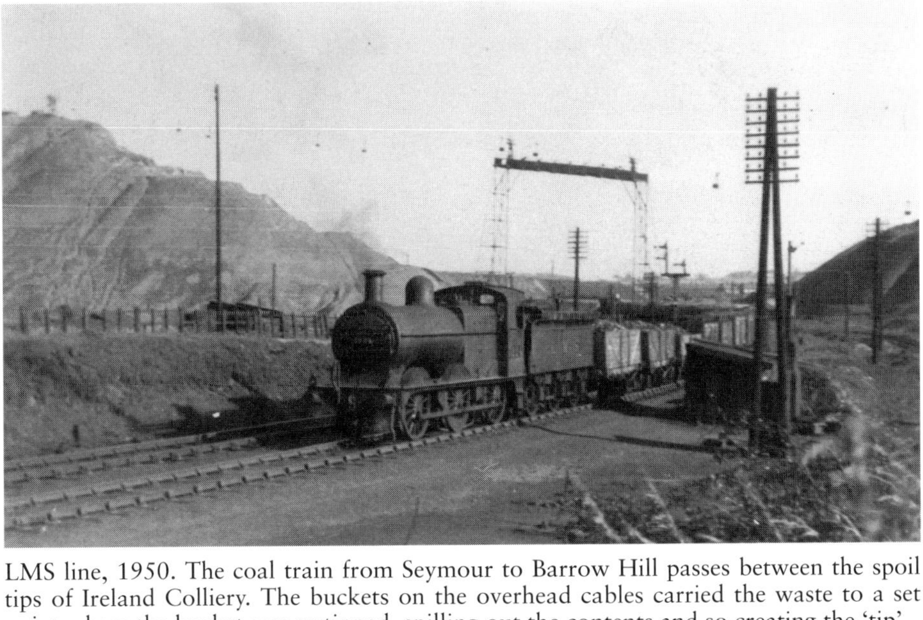

LMS line, 1950. The coal train from Seymour to Barrow Hill passes between the spoil tips of Ireland Colliery. The buckets on the overhead cables carried the waste to a set point where the bucket was uptipped, spilling out the contents and so creating the 'tip'.

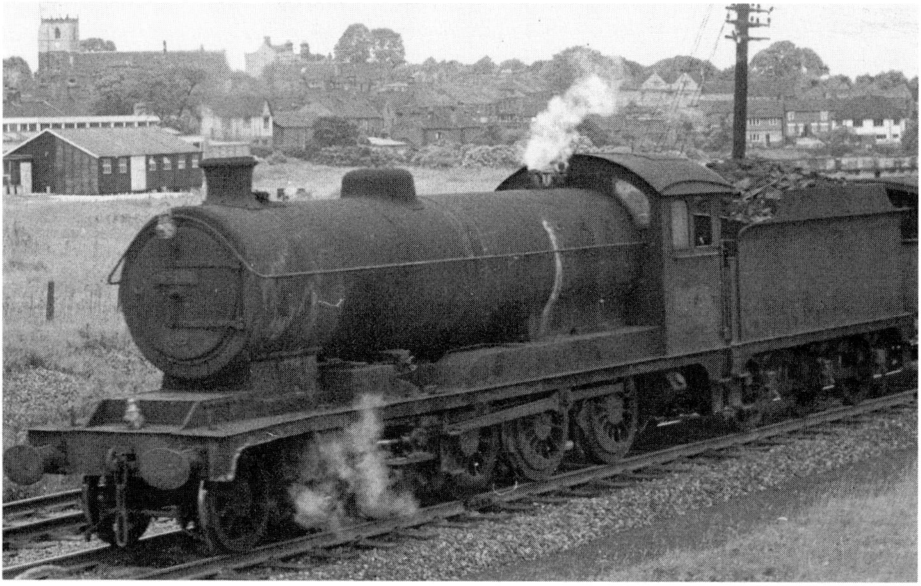

The Chesterfield branch line, 1950. This is interesting because of the buildings that can be seen behind the engine. Hunstan House and the Roman Catholic School on Duke Street are visible over the funnel, and the white house to the right hides Buttermilk Row. These have all been knocked down and the sites re-developed.

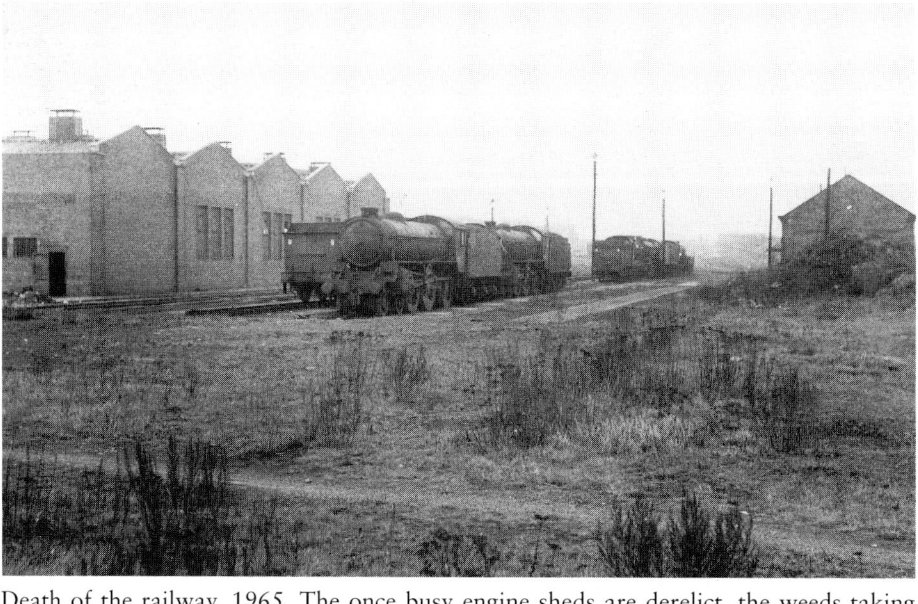

Death of the railway, 1965. The once busy engine sheds are derelict, the weeds taking over where once the tracks ran, and the few remaining engines are waiting for the scrapman. Today the line is a nature trail from Arkwright to Rother Valley Park.

SECTION SIX

Coal and Iron

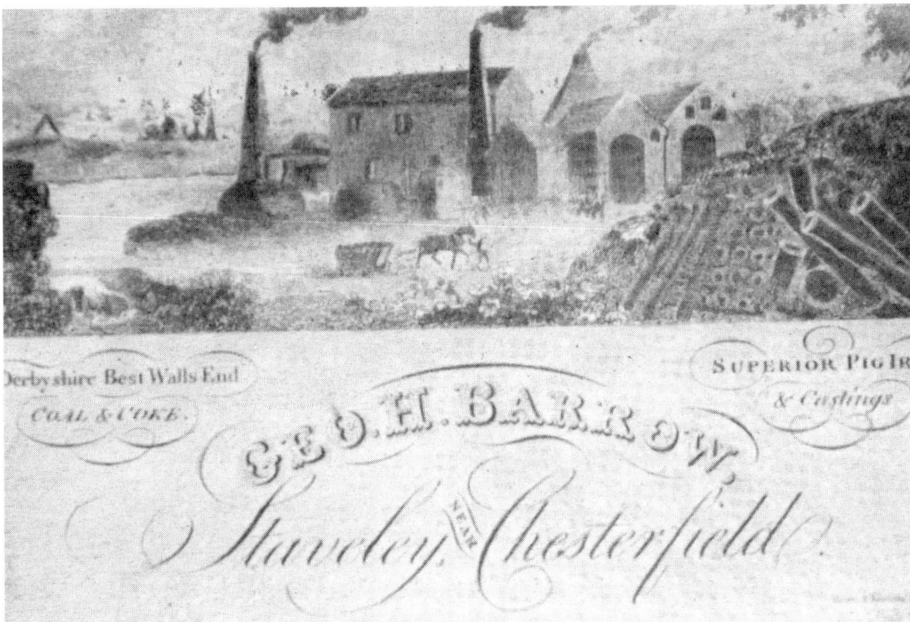

Mr George H. Barrow's business card, showing the Staveley Works, 1832. A furnace and forge can be traced back to the time of the Frechevilles in the 1660s. The works came into the Barrow family through marriage and in 1840 it passed into the hands of Mr Richard Barrow.

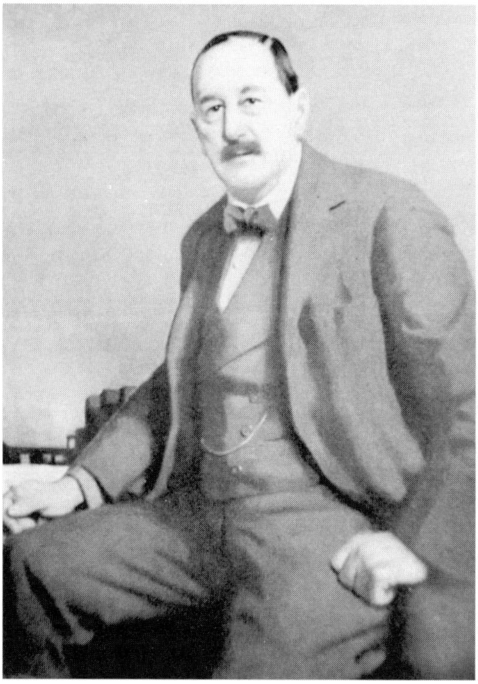

Charles Paxton Markham, 1865–1926. The well-loved ironmaster who, on his father's death in 1888, was elected to the board of the Staveley Coal & Iron Company. On becoming chairman in 1903 he created the Devonshire Works; he was also the owner of Markham and Company, Chesterfield; and for three terms he was Lord Mayor of Chesterfield. A tireless worker in both expanding Staveley Company and improving the lot of the workers, his sudden death was a great loss to all.

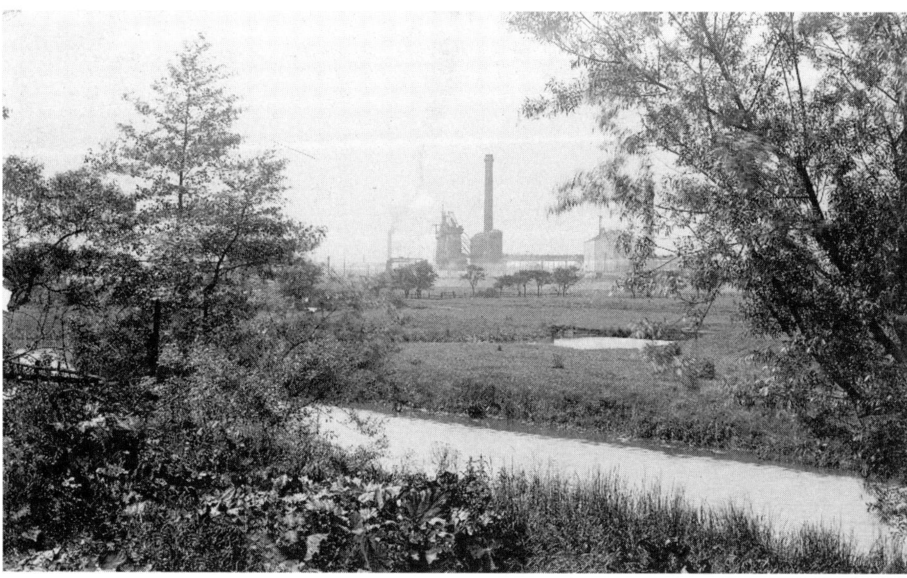

Staveley New Works, 1908. A postcard by Crowther Cox of the view from the banks of the canal clearly shows that Staveley Works was not all dirt and smoke.

The Staveley Coal & Iron Co. Limited.

Telegraphic Address "Staviron" Barrow Hill

Works Established over 100 Years.

Gas & Water Pipes. Pig Iron. Cylinders, Columns, & Heavy Castings of Every Description.

Colliery Proprietors. Steam House & Cannel Coals. Shippers of all descriptions of coal.

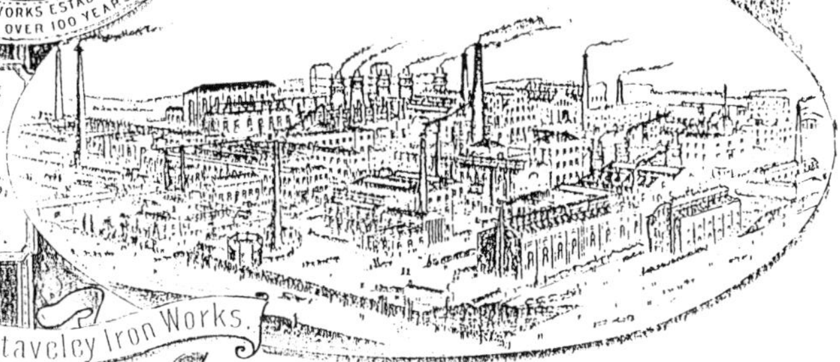

Staveley Iron Works.

Nr Chesterfield. Nov 2nd 1914.

National Telephone No 251.

In your reply refer to Foundry Dept. JL/AB.

C. W. S. Oldham Esq
Waterworks Offices
Waterworks Street
Ipswich.

Dear Sir

Flange Pipes & Specials. Ref PCS.

We are in receipt of your letter of the 29th ult. re delivery of above and beg to inform you that we have the order well in hand and will push on with all speed.

Yours faithfully

Pro The Staveley Coal & Iron Co Limited

Douglas G. Cochrane

An example of the Staveley Coal & Iron Company letterhead, 1914. The company was formed in 1864 and at its height covered an area of over 200 acres, with 4,000 men employed. The company also owned eight collieries employing about 13,000 men. Among its products were pig-iron, cast-iron pipes, ammonia and coal tar products, various acids and sodas, and many tons of tarred slag.

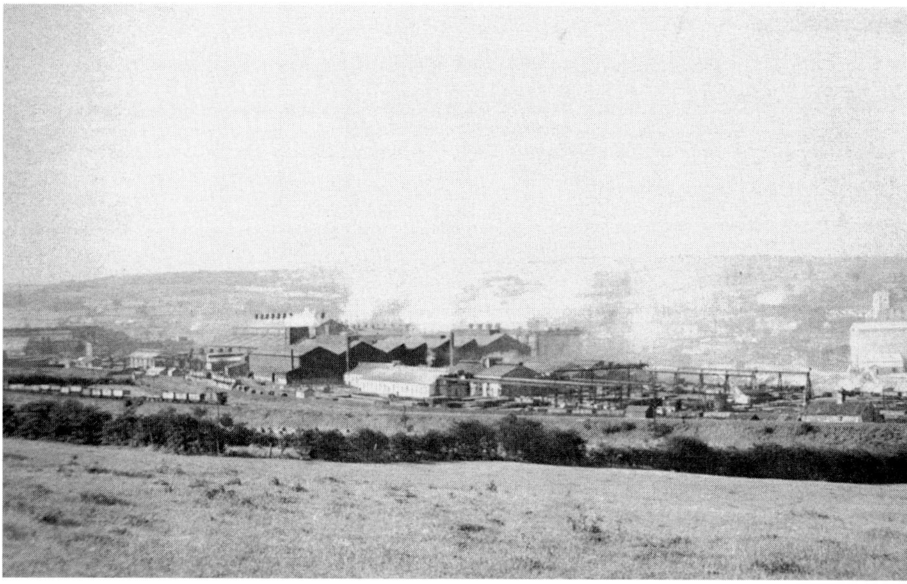

The Devonshire Works, viewed from the Chesterfield Road, 1965. The Chesterfield loop line runs through the centre of the picture, with the canal just over the embankment. The roof of the Canal Tavern can be seen to the right.

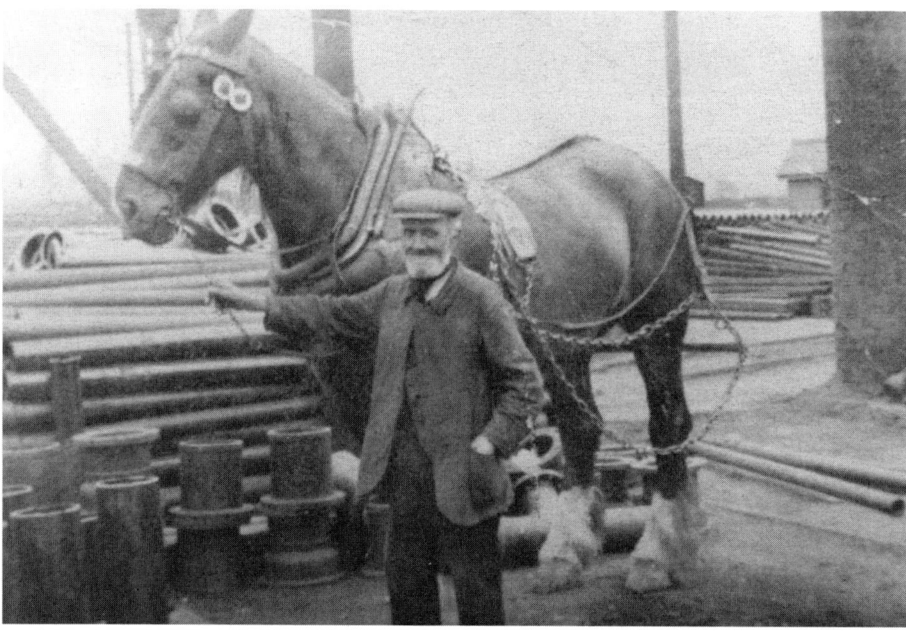

Thomas Dunkley and horse, the dipping tank team, near the coating plant, *c.* 1930. After casting, inspection and testing, pipes are transferred to the coating plant to be either dipped or externally coated with a bitumen tar as protection against the weather.

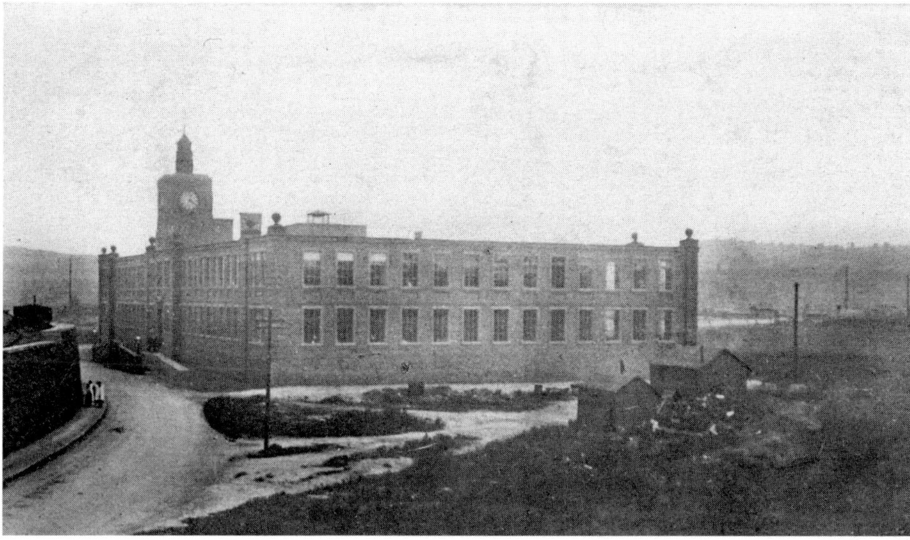

General Offices, Staveley Works, 1914. This new block on the Barrow Hill road, incorporating the old clock from the early offices which stood in the foundry yard, was opened in 1913. The staff then worked from 9.00 a.m. until 6.00 p.m., with one hour for lunch.

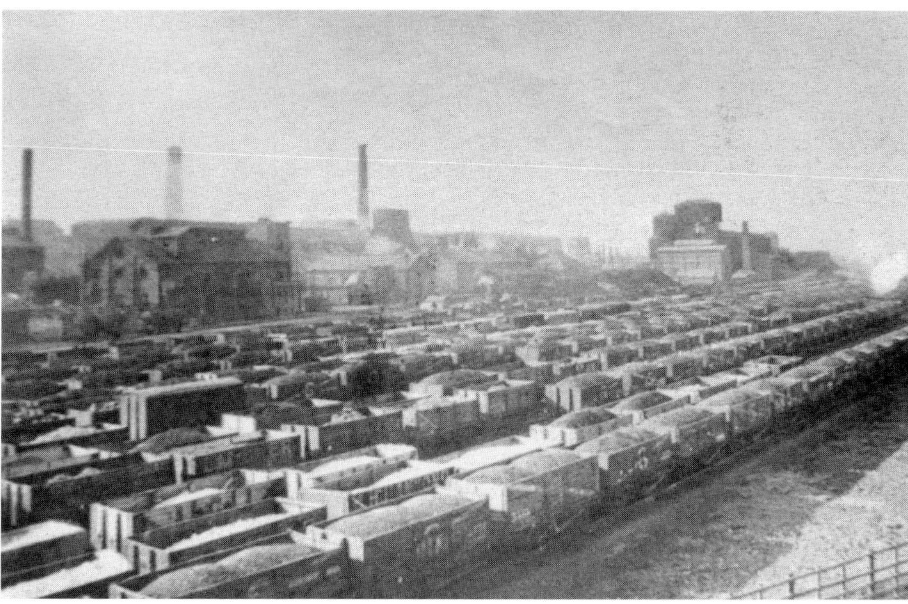

Part of the sidings at the Devonshire Works, 1949. The sidings were planned by Mr C.P. Markham to take advantage of the natural gradients so that gravity favoured the full wagons. Staveley Company at one time owned 7,000 wagons.

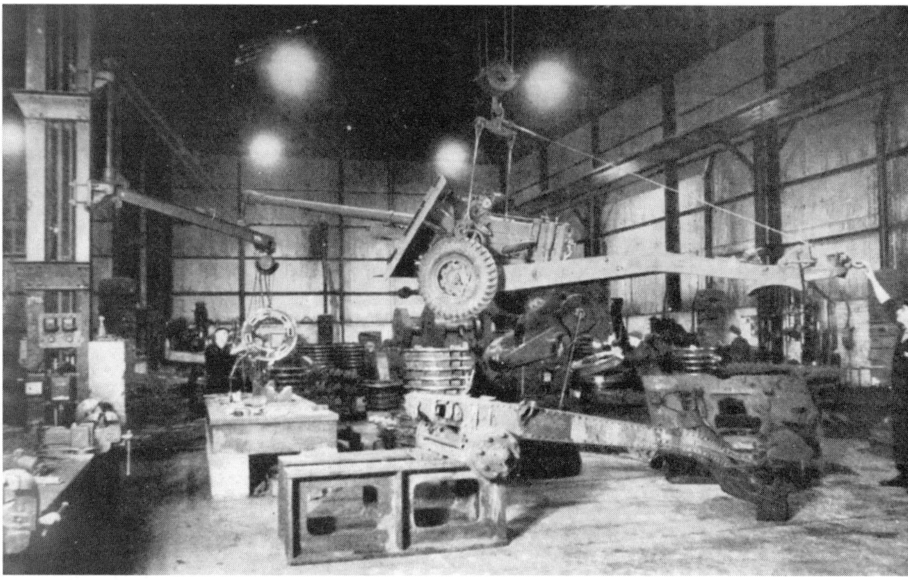

Staveley Works in wartime, 1939–45. It supposedly took fifteen men and women in factories and on transport to keep each soldier fighting at the front; these four photographs show some of Staveley's contribution. Above, a 17-pounder anti-tank gun is ready for despatch.

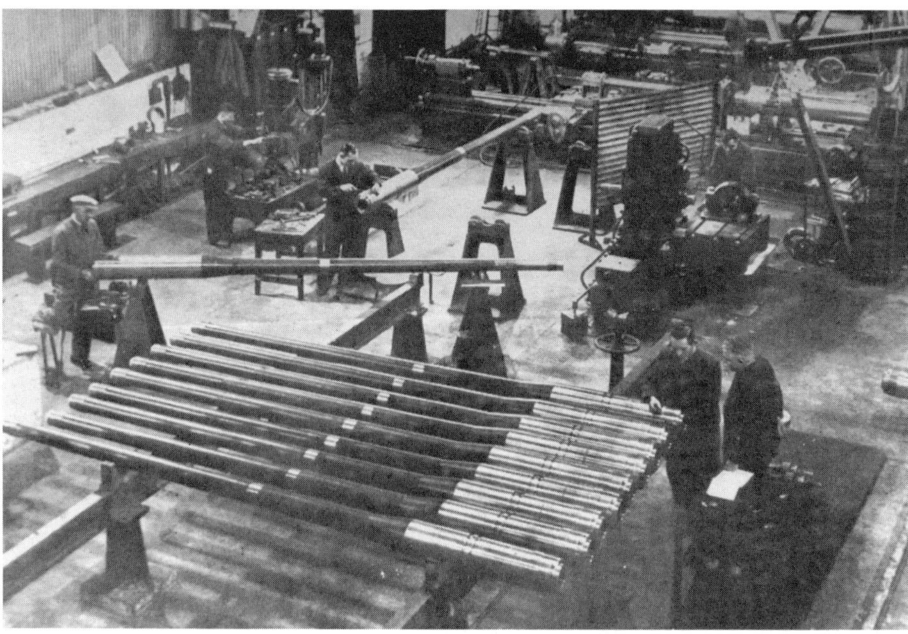

The finish and inspection of the 17-pounder gun barrels. Staveley played a leading part in the production of these anti-tank guns.

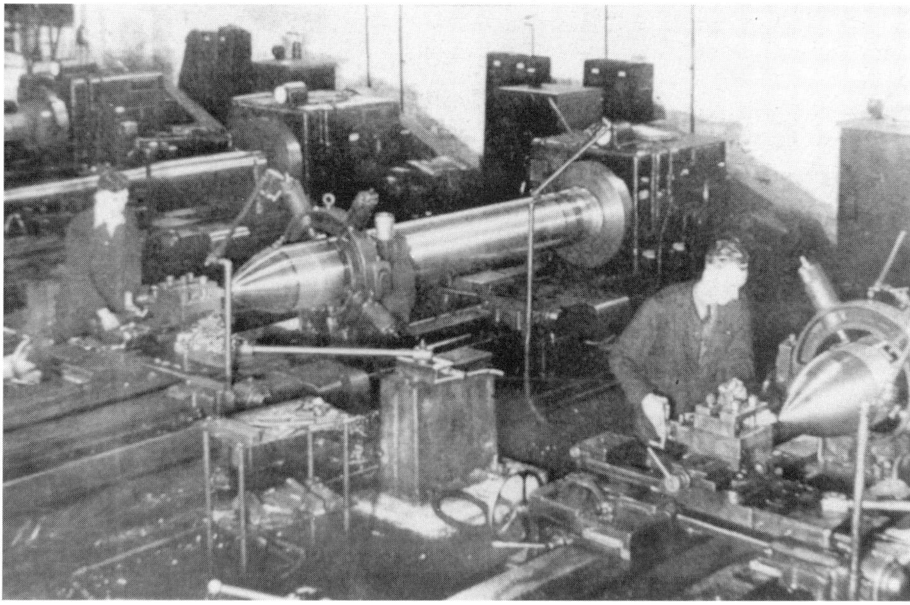

These men are making the noses of the 4,500 pound bombs. Staveley also made shells and smoke bombs in the chemical works, with the primers to fire them.

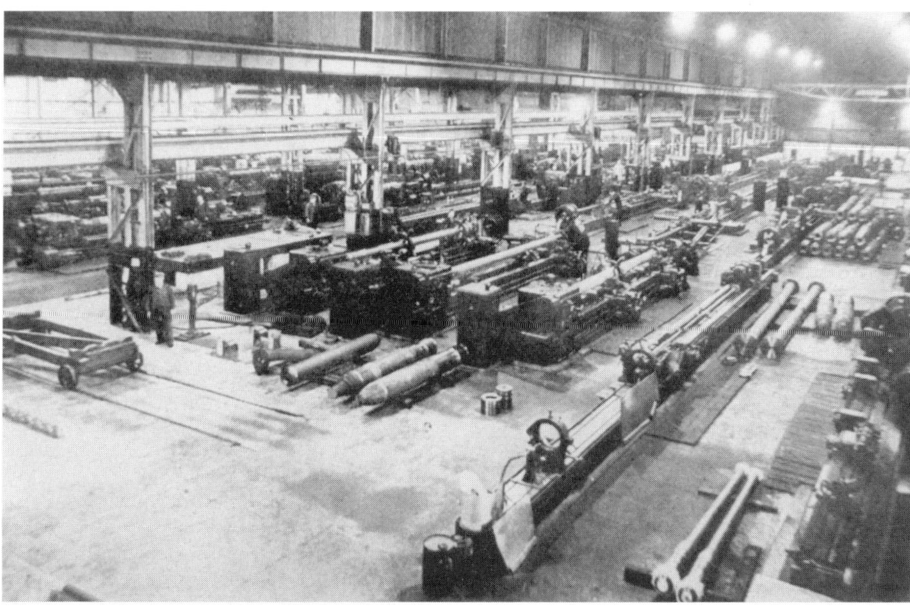

Production of the 17-pounder gun barrels, 4,500-pound bombs, and corvette and frigate shafts. A firing range was built to enable the gun carriages to be tested.

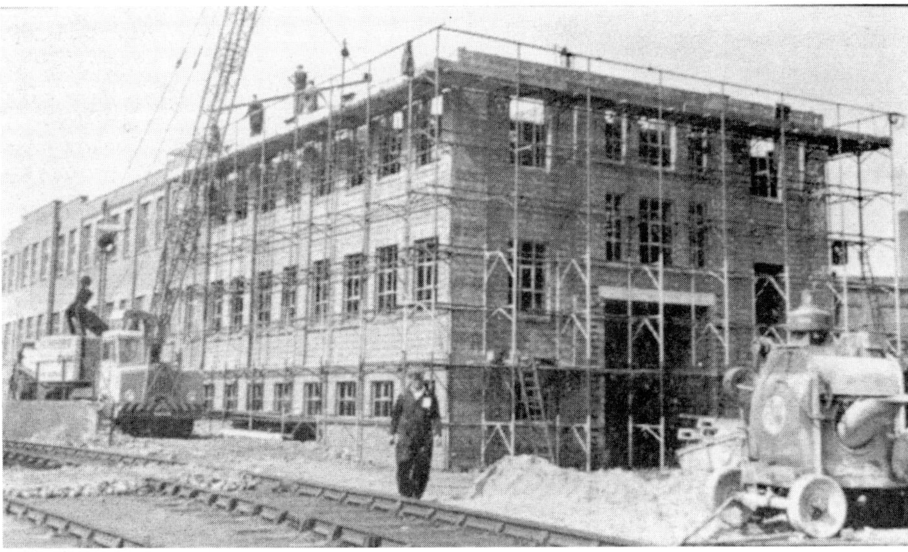

The 1958 extension to the foundry offices. With never enough room to accommodate all the business, the offices were forever expanding. This new block, completed in 1925, took the overflow from the earlier 'new' block opposite the New Works. The extension provided a home for the Research Department.

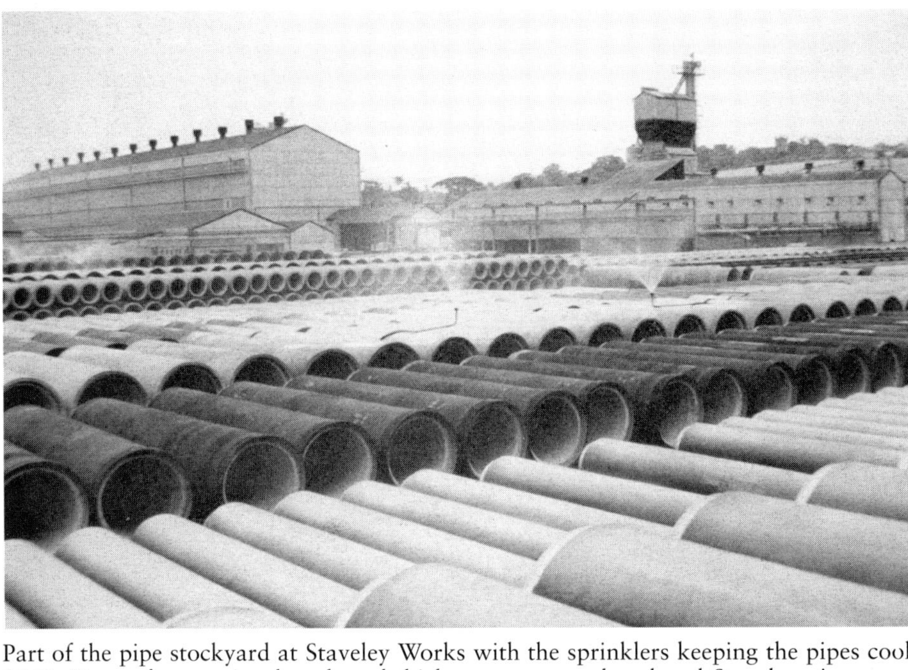

Part of the pipe stockyard at Staveley Works with the sprinklers keeping the pipes cool, 1950. Pipes of every size, length and thickness were produced and Staveley pipes were seen all over the world.

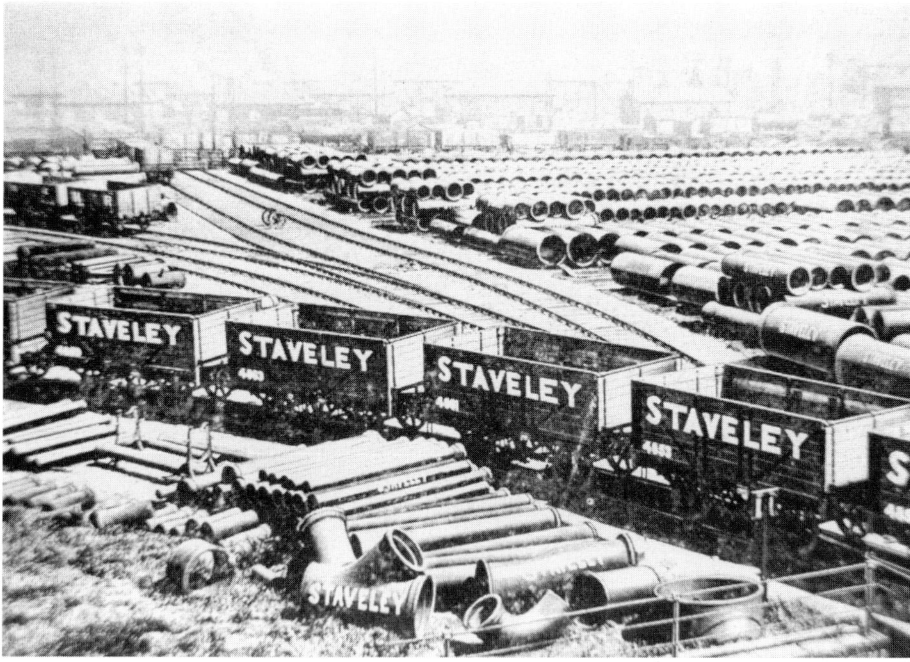

The stocking ground, 1940. This is another portion of the extensive stockyards of Staveley Company and shows the interweaving of the railway as well as the close proximity of Barrow Hill.

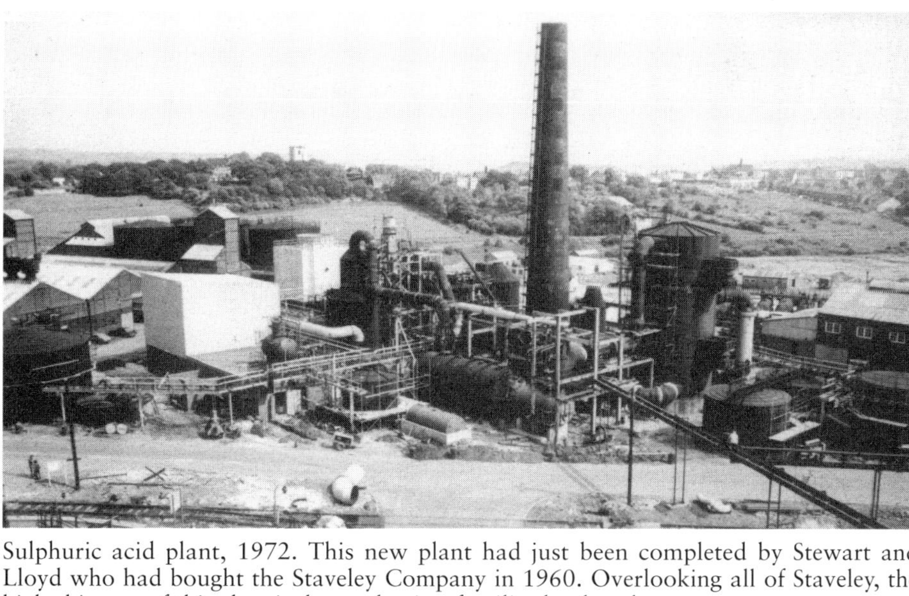

Sulphuric acid plant, 1972. This new plant had just been completed by Stewart and Lloyd who had bought the Staveley Company in 1960. Overlooking all of Staveley, the high chimney of this chemical complex is a familiar landmark.

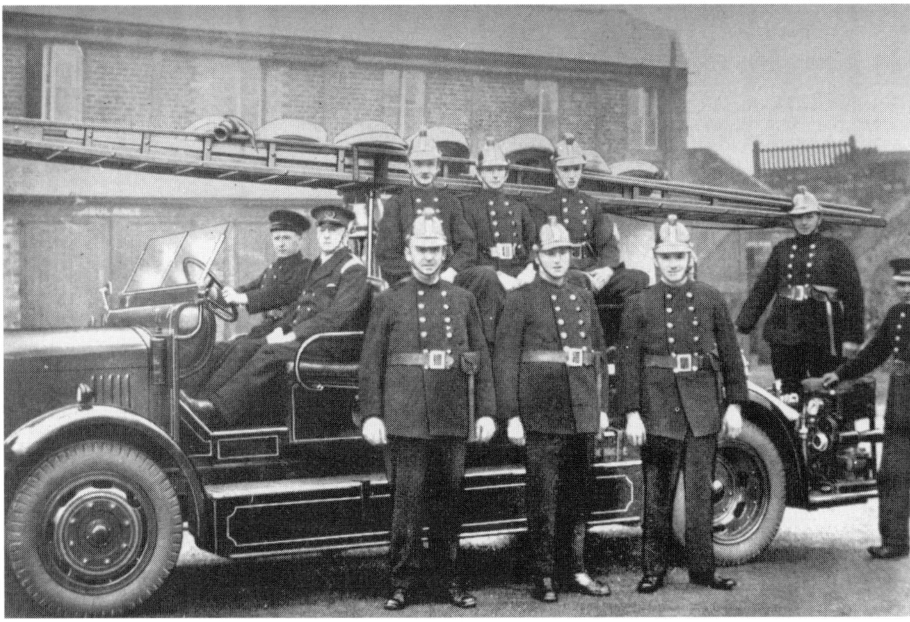

Staveley Company's own fire brigade, 1935. Being the type of industry that it was, the works had always provided their own firemen and their own fleet of ambulances and crew.

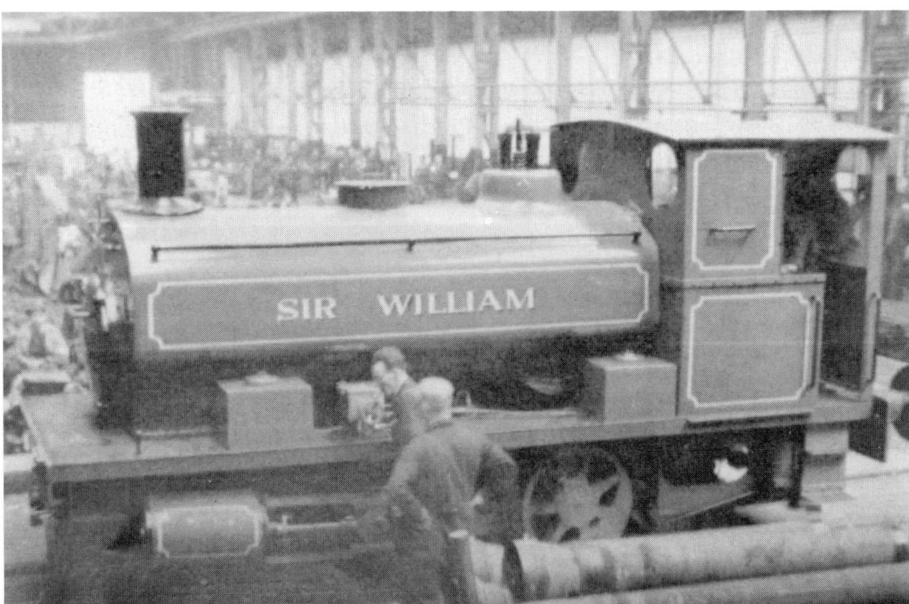

Works locomotive *Sir William* in the fitting shop for a major overhaul, 1955. *Sir William* was built at the Caledonia Works of Andrews, Barcley and Sons at Kilmarnock in 1930.

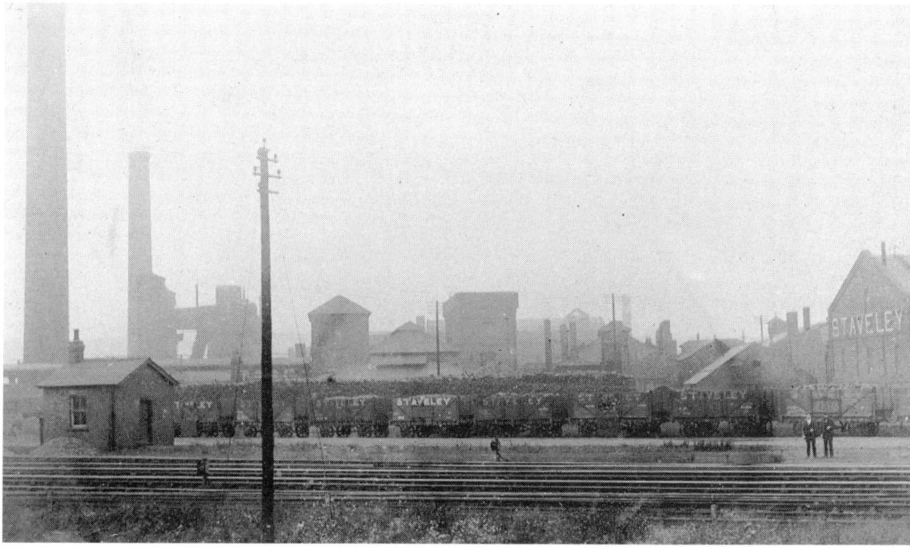

Staveley Works, 1913. Described as the largest chemical works and blast furnace complex in the country the works was self-contained, owning collieries and brick-works, generating its own electricity, using water from the River Rother, and even possessing a wagon building and repair shop.

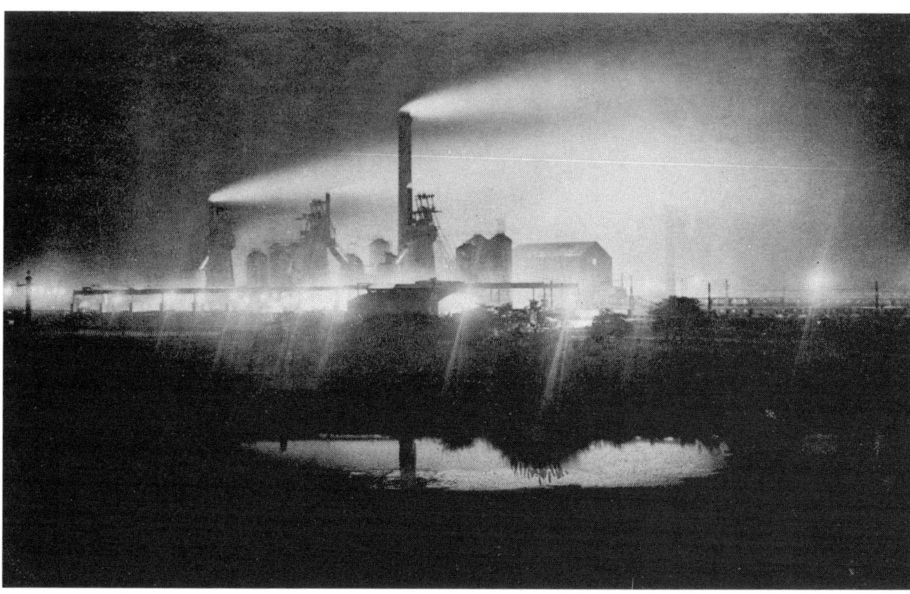

Devonshire Works, 1914. At 9 o'clock at night the open-topped furnaces light up the sky over Staveley. In Staveley a red sky at night meant that the molten waste slag was being tipped on the spoil heaps.

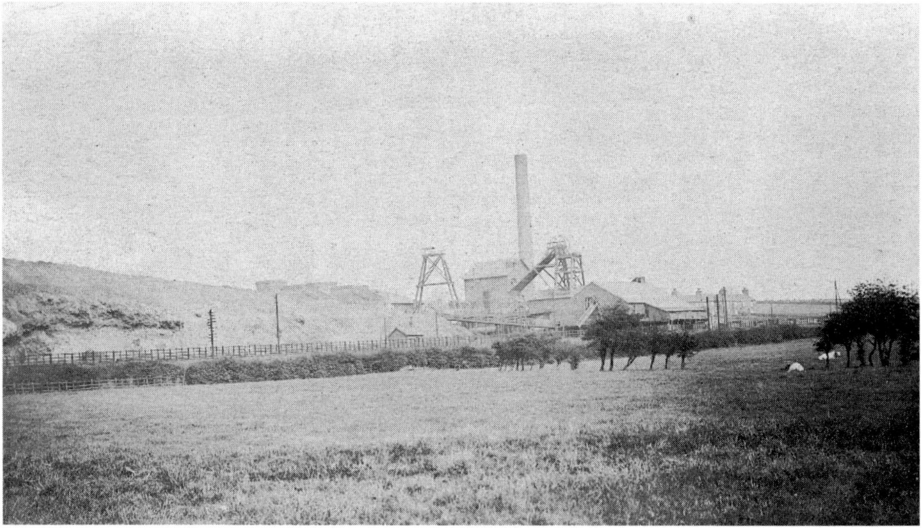

Hartington Colliery, 1905. Standing to the north of Staveley centre, by the side of the Chesterfield Canal, this was one of the collieries owned by the Staveley Coal & Iron Company. Sunk in 1858, the Hartington pit at 218 yards was the deepest in the area.

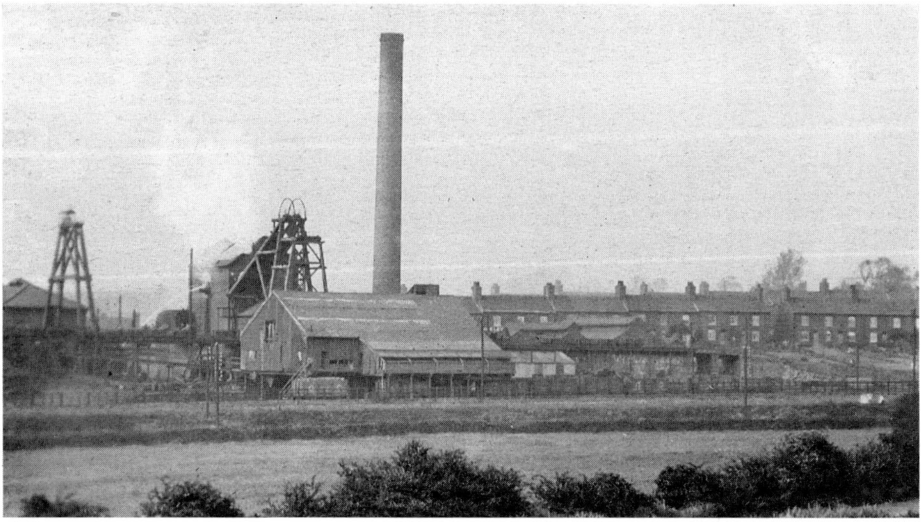

Fire at Hartington Colliery, 1907. The smoke from the underground fire can just be seen to the left of the winding shaft. Hartington Cottages, their gardens running down to the railway line, stretch right to the Eckington Road. The hedges in the foreground line the canal path.

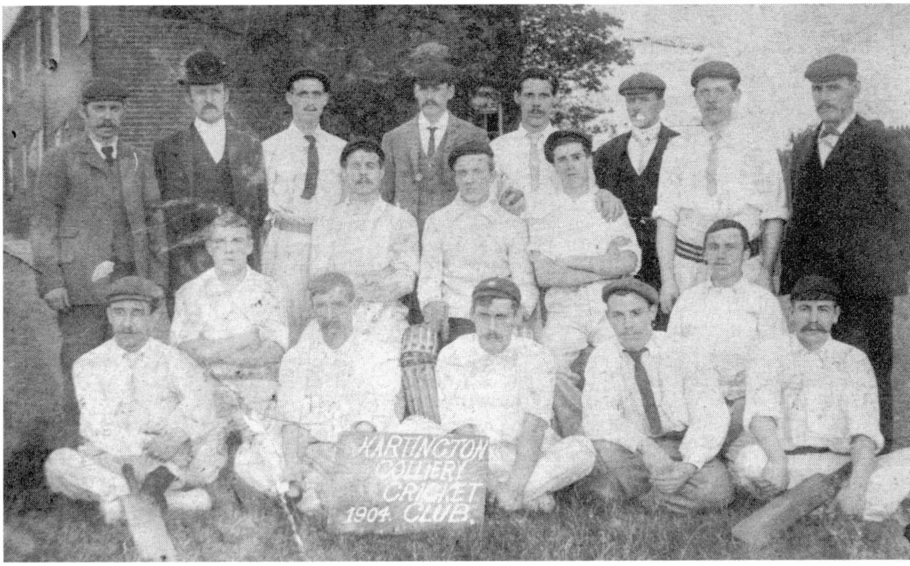

Hartington Colliery Cricket Club, 1904. Back row, left to right: W. Townsend, Ed Davies, F. Johnson, Wm Rudd, A.E. Onions, J. Goring, T. Hill, G. Horner. Middle row: A. Goodwin, Ray Townsend, Joe Lowe, A. Thrall, Edgar Bull. Front row: H. Watson, Sam Turner, F. Onions, F. Williams, Geo. Cowlishaw.

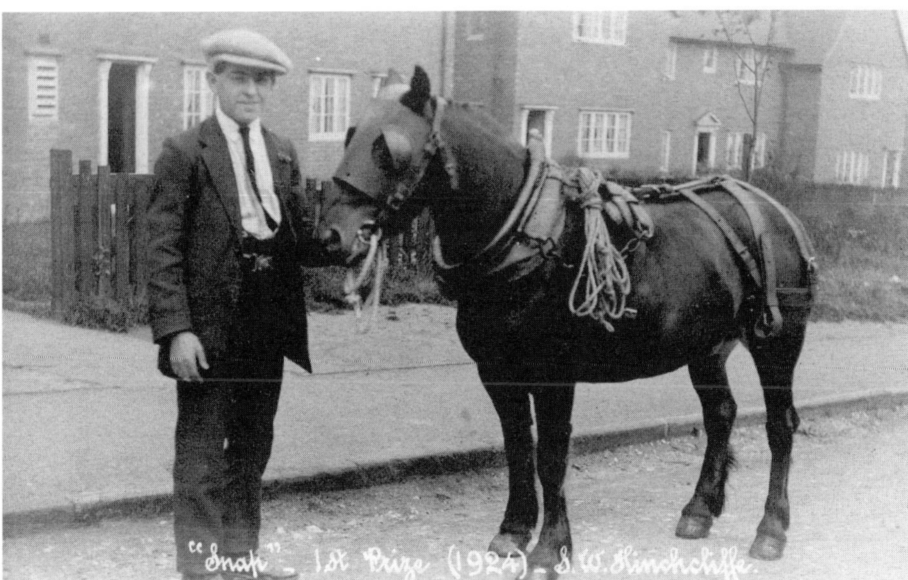

Mr Hinchcliffe with Snap, a first-prize winner, 1924. The pit ponies played an important part in the colliery, having their own whitewashed standing area, a horse-keeper and daily checks by a farrier. In summer a few of the ponies would be shown around the local and national shows, winning many cups and rosettes.

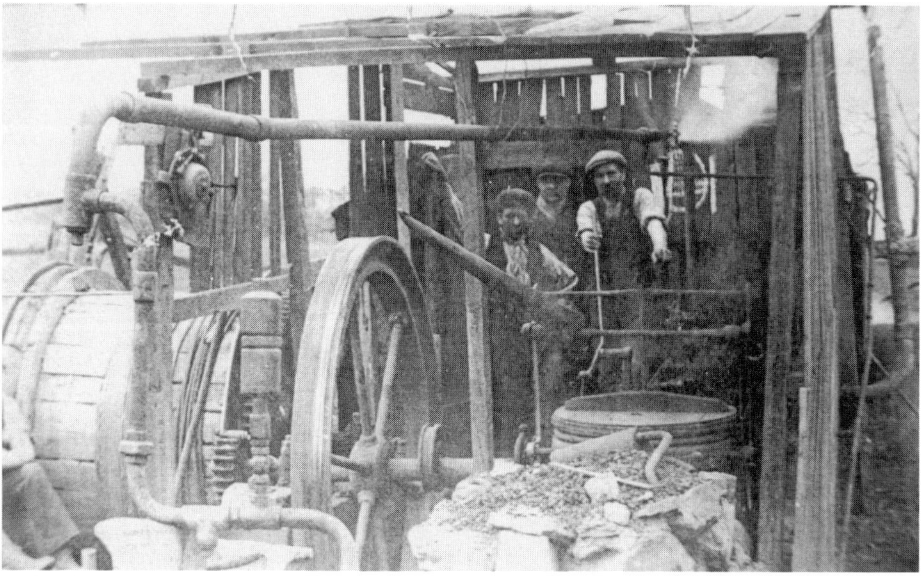

The men at the Woodthorpe Footrill, 1902. Sited just off the Norbriggs Road this small colliery was known as 'Wangem Main' or Wagon Main. These workers – Arthur, Ernest, John and Frank – are all from the Lowton family.

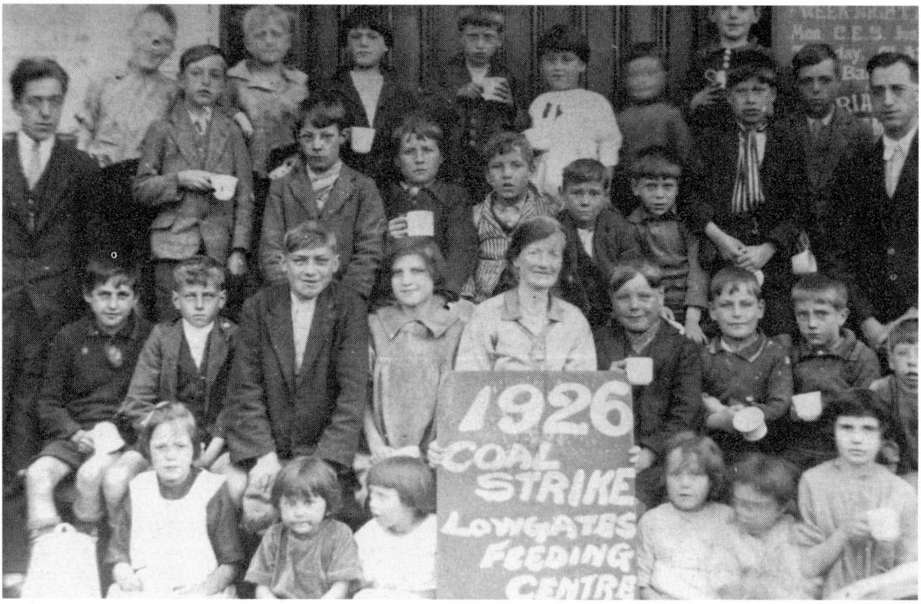

Lowgates Feeding Centre, 1926. Miss Brodie, one of the Lowgates Chapel stalwarts, poses with some of the visitors to the feeding centre during the miners' strike. As in the 1912 strike families suffered terribly trying to feed themselves with no money coming in. Soup kitchens, quite often the last resort, were a life-saver.

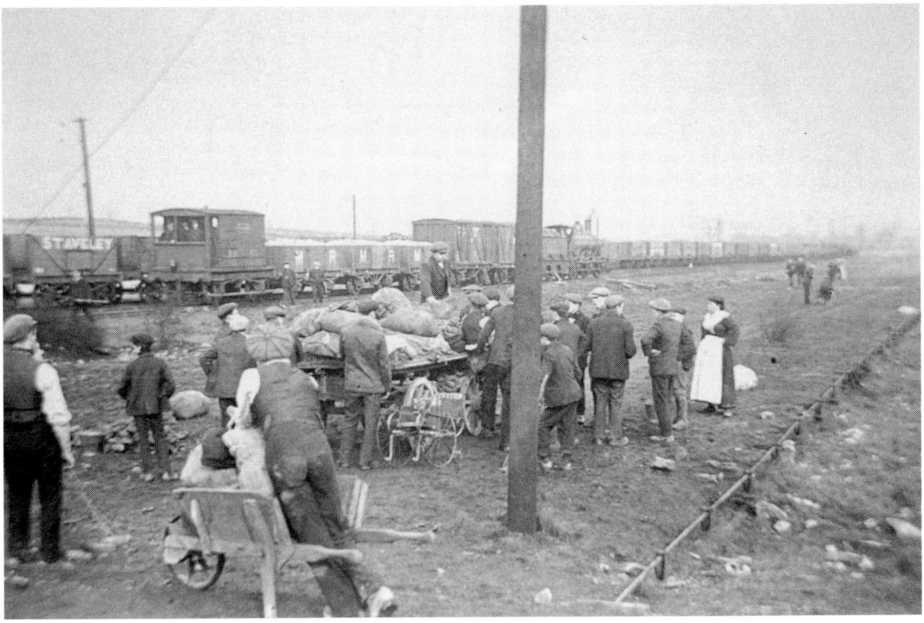

The 1926 coal strike. In an effort to keep the home fires burning, the miners' families struggle with bags and barrows after picking up the pieces of coal that have dropped off the coal trains at Poolsbrook.

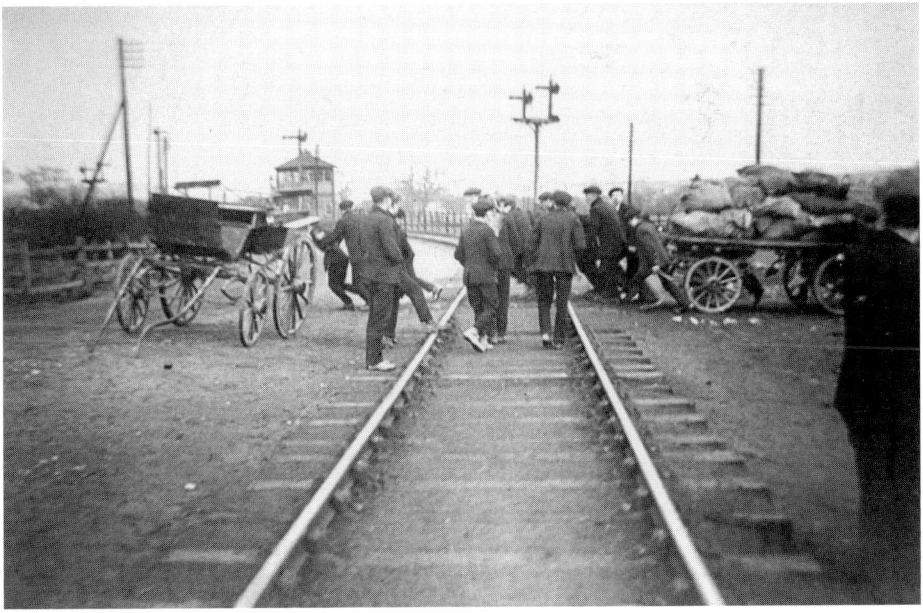

The men join forces to pull a loaded cart full of coal bags over the railway lines at Poolsbrook.

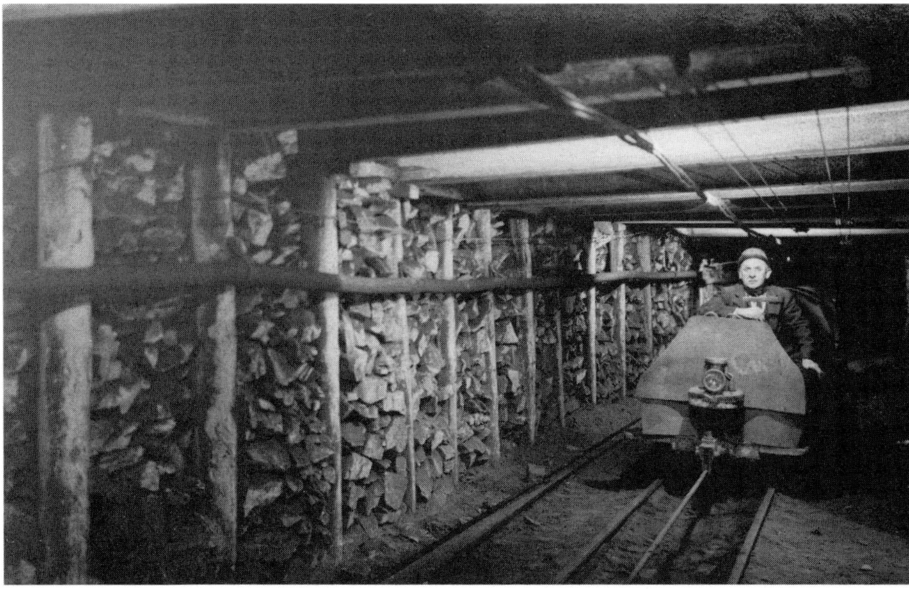

Tommy Liversidge drives the paddy train underground at Ireland Colliery, 1940. The well-supported roof and walls are evidence of improved conditions since the early days of mining, when hands and picks were used and children carried coal to the surface.

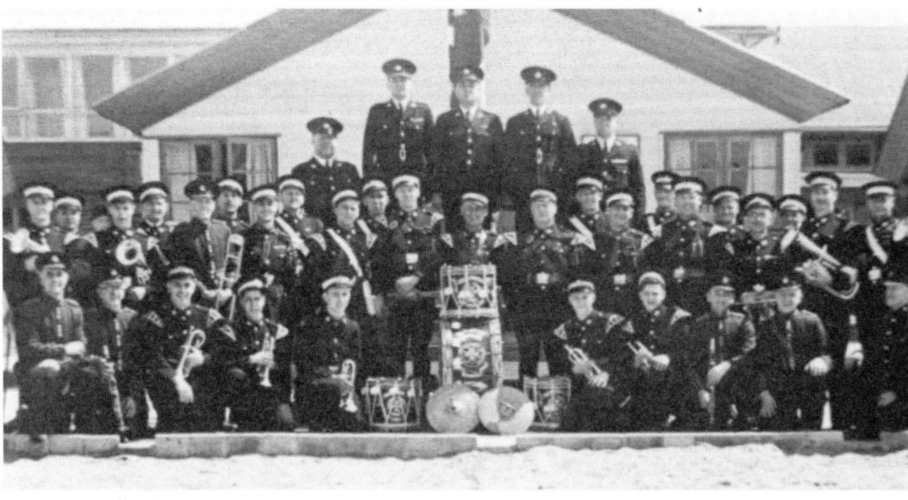

Ireland Colliery St John Ambulance Brigade, 1949. Ireland Colliery has had a SJA division since its official sanction in 1911. This photograph was taken at the Skegness Miners' Holiday Centre camp. Before the war the annual camp was always under canvas.

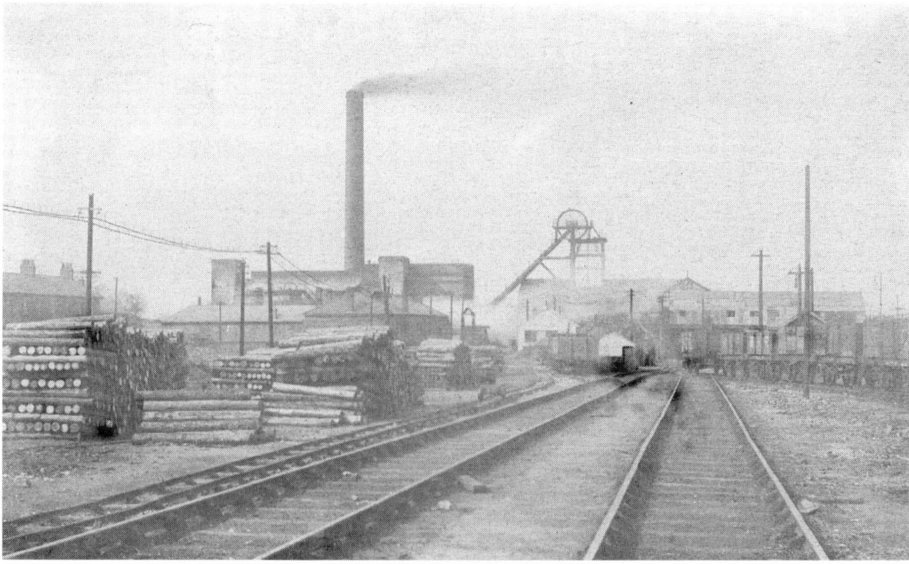

Looking down the rails into the pit yard of Markham Colliery, 1918. The houses showing above the wood stack are where the main road runs through the colliery. Markham, like Ireland, was demolished.

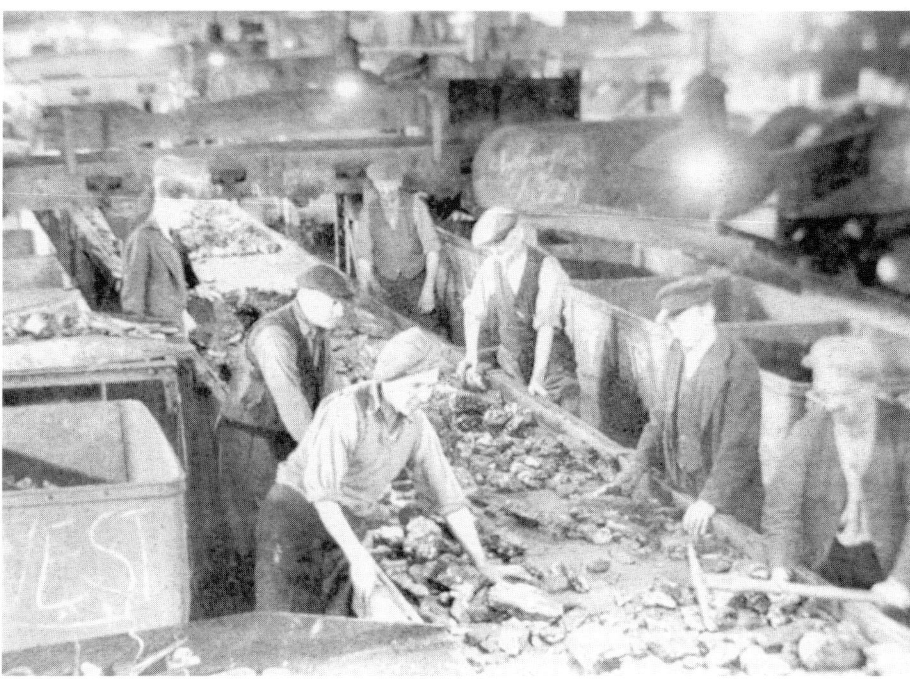

Markham Colliery, 1949. These men are picking out by hand the waste and rubbish on the No. 1 screens.

In Loving Memory

of the Miners who lost their lives in the terrible Pit Explosion, at the Markham Colliery, Chesterfield, Derbyshire, Tuesday, May 10th, 1938

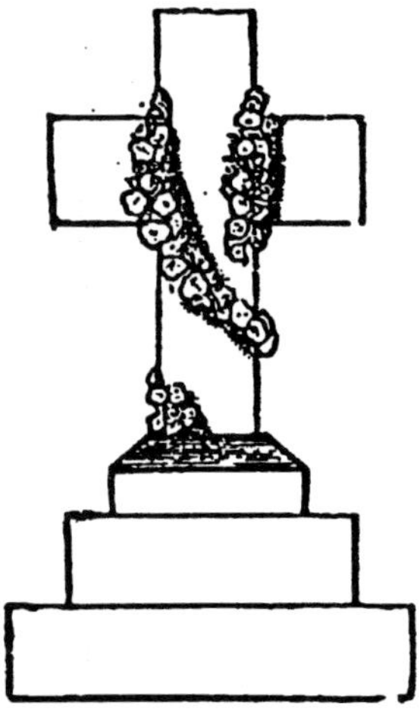

In health and strength they left their homes,
Not thinking death so near;
It pleased the Lord to bid them come
And in His sight appear.

Death to them short warning gave,
Therefore be careful how you live;
Prepare in time, make no delay,
For who may know their dying day.

In prime of years they were cut down,
No longer could they stay;
Because it was their Saviour's will
To call them hence away.

'Tis hard to part with those we love,
Tho' parting days will come;
Yet let us hope to meet above,
For this is not our home.

There is no Death! what seems so is transition;
This life of mortal breath
Is but a suburb of the life elysian,
Whose portals we call death —*Longfellow.*

The memorial leaflet for the 1938 Markham disaster in which seventy-five men died and thirty-eight were injured. The explosion at the coal-face at the end of the night shift caught 160 men in the pit unawares while preparing to leave.

H. ALBERRY,
J. ALLEN,
L. ATKIN,
J. T. BROWN,
H. BRADFORD,
G. BUCKLEY,
H. BROUGH,
W. BLUER,
A BELL,
C. BOWN,
A. BRAY,
S. BRAY,
D. BANN,
W. COMMONS,
G. COWLEY,
Ar. CARTER,
T. DAVISON,
A. FURNISS,
W. FROST,
B. GREGORY,
R. GREGSON,
J. GEARY,
A. GARLAND,
A. GRAINGER,
T. GRAINGER,
R. E. GRAINGER,
L. HARGREAVES,
H. HARGREAVES,
H HARGREAVES, Junr.
J. HADLEY,
W. HAYWOOD,
H. HUDSON,
J. HARDY,
C. HILL,
A. HENSON,
J. HIBBARD,
G. H. JACKSON,
L. JACKLIN,
E. JONES,
T. JONES,

F. JONES,
S. KERRY,
R. KIRK,
A. KELLER,
J. LILLEY,
F. LINATHAN,
W. LAMB,
S. LODGE,
H. LAVENDER,
W. LIEVESLEY,
F. MONKS,
J. McCONNON,
A. MAY,
C. G. PEMBERTON,
G. PETHER,
C. PALMER,
W. PICKERING,
J ROWLANDS,
M. RICHARDS.
A. RODGERS,
A. ROPER,
F. SMITH,
R. SIMMS.
C. SILCOCK,
W. SHERWIN,
E. SALT,
H. TAYLOR,
F. TAYLOR,
D. WHELPDALE,
G. WHITLEY,
M. WILLIAMS,
H. WALE,
R. WHITEHEAD,
W. WATSON,
R. WOOD.
W. WELPTON,
T. G. YATES.
B. WALLACE,

A BROWN, died in Hospital

The names of the men killed in 'The Worst Disaster in the History of the Derbyshire Coalfield'. Truly the price of coal.

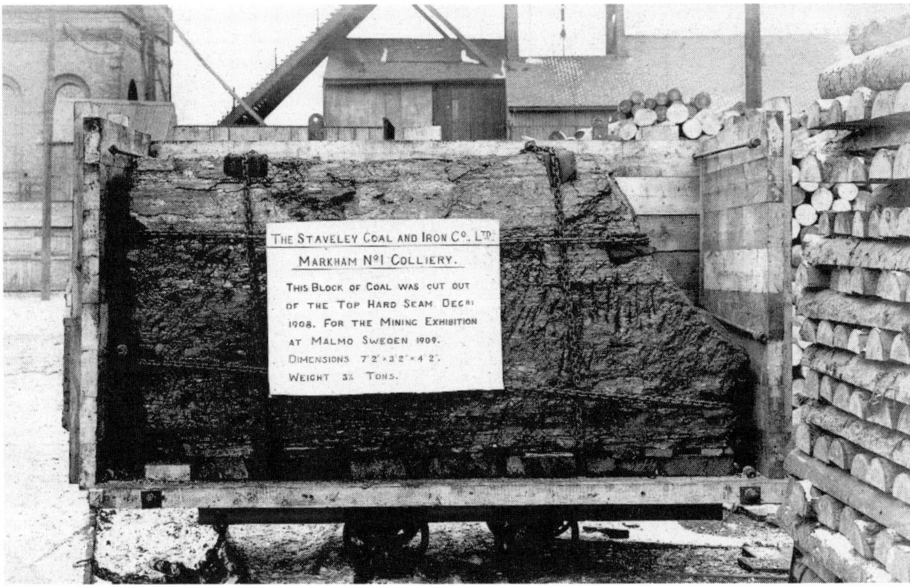

The 3½-ton block of coal cut out at Markham for an exhibition in Sweden, 1908. These large blocks of coal were quite a feature of many exhibitions. Ireland Colliery also sent a 3-ton block to the British Empire Exhibition at Wembley in 1924, the second piece; the first one broke while being taken out.

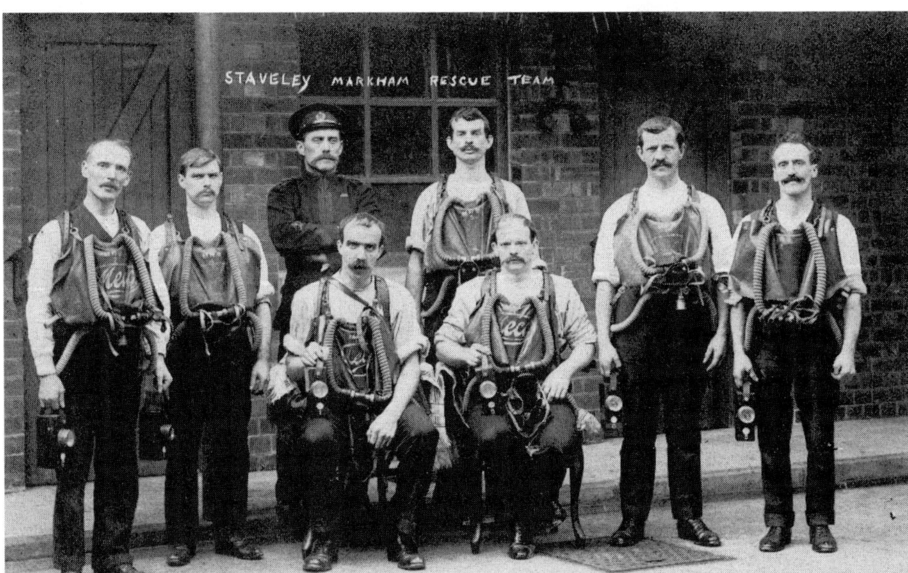

The brave men of the Markham Colliery Mines Rescue Team, 1908. Indispensable in any emergency, they were always the first on the scene with their expertise.

SECTION SEVEN

Barrow Hill and Poolsbrook

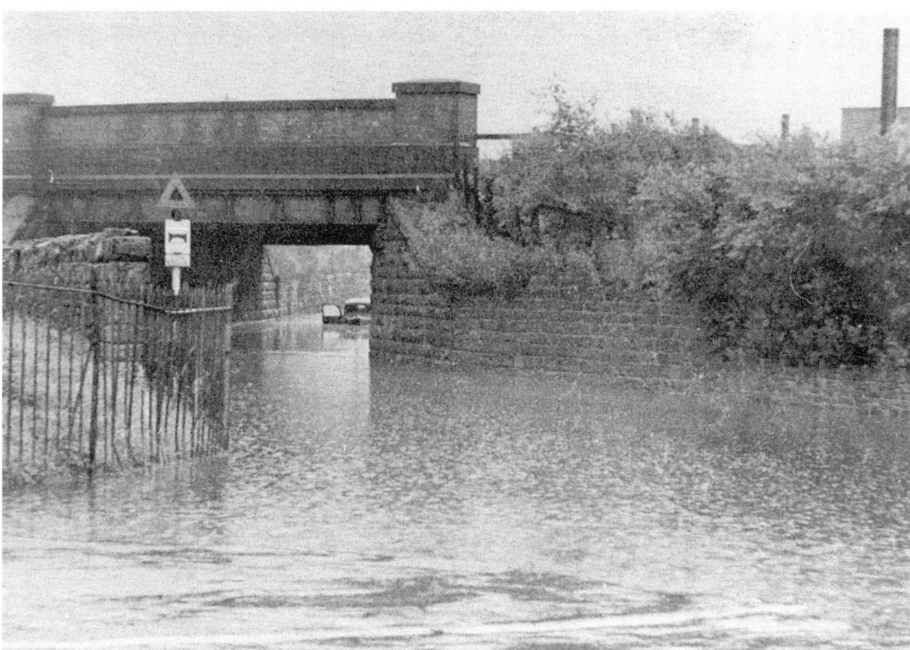

The flooded road to Barrow Hill, 1940. The car has just left Barrow Hill on the way to Hollingwood. The floods were a regular occurrence, making the road impassable and spreading out into the works yards of the Staveley Company.

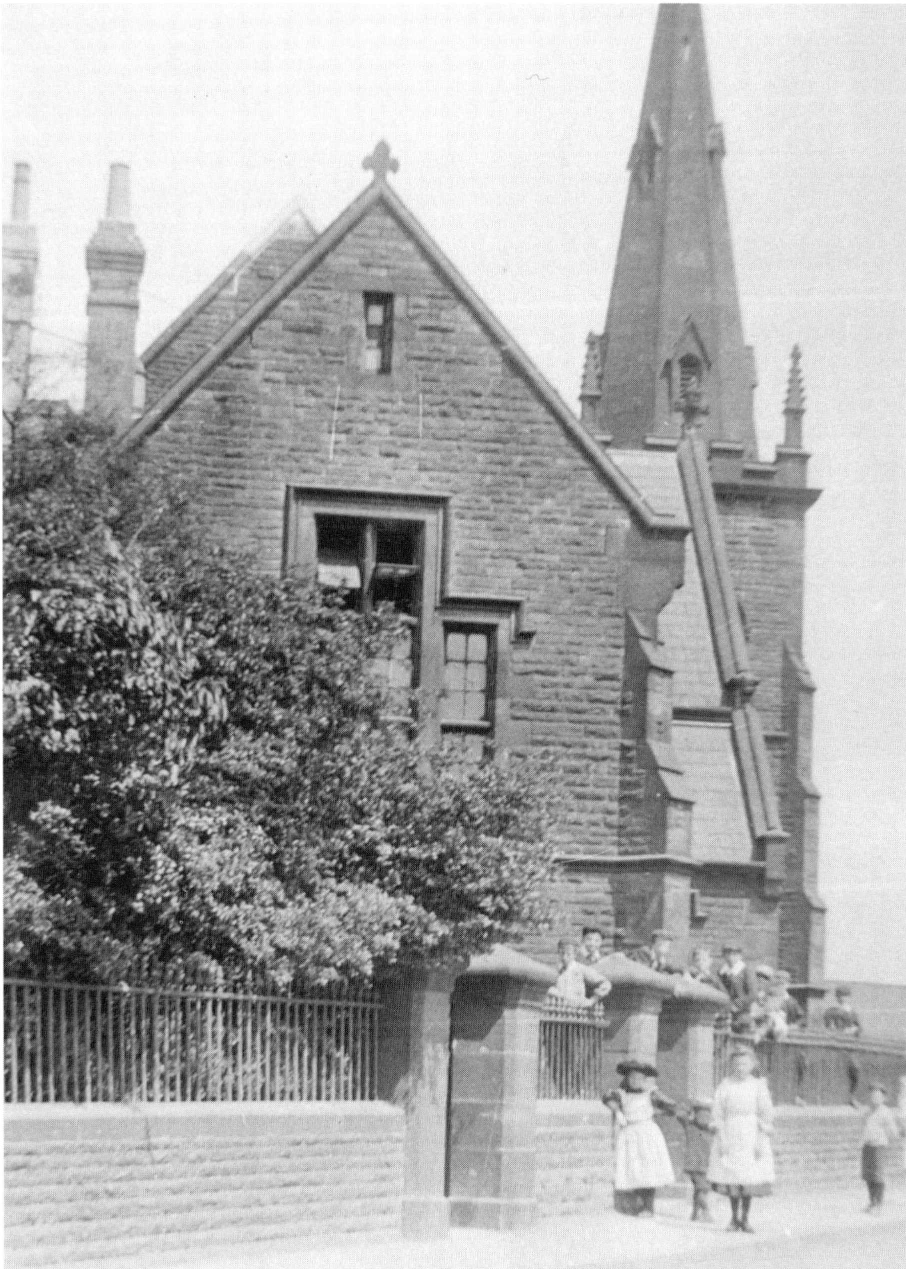

Barrow Hill School, 1912. The school, which was built in 1856 by Mr Richard Barrow for the children of Barrow Hill, stands in a prominent position at the top of Station Road. When new, the school was presented with an organ costing £200 and a full-length portrait of its benefactor.

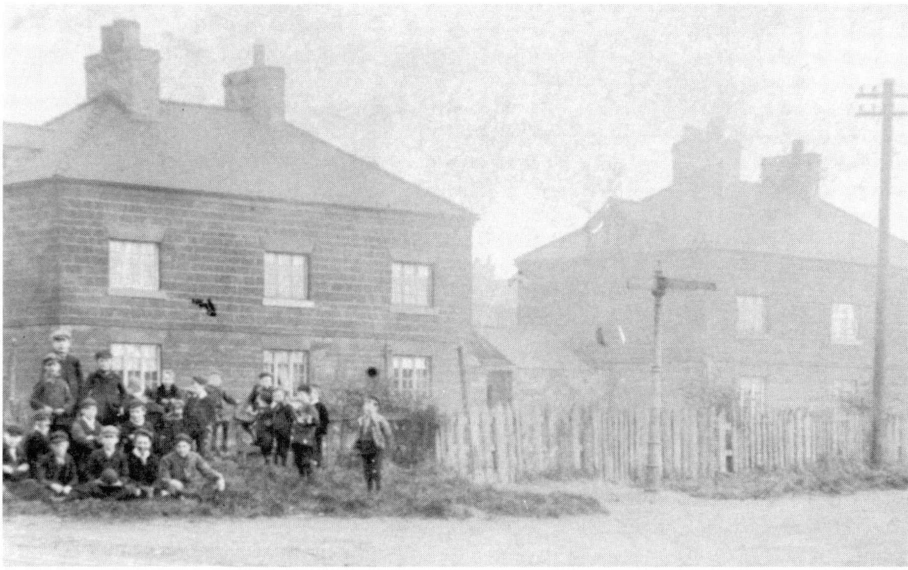

Barrow Hill crossroads, 1918. The boys are gathered at the junction of Station Road and Staveley Road, posing for the photographer in suits and caps and clutching their football.

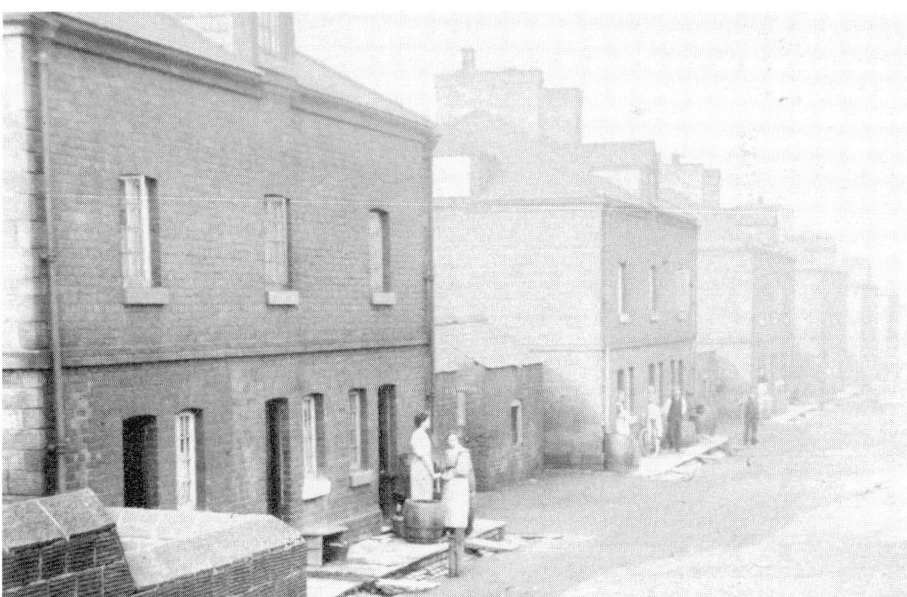

Barrow Hill blocks, 1918. Richard Barrow built 200 houses in blocks of three for his workers at Staveley Works, all with water laid on, a facility the ladies with the washtub had probably been making use of. Almost all Barrow Hill has been replaced now with more modern housing.

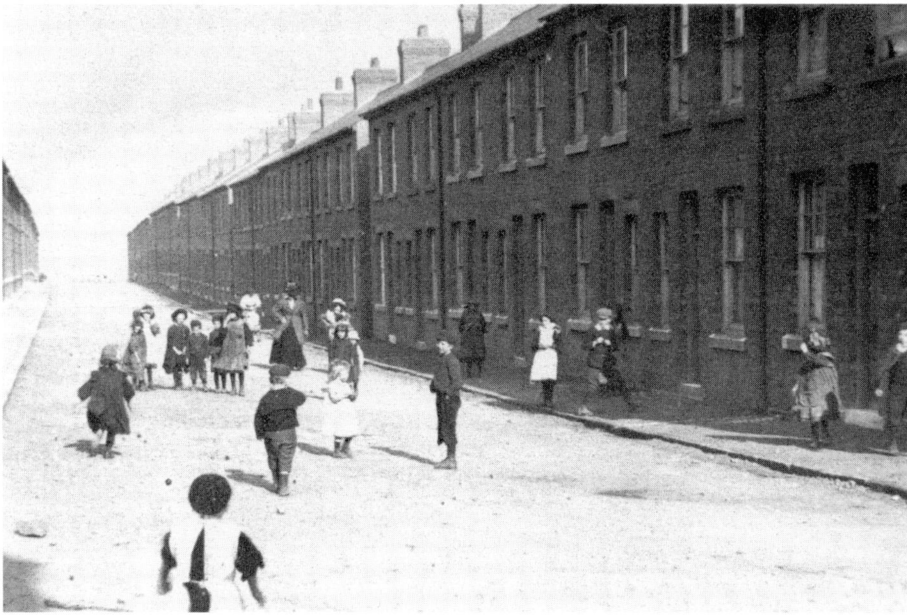

Devonshire Cottages, Barrow Hill, 1918. The children are playing in front of the only houses not owned by Richard Barrow. These railway-owned rows were built on the site of a planting of trees. After a short occupation some tenants had to move out because the roots had begun to grow again and push up the floors.

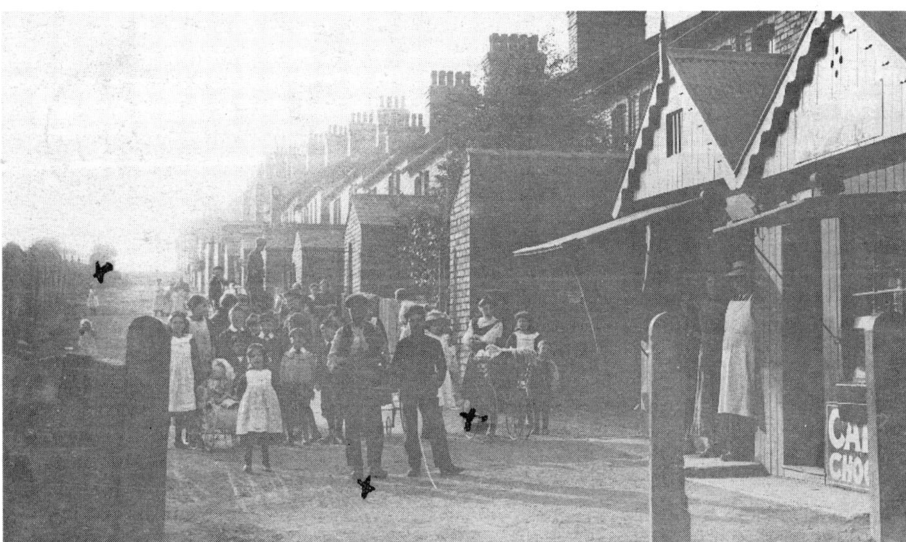

Barrow Hill, 1908. The residents of Traffic Terrace are standing at the bottom of the row. The houses are still there today, but the butcher's and confectioner's shops have gone.

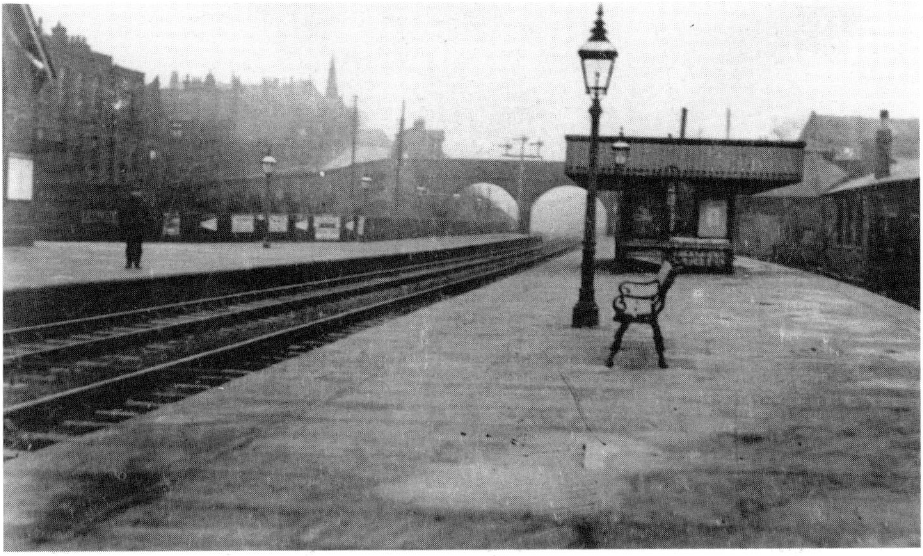

Barrow Hill station, 1910. This photograph clearly shows the position of the station on the main road through Barrow Hill, with the spire of Richard Barrow's school on the skyline. The bridge led over the rails to the Methodist chapel and Devonshire Cottages.

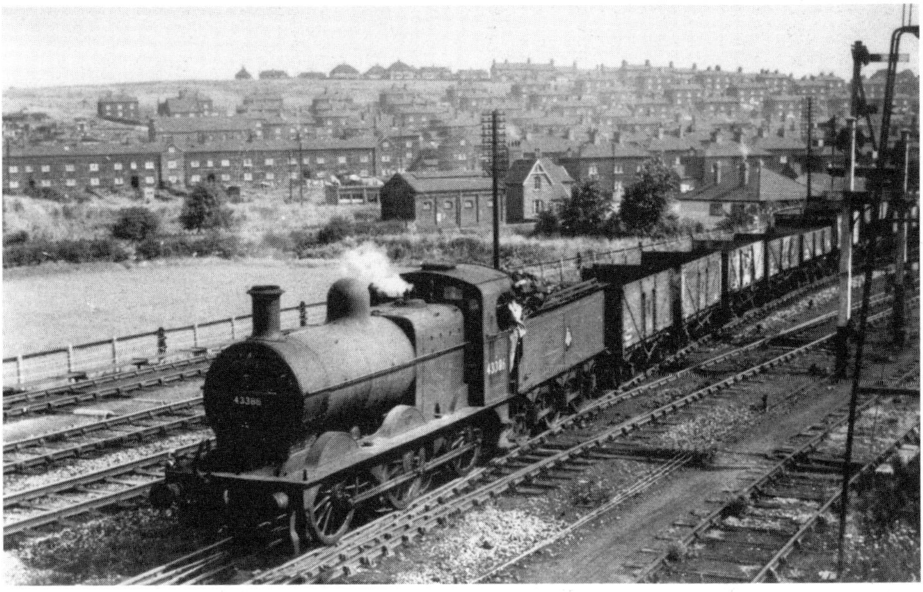

A coal train on the Sheffield to Chesterfield LMS line, 1960. The Staveley Company's houses are on the hillside with the chapel on Campbell Drive just visible over the left-hand cottages. It was known as the 'sheds' chapel because of its closeness to the engine sheds.

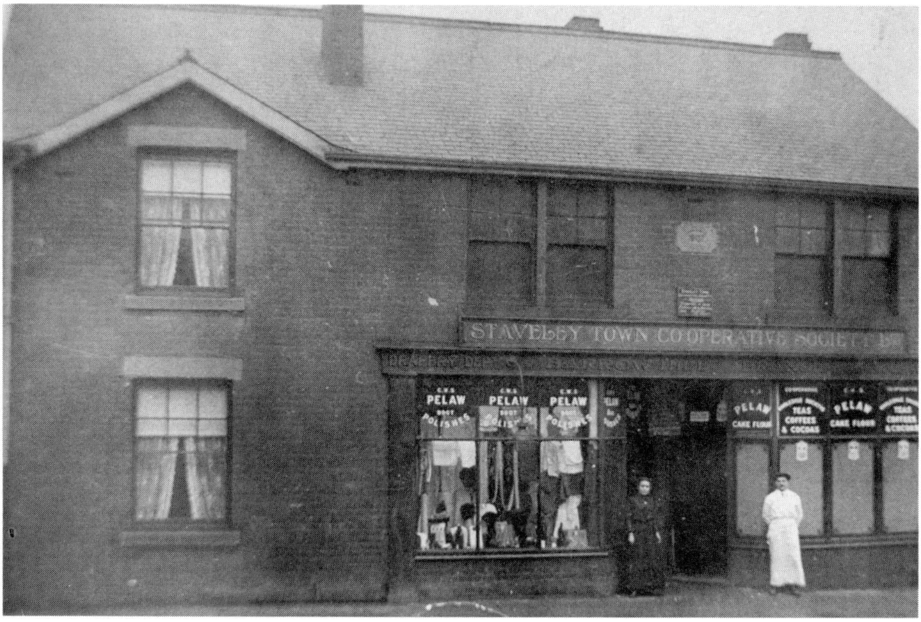

Staveley Town Co-operative, Barrow Hill branch, 1907. The manager, Mr W. McCabe, stands outside the recently opened shop. The co-operative shops always sold a wide variety of goods from the one large room, all from different counters.

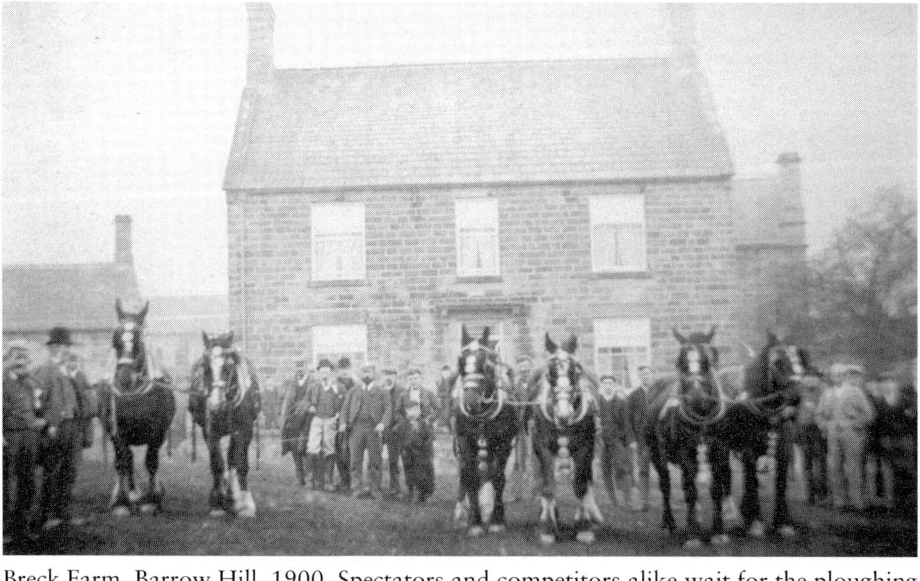

Breck Farm, Barrow Hill, 1900. Spectators and competitors alike wait for the ploughing match to start at George Smith's farm on Wildgoose Lane. Leading down from the Hall Lane crossroads, past the Breck and White Lodge farms and into Foxon Wood, the lane then continues into Eckington.

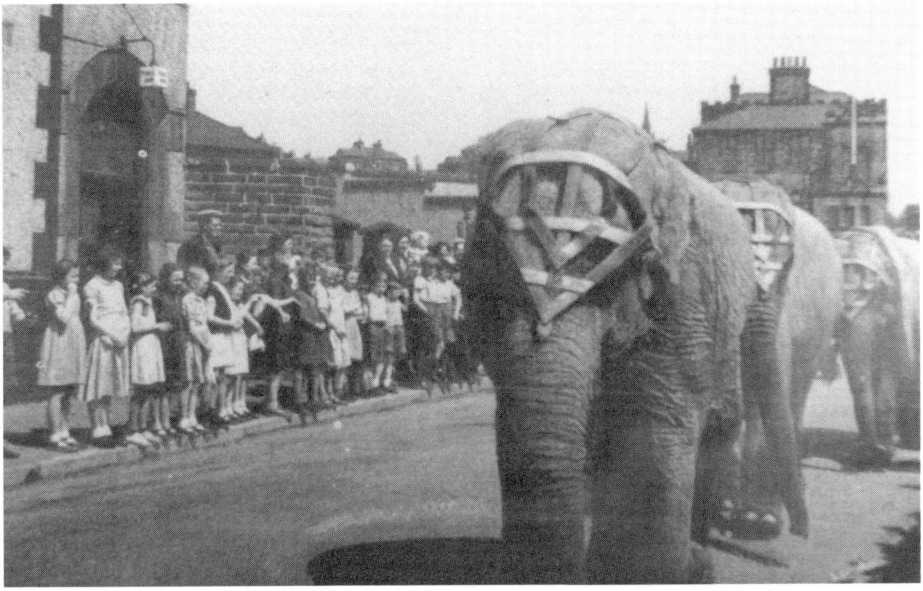

Chipperfield's Circus comes to Barrow Hill, 1954. The children are gathered outside the station to watch the elephants disembark. It was quite usual to transport the animals by rail and provided good advertising as they marched through the town.

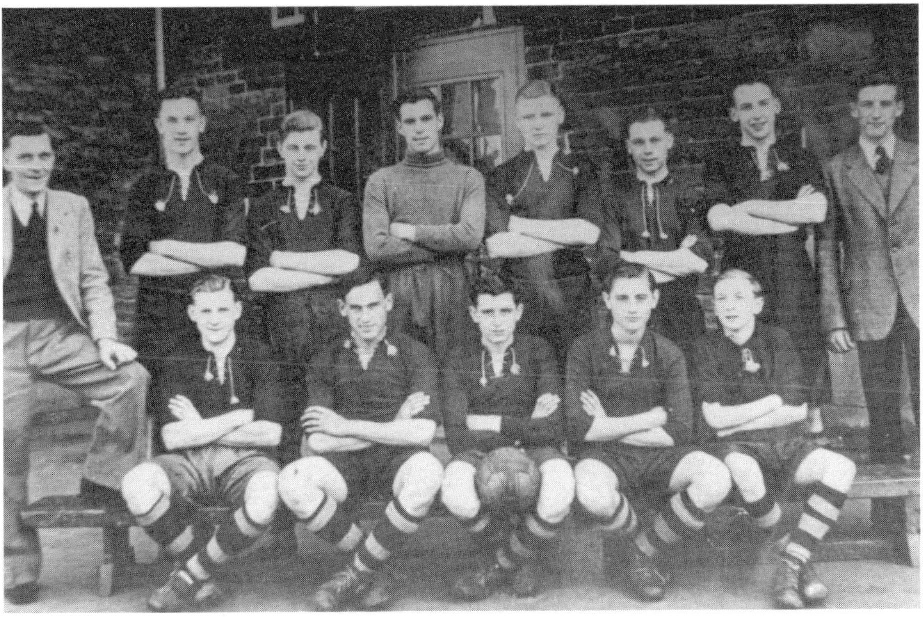

Barrow Hill Youth Club Football Team, 1950. Standing, left to right: Wilf Cooper, Alan Jukes, Colin Shaw, Wilf Day, Jock Oxley, Archie Renshaw, Dennis Clark, Will Sutherland. Seated: Eric 'Fudge' Fuller, Tommy Adams, Roy Thacker, Horace Bird, -?-.

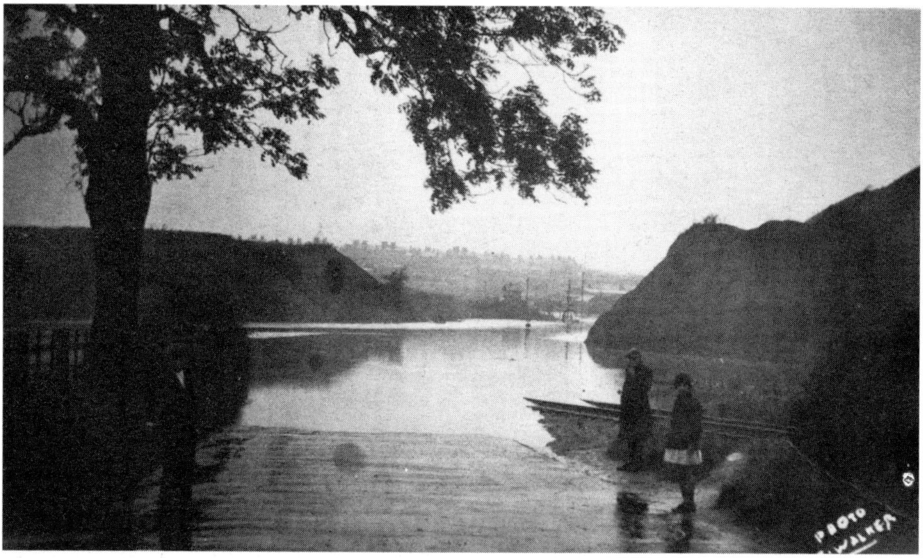

The road to Poolsbrook, 1931. Staveley is unattainable in the distance as the road between the two Ireland Colliery tips floods once again. The road frequently became impassable because of the overflow from the Pools brook.

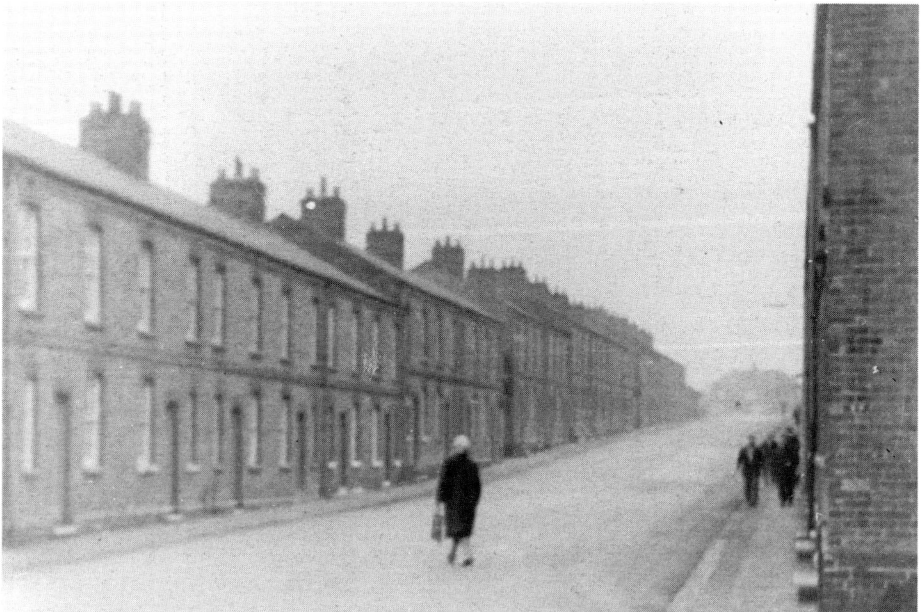

Poolsbrook, 1930. These parallel rows of cottages, with a school, were built by the Staveley Company in 1892 for the workers of the nearby collieries. There were six rows in total, with outhouses in between each two rows.

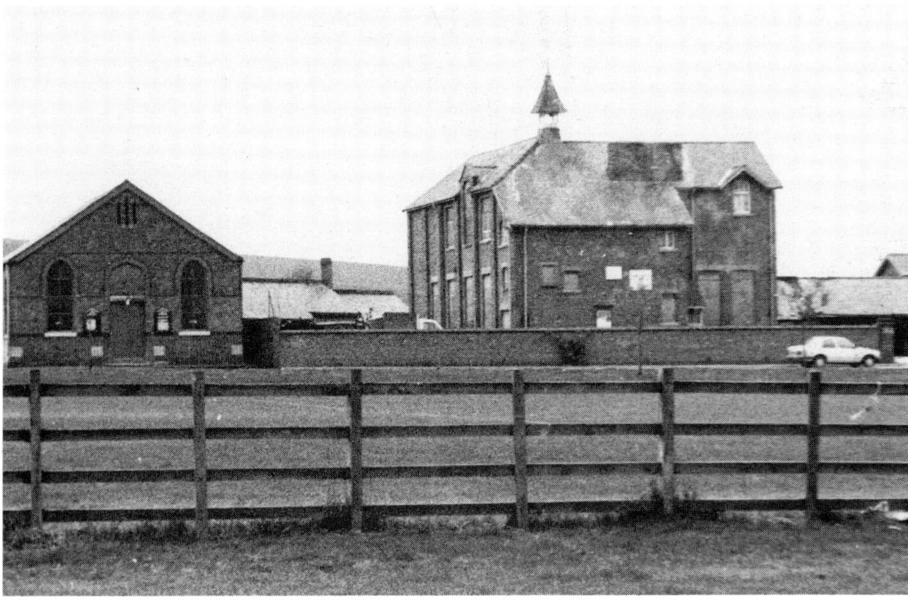

The Junior School at Poolsbrook, 1960s. Built to the back of the rows, with the Methodist chapel on the left, the school has now been replaced by a new open-plan school to serve the community.

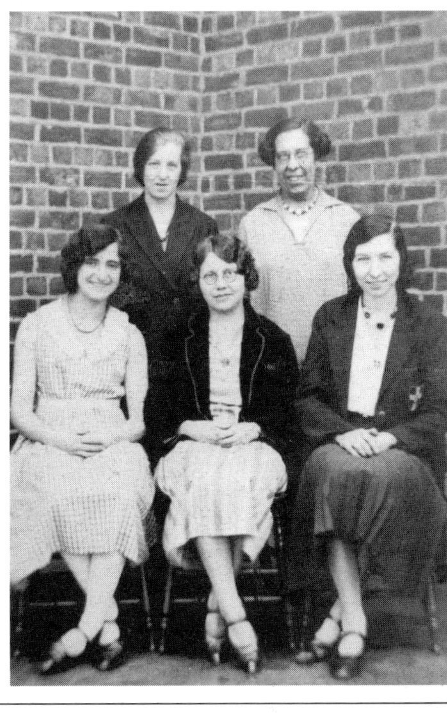

The ladies of Poolsbrook Infant School, 1926. Standing: Miss Webley (left), Mrs Andrews. Seated: Mrs Freeman, Miss Cable (headmistress) and Miss Broadhead.

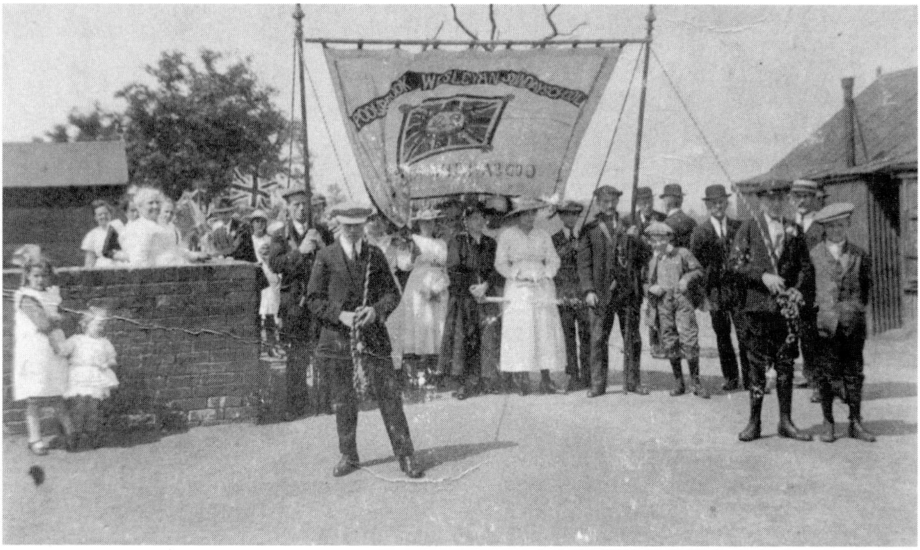

Poolsbrook Wesleyan Sunday School elders, with their banner, preparing to take part in their annual parade, 1908.

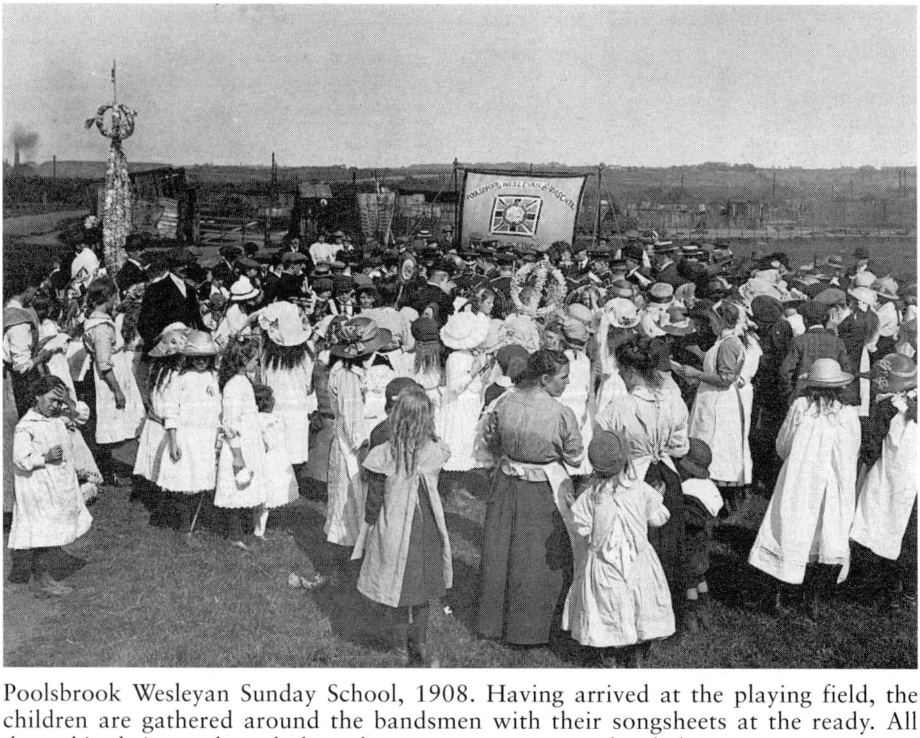

Poolsbrook Wesleyan Sunday School, 1908. Having arrived at the playing field, the children are gathered around the bandsmen with their songsheets at the ready. All dressed in their very best clothes, almost everyone wears a lovely hat.

Poolsbrook Methodist Chapel, 1894. Until the provision of this newly opened chapel, built on a site leased from a Mr Arkwright, prayer meetings were held in the local houses.

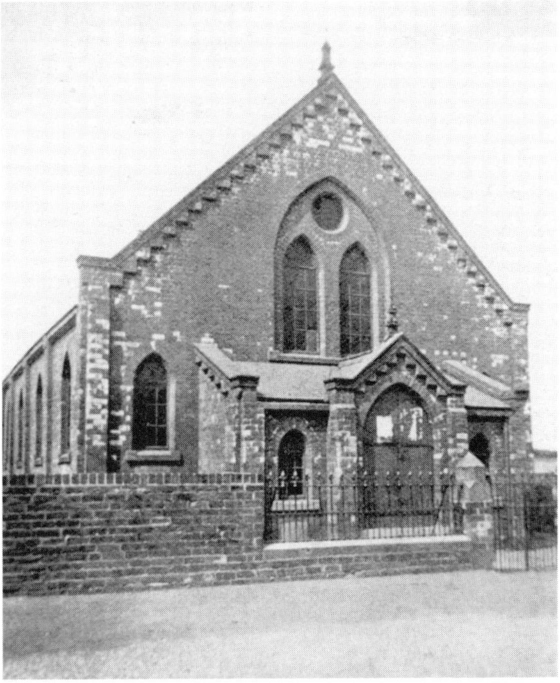

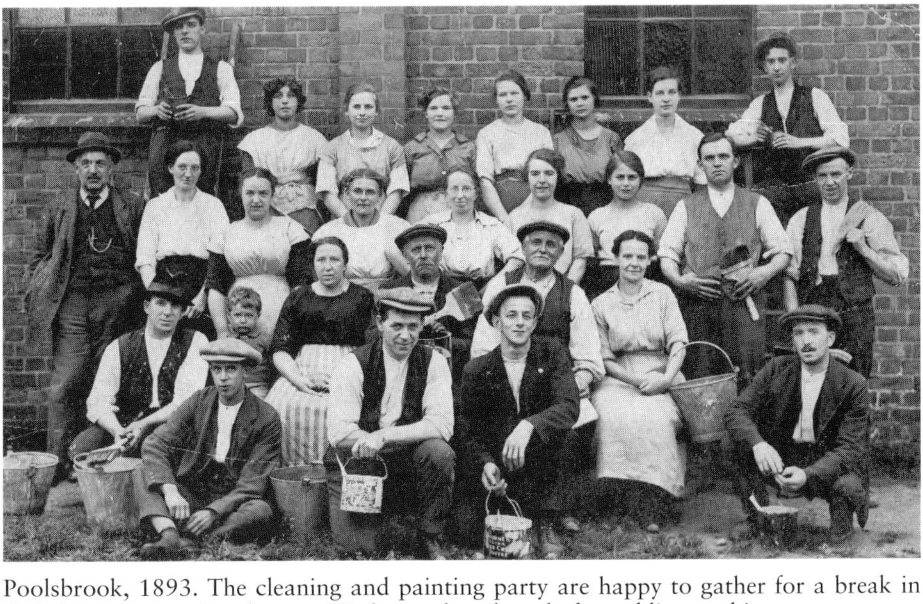

Poolsbrook, 1893. The cleaning and painting party are happy to gather for a break in their labours – getting the new Wesleyan chapel ready for public worship.

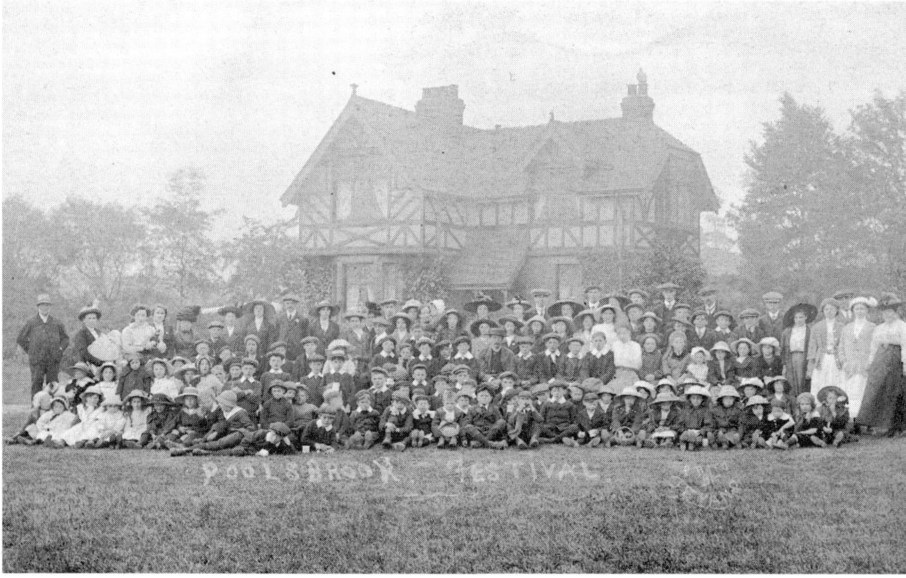

Poolsbrook Festival, 1906. During a lull in proceedings the children and adults have gathered for the cameraman to record the day they came to the pleasant Queen's Park in Chesterfield.

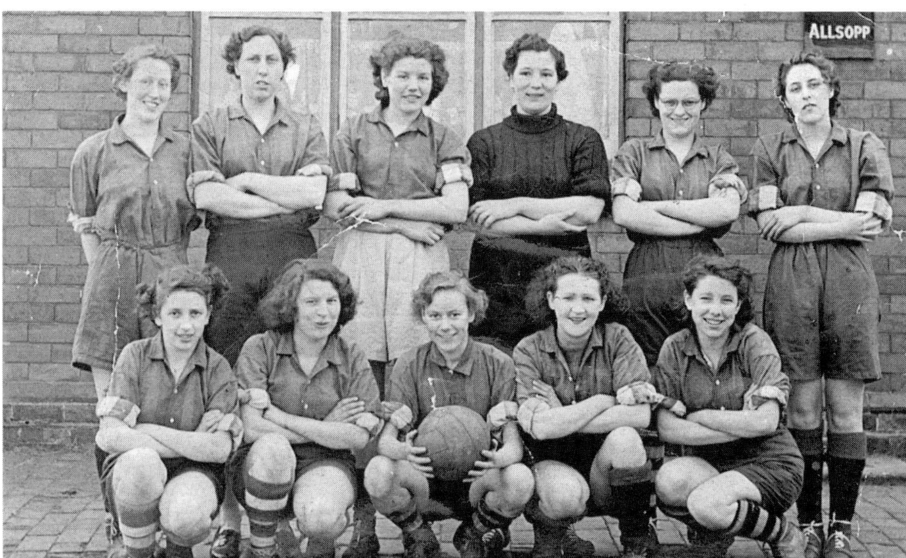

Poolsbrook Ladies Football Team, 1940s. Back row, left to right: Margaret Page, Rosie Middleton, Esme Kennon, Lois Richmond, Dorothy Walker, Audrey Walkers. Front row: Jean Bannister, -?-, Pat Evans, Elsie Fenn, Marina Dickinson.

SECTION EIGHT

High Days and Holidays

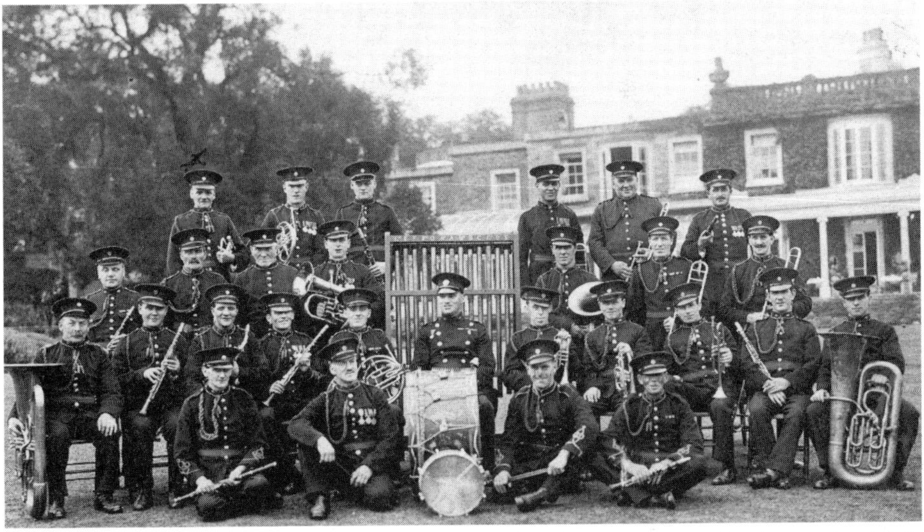

Staveley Military Band outside Ringwood Hall before a concert in the park, 1928. Among those playing are, back row, second from left, 'Digger' Stanley, third Kenneth Dean (clarinet player). Third row, first from left, James Booker, third 'Bendy' Hayes (who was the last town cryer). Second row, first from left, Tommy Thompson, third Frederick Bowerfield, fourth Paddy Burke (a founder member); third from right, Teddy ?. Front row, second from left, Ben Parsons, third Aubrey Hodson. The band usually practised in the Markham Hall on a Sunday.

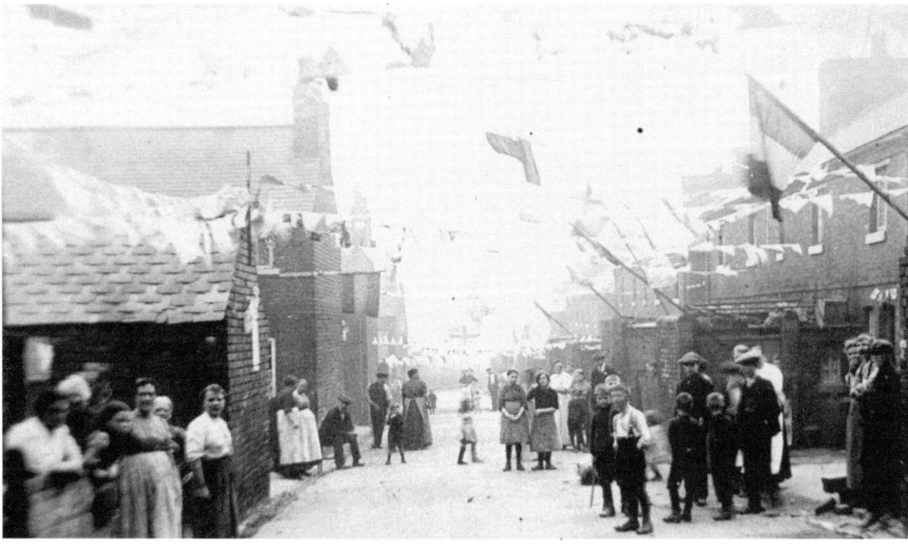

Speedwell Terraces, 1919. The flags are out and the people of the Terraces are preparing to celebrate the end of the First World War. This photograph was taken from the Inkersall Road looking down towards Ireland Colliery, which stood a few yards beyond the end of the row.

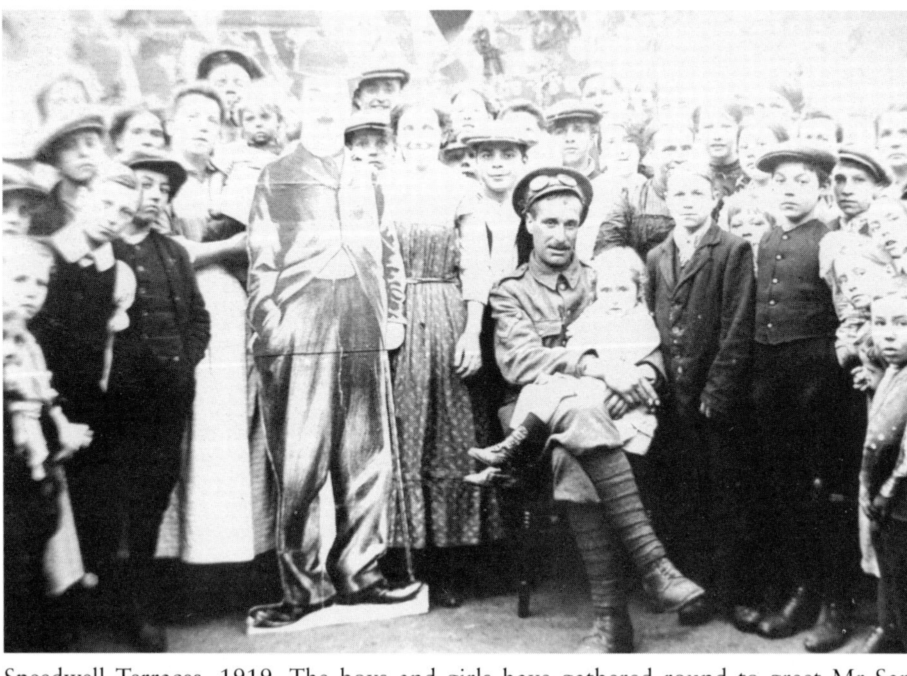

Speedwell Terraces, 1919. The boys and girls have gathered round to greet Mr Sam Waddoups on his safe return from the war. Does anyone have an explanation for the cardboard cut-out of Charlie Chaplin?

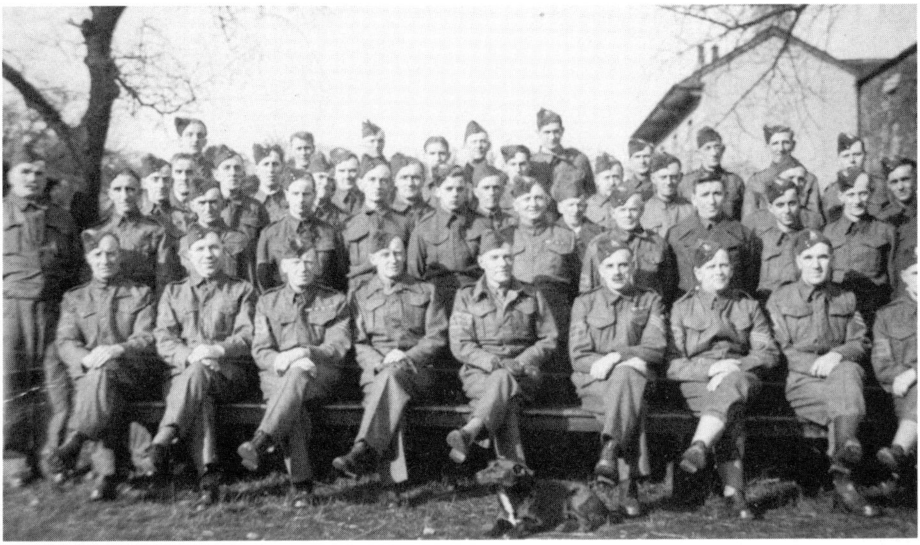

Staveley Town LNER Platoon, D. Company, 7th Battalion, 1944. Among those present in the grounds of Leyfield House are S. Rimmington, K. Bacon, F. Addy, W. Mosley, H. Fountain, R. Webb, A. Trevor, W. Smedley, E. Cutts, F. Wood, T. Bennett, J. Baker, T. Jackson, J. Abbott, J. Andrews, J. Woodward, R. Gill.

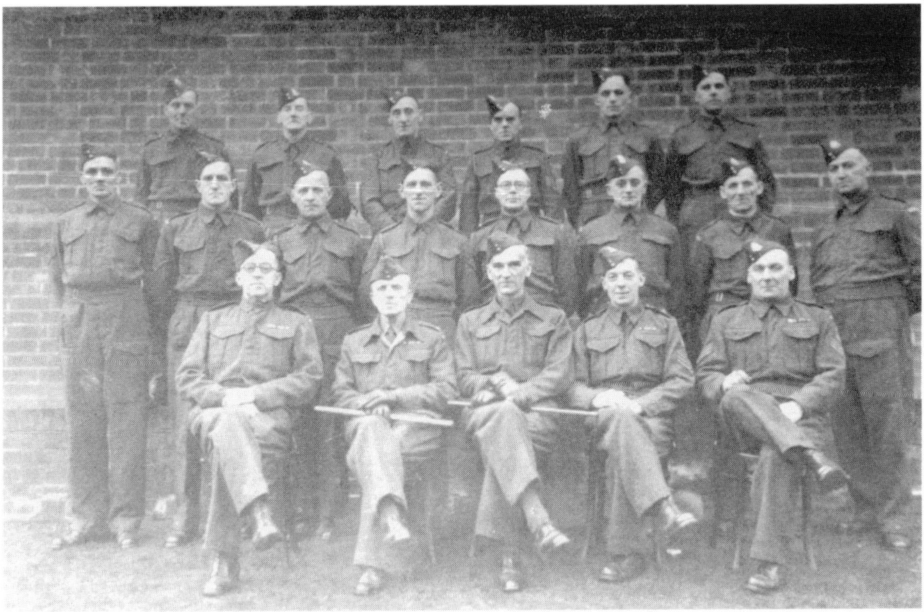

Staveley Lowgates Home Guard, 1944. Back row, left to right: A. Hodson, -?-, Tommy Nuttall, W. Winters, Ben Nuttall, Alf White. Middle row: John Pollard, -?-, Clarence Jones, Len Brownlow, E. Peabody, K. Geary, -?-, -?-. Front row: T. Cammel, S. Rooney, A. Munday, ? Derricot, ? Smith.

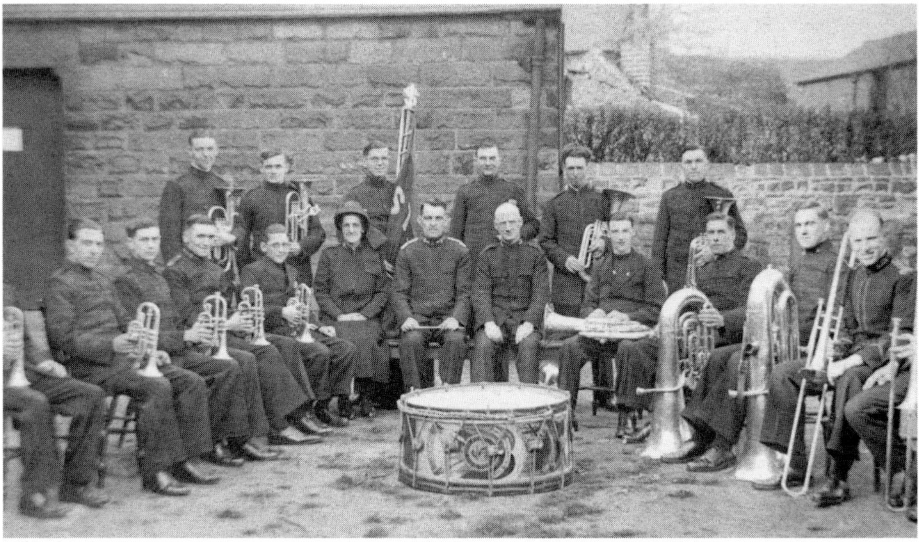

The Salvation Army Band, 1938. Once a very active group in Staveley, always in the forefront at the parades, their numbers waned in later years and the Army Hall was closed. With the band are Wilf (centre front, with baton) and Bill Hinchcliffe, Tommy Bennett and Mr ? Speed.

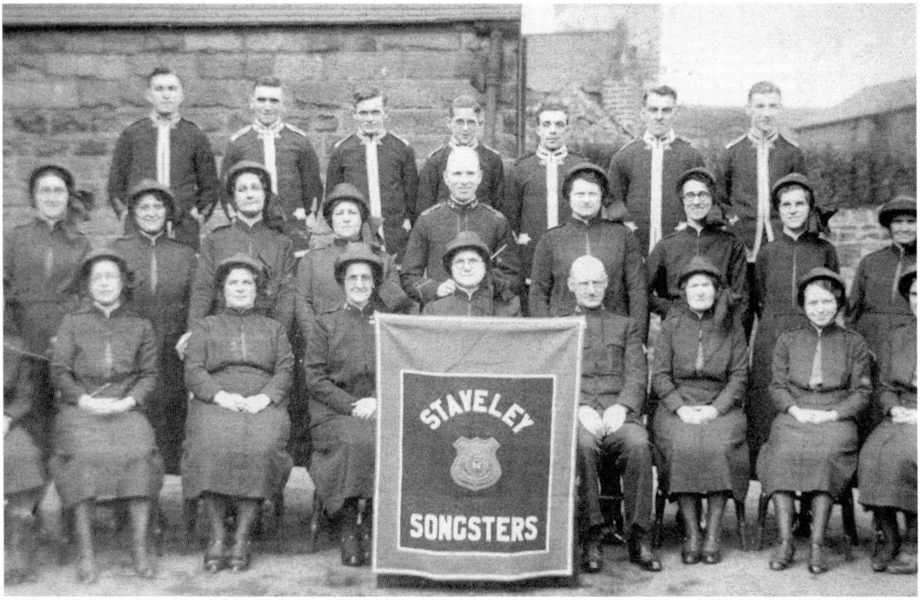

Staveley Salvation Army Songsters, 1938. Wilf and Bill Hinchcliffe were once again keen supporters, with help from Aggie Bennett, Frances, Olive and Edie Speed, Mrs Day and others. For many years they sang carols around the streets at Christmas and are still fondly remembered.

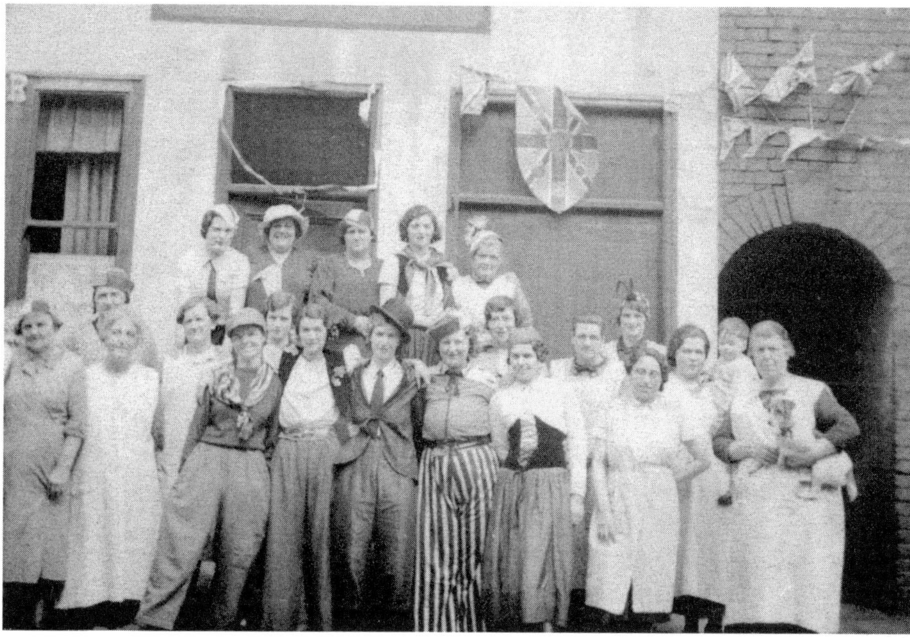

The New Inn, New Street, 1945. Outside the 'Drum and Monkey' Mrs Marlow, Bella Hart, Mrs Wheeldon, Una Wheeldon, Nell Brough, Lil Griffiths and others have a break from the festivities of VE-Day.

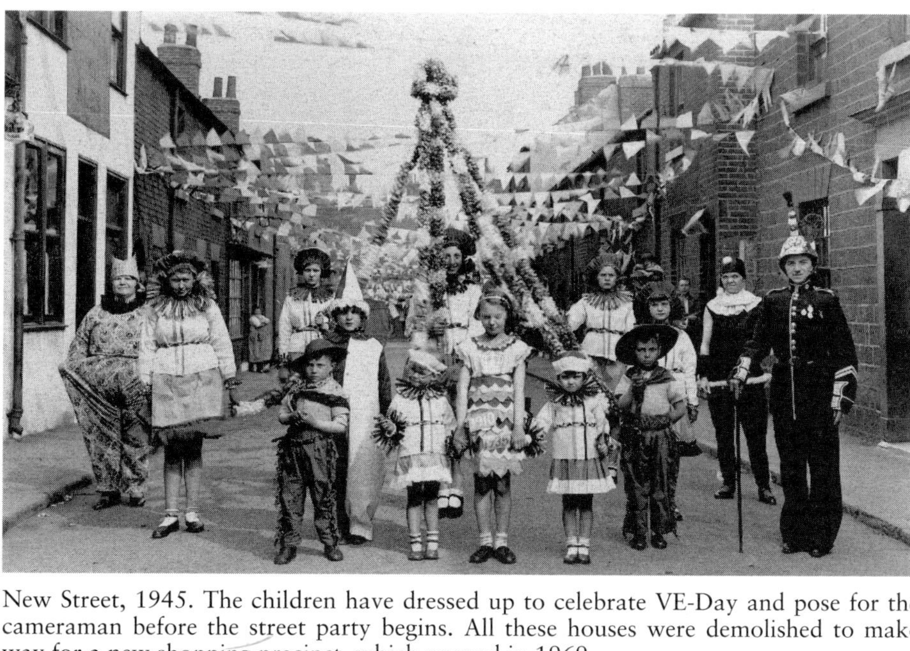

New Street, 1945. The children have dressed up to celebrate VE-Day and pose for the cameraman before the street party begins. All these houses were demolished to make way for a new shopping precinct, which opened in 1969.

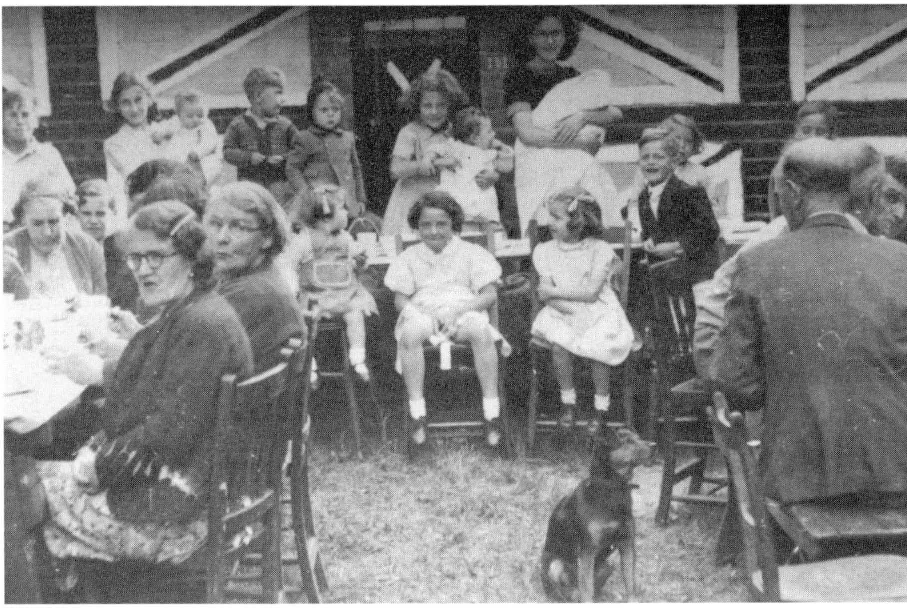

The party in The Poplars, 1945. Mrs Taylor, Mrs Baguley, children and dog share a victory tea in this small cul-de-sac of twenty-three houses which led off Market Street. Flats are now built where these once stood.

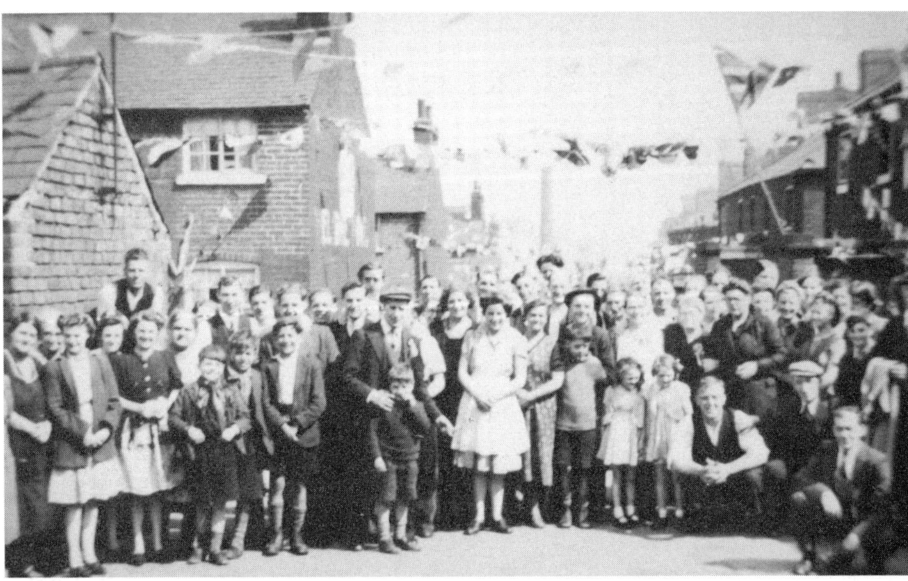

Speedwell Terraces, 1945. A photograph taken from the same point as the First World War celebration picture on p. 110, but this time the smiling faces are for VE-Day. Among those present are Stan Kaye, Lou Palmer, Tate Turner, Alice Parsons, Frank Smith, Jack Kaye and Laura Parsons.

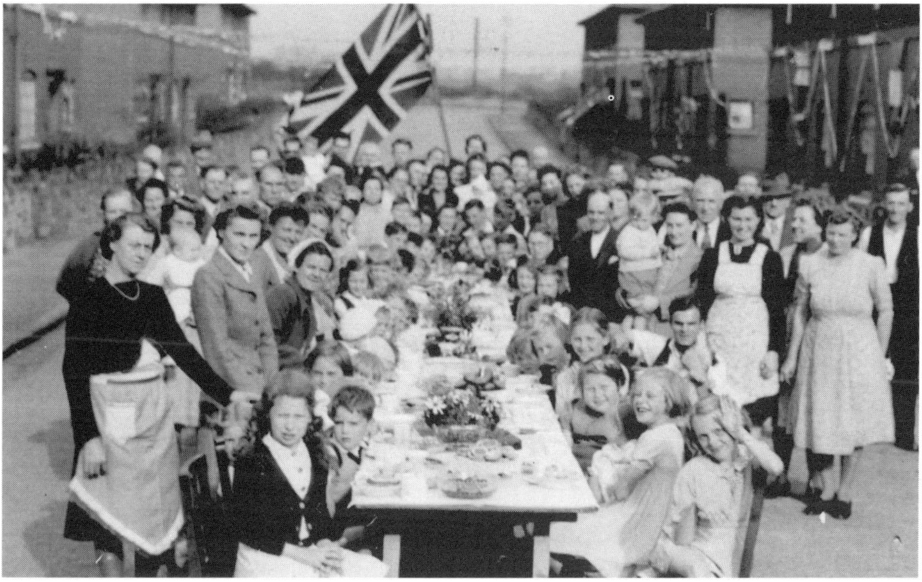

Whitehead Street, Fan Road, 1945. This street party to celebrate the end of the war was provided by Mrs Prentiss, Mrs Baguley, Mrs Wood, Mrs Samuels, Mrs Houghton, Mrs Brownlow, Mrs Shaw, Mrs Swain, and the Cottage girls, with a little help from the gentlemen of course.

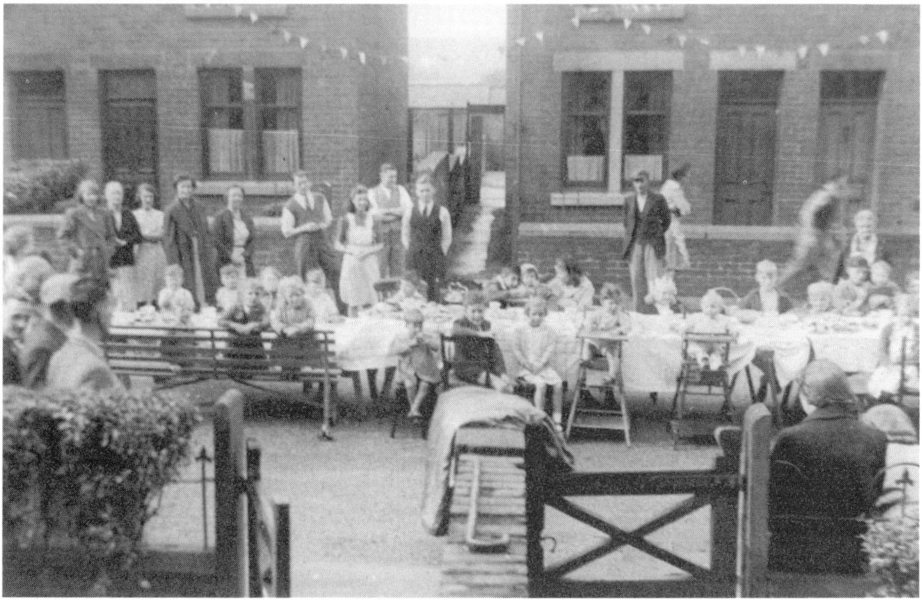

Victoria Avenue, Lowgates, 1945. Mr John Churm (in cap) is watching proceedings at the victory street party. All the families helped in preparing the food and drink, and each child brought along his or her own cup, plate, knife and fork.

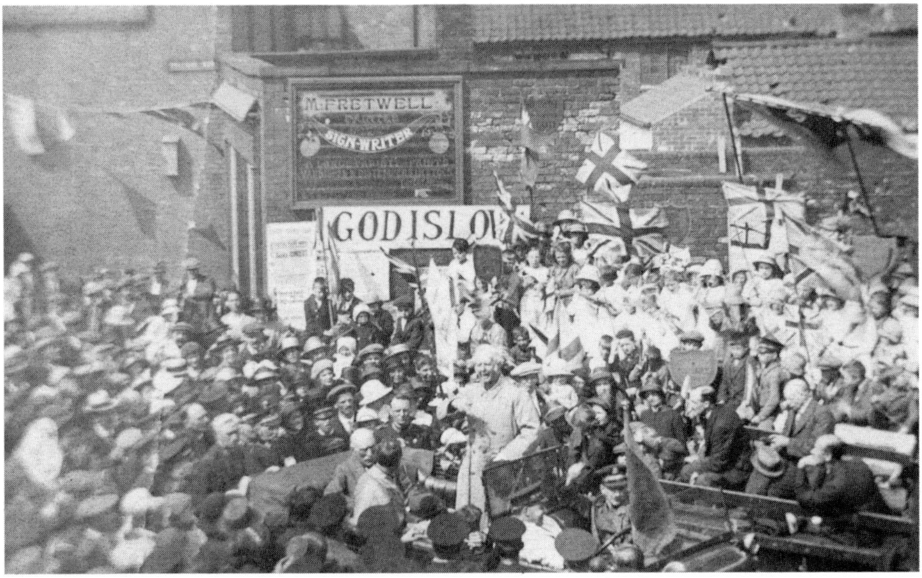

The Cross, Market Street, 1923. The crowds have gathered to hear General Booth, the Salvation Army leader, speaking. Sir Josiah Court listens in the back of the chauffeur-driven car.

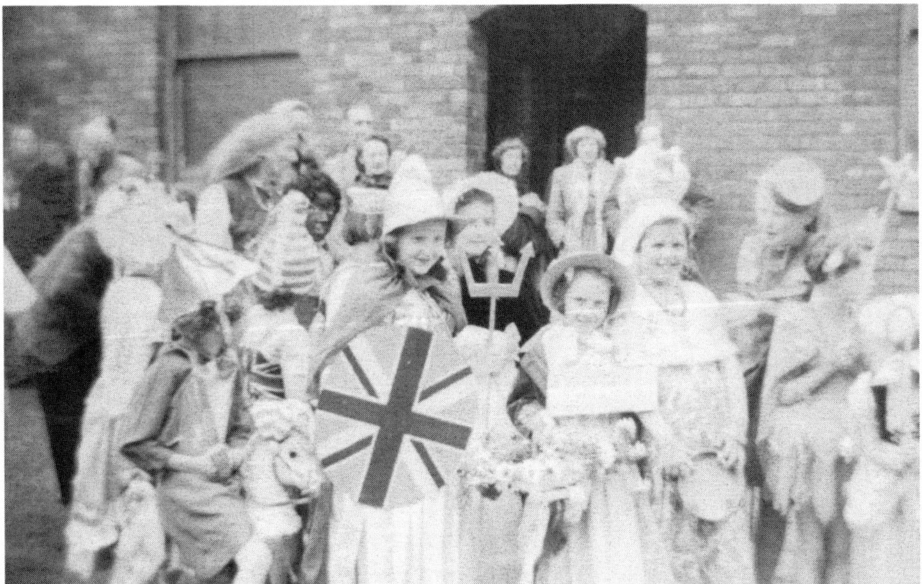

Outside the ambulance room at Hartington Colliery, 1953. The children have gathered in their fancy dress, watched by Mr and Mrs Brailsford, ready for a parade and party to celebrate the Queen's coronation.

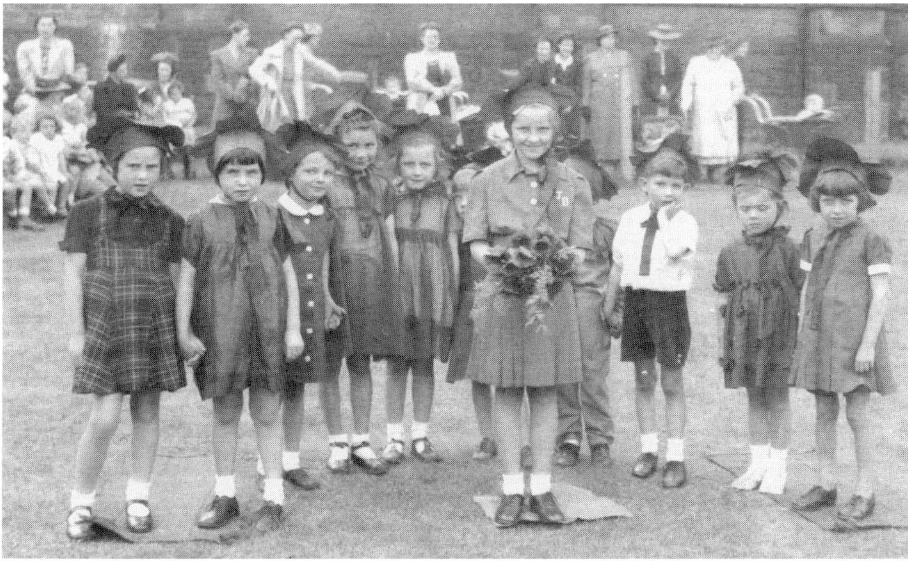

The Poppy Queen, 1943. As part of the Rose Queen Pageant, performed annually by the pupils of the Church School, Rose Queen and attendants were chosen – accompanied by four Flower queens with their attendants. Jill Brownlow is attended, from left to right, by: -?-, Shirley Keller, Fay Turner, -?-, Pam Caudwell, -?-, -?-, Roy Johnson, Margaret Bradshaw, -?-.

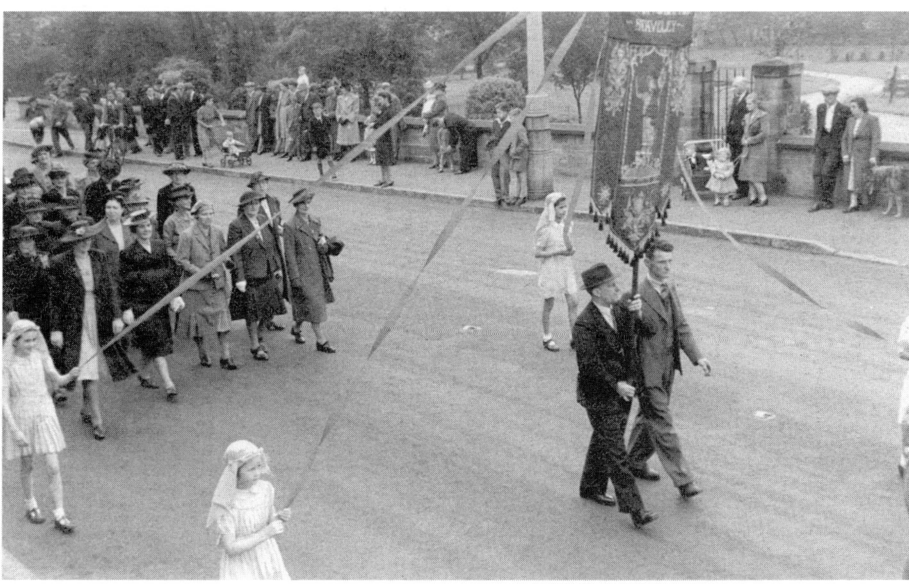

A Whit Sunday Church Parade, 1944. Carrying the banner of St John the Baptist past the Garden of Remembrance, the churchwardens and girl attendants are followed by the Church Ladies Guild.

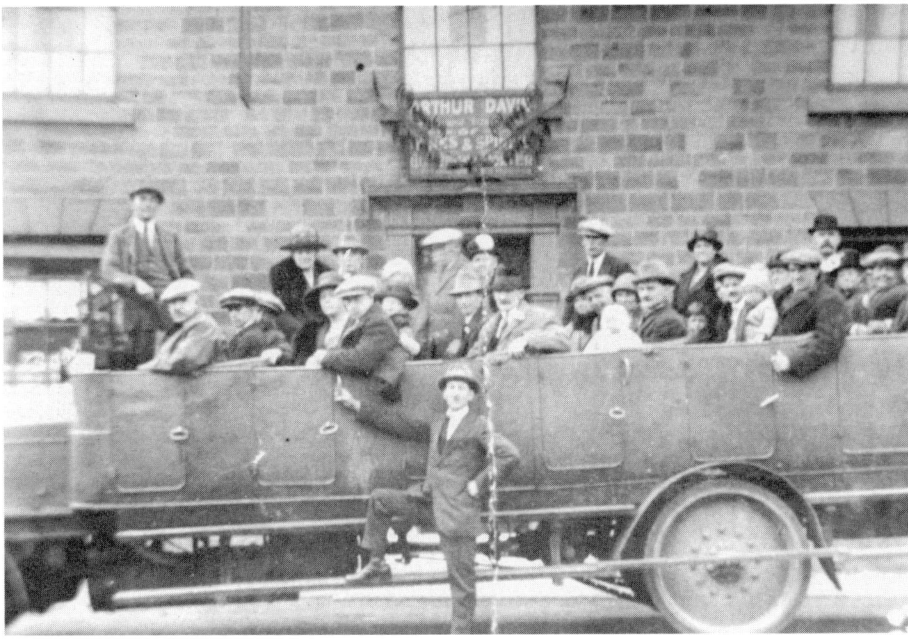

A charabanc outing from The Crown, The Cross, 1925. There were two charabanc proprietors trading in Staveley, Percy Palmer on Devonshire Street, and Shore and Girdham at Netherthorpe.

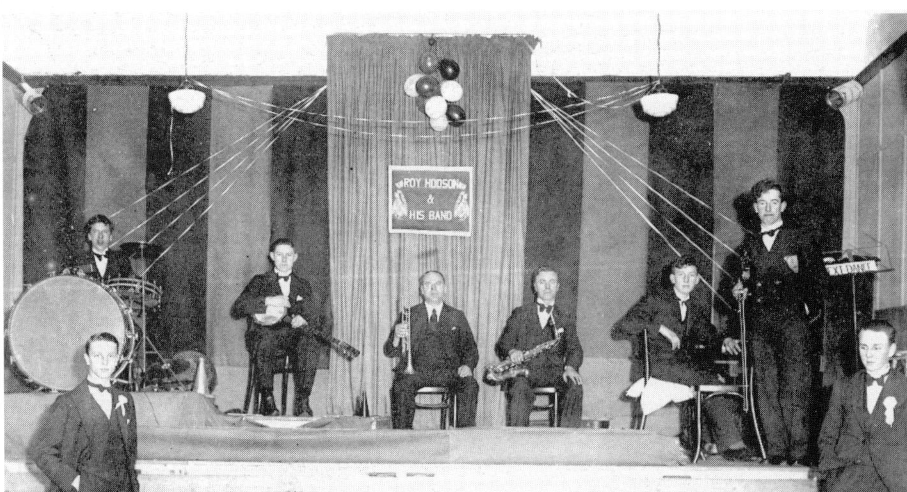

Roy Hodson's Band, 1930. On stage, from left to right, are: Bill Taylor, Joe Hodson, Chas Norris, Joe Walsh, Ernest Hallam, Lance Naylor, with Frank Turner standing front left, who were all members of this well-known band, which was a favourite at the dances and *soirées* held in the Markham Hall.

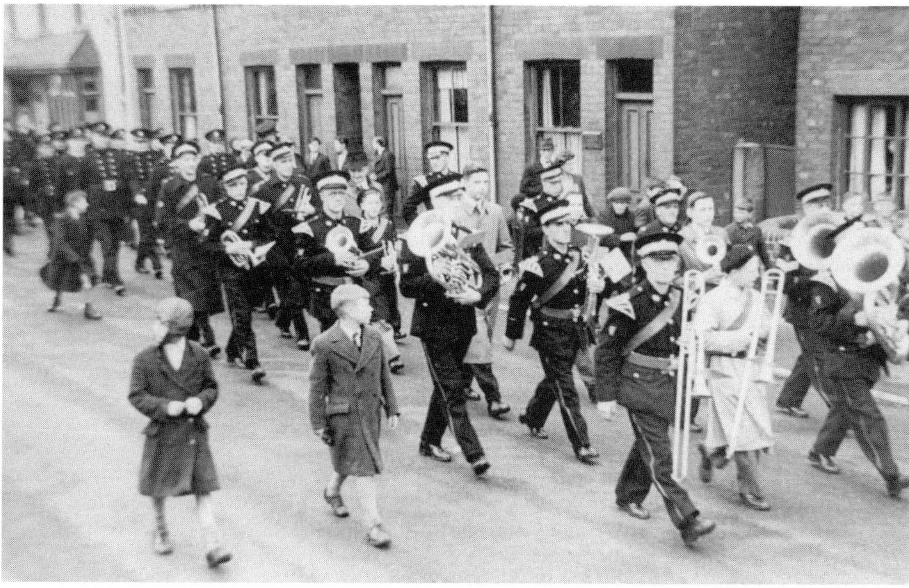

The St John Ambulance Brigade Band, followed by the Staveley Fire Service in the Victory Parade to the church for a thanksgiving service, 1945. Twenty-four local groups took part in the march, with a little help from most of the small boys in Staveley!

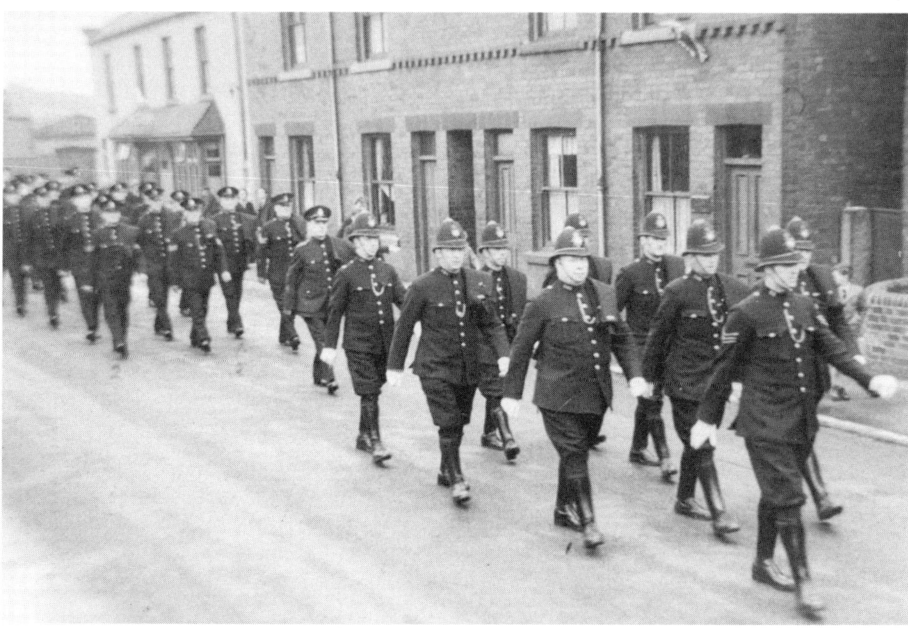

Victory Parade, 1945. 'Bobby' Buck, a well-known member of the Staveley Police Force, marches behind the sergeant past the Nag's Head, followed by the men of the Special Constabulary.

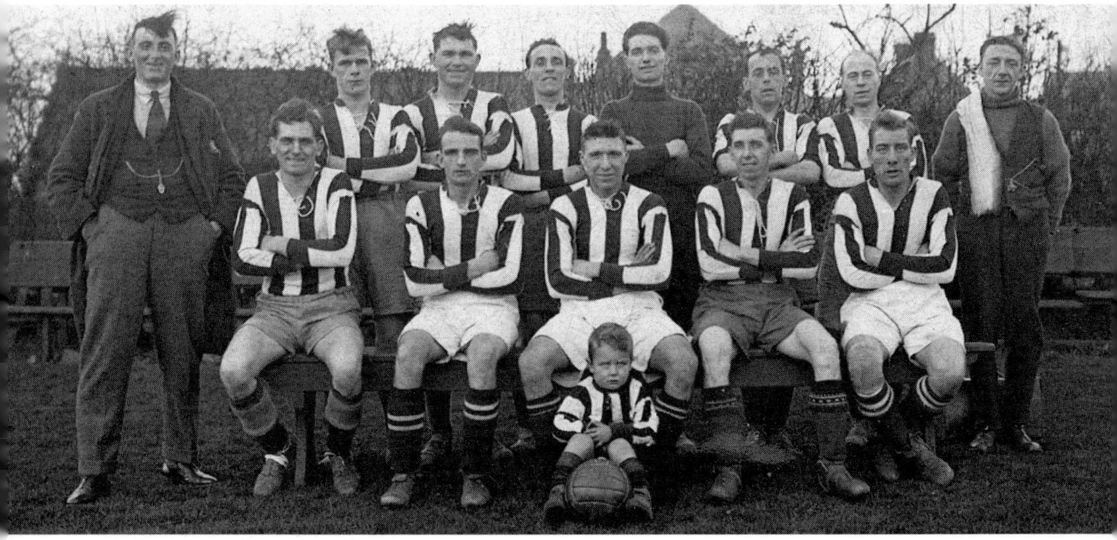

Speedwell Old Boys, 1932–3. Standing, left to right: G. Harding (secretary), A. Fogg, J.W. Goodwin, O. Birch, A. Griffiths, G. Arblaster, E. Griffiths, S. Rimmington (trainer). Sitting: S. Evil, C. Brooks, A. Higginbottom, E. Wright, R. Poxton. The little boy's name is not known.

When I was a kid the most wonderful sight
Were the stripes of the Old Boys, black and white.
This was truly a marvellous side,
For each young fella wore his shirt with pride.

Hat-trick Atty, the pride of them all,
Nothing this lad couldn't do with a ball,
The best centre forward ever seen,
Except maybe for Dixie Dean.

With goalkeepers too this team was blessed,
I remember four of the best.
Oliver Birch was never at fault,
Nor were the Turners, Harry, Arthur or Walt.

Watch these lads fly down the wing,
The ball must be tied to their boots with string.
Harry Griffiths, Sam Evil, Stan Hardin', Wag Brooks,
All good enough for Arsenal's books.

In defence, very few cracks,
With Bunt and Ern Griffiths, full-backs.
Zia Morris, Harry Limb, Mag Goodwin, Harry Wright,
Ern Mansell, Herb Pendleton, heroes all in black and white.

An extract from a poem by an unknown Speedwell Old Boys football fan who watched the team when he was ten years old.

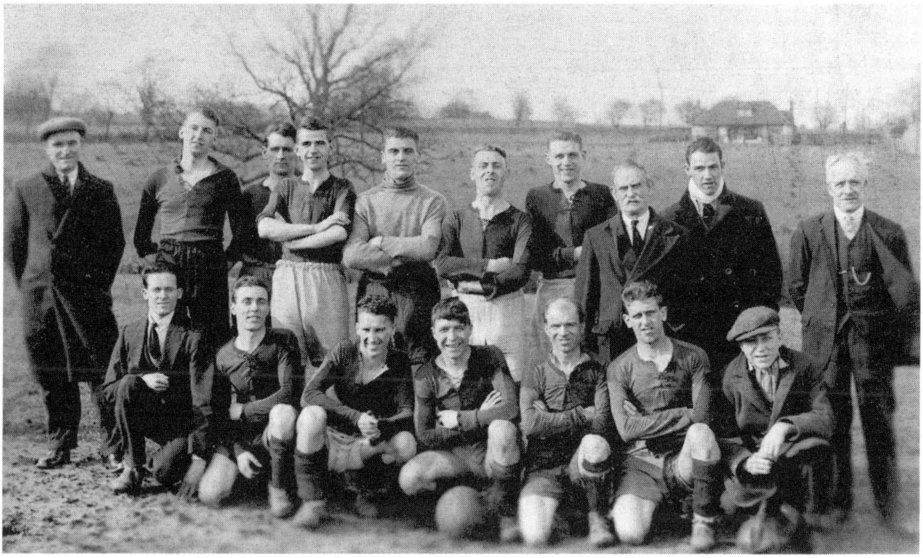

Speedwell Mission Football Club, 1931. Chesterfield Church League winners and Medal Final runners-up. Back row, first from left, Walt Barrow, fourth Billy Pearson, fifth Arthur Turner, seventh Jack Lancaster, ninth Albert Bendall, tenth Mr Higginbottom. Front row, second from left, Arthur Griffiths, fourth Alf Higginbottom, fifth Tony James, seventh ? Fox.

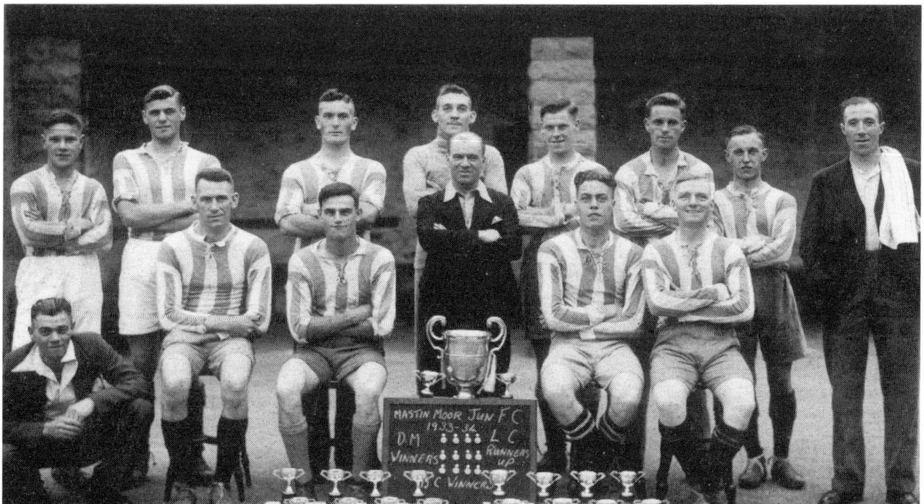

Mastin Moor Football Club with some of their trophies, 1933–4. Back row, left to right: Tommy Nuttall, John Wickins, William Church, Billy Speed, John Harold Lane, Wilfred Mosley, Edward Royal, Harold Church (trainer). Front row: Charley Mellor, Charley Speed, Stanley Mellor, Johnny James, George Lowe, George Hancock.

STAVELEY TOWN F.C.

OFFICIAL PROGRAMME.

ISSUED BY THE SUPPORTERS' CLUB.

PRICE 1d. Prize given for numbered programme

CRAGG BROS.,

THE Printers.

Stationers, Tobacconists.

WHOLESALE AND RETAIL. **HIGH STREET.**

AFTER THE MATCH—CALL AT THE

Elm Tree Hotel,

Chesterfield's
FINEST ALES
on DRAUGHT,
Wines & Spirits.

Proprietor : C. TONKS.

CONNIE BROOKE'S CAFE

TEAS & LUNCHEONS.

HIGH STREET.

Hair Tonics. Brilliantines, etc.

For a Good Clean Shave & Haircut,

Call at

JACQUES.

MARKET STREET.

THE MISSES SMALES,

31, HIGH STREET,
STAVELEY.

Wool, Needlework, Haberdashery.

Our own Hand and Machine Knitting a Speciality.

Orders Taken and Executed Promptly.

R. HINDE.

High-Class Grocer,

HIGH STREET, STAVELEY

Specialist in Poultry Foods.

The 1928 official football programme for the Staveley Town Midland League, with advertising for some local shopkeepers. Most of the players mentioned appear in the photograph on p. 124.

Saturday, April 28th. *No.*204

STAVELEY.

RIGHT. **Crookes.** LEFT.

Hamby. **Eggleshaw.**

Weaver. **Adlington.** **Jones**

Burton. **Tremelling.** **Meads.** **Clarke.** **Chapman.**

Kick off 3-30.

Dennis. **Keeton.** **Smalley.** **Spaven.** **Watson.**

Pearce. **Waterall.** **Cooke.**

Derrick. **Yoldren.**

LEFT. **Walker.** RIGHT.

GRANTHAM.

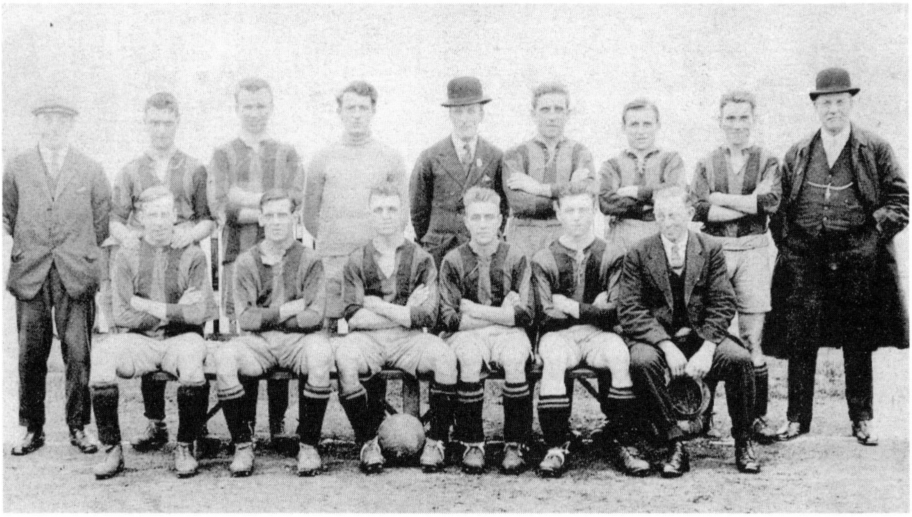

A postcard by Cragg of Staveley Town Midland League Team, 1927–8. Back row, left to right: S. Payne (trainer), Templey, Hamby, Crookes, Colquhoun (secretary), Adlington, Eggleshaw, Jones, Cragg (selection committee). Front row: Burton, Tremelling, Meads, Clarke, Chapman, A. Dunks (selection committee).

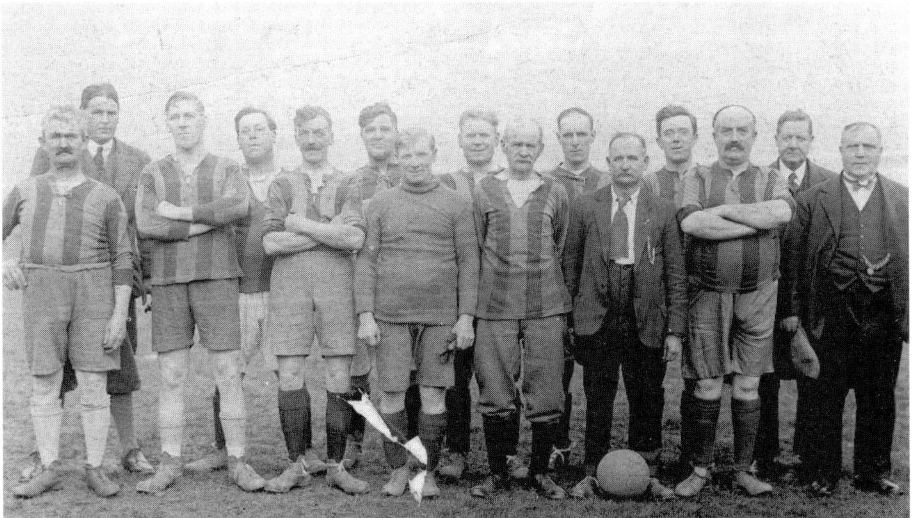

Jack Baguley's Eleven, early 1920s, including some well-known Staveley faces. Left to right: Mr Senior, -?-, Mr Fowler, Norman Onions, P. Hopkinson, Jack Baguley, H. Holt, Henry 'Pip' Richardson, ? Kerry, Barry Howells, Aaron Dodd (landlord of the Speedwell Inn), Robert Marriot, Teddy Williamson, -?-, -?-.

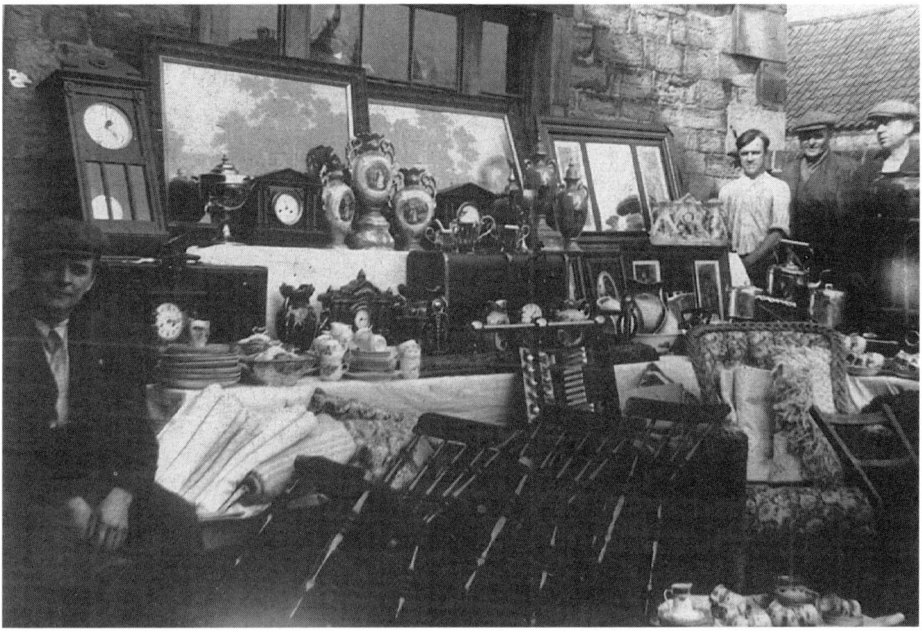

The Railway Inn, Netherthorpe, 1925. Messrs Perkins and Townsend, with Jack Hay the landlord, show off the wonderful variety of prizes for the Fishing Club. This building, which was made of stone with huge external stone buttresses from floor to roof, was replaced by the present inn in 1931.

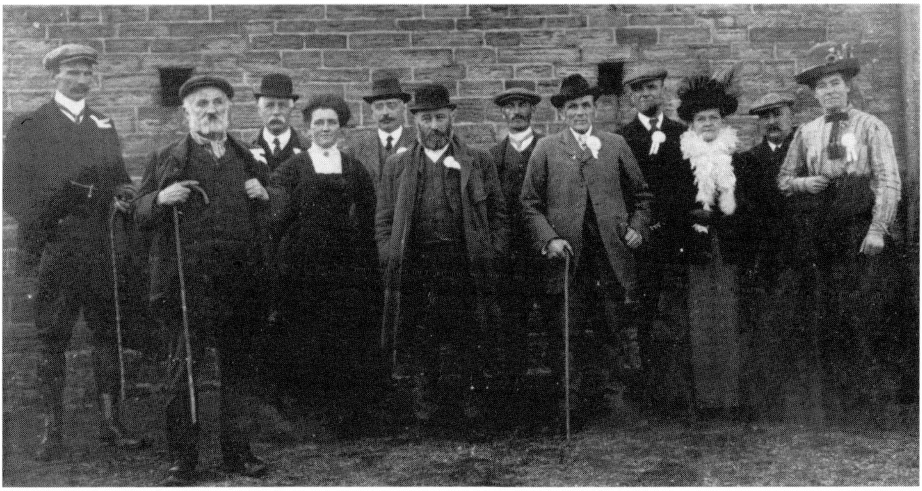

The ploughing match at Belle Vue Farm, Nether Handley, November 1911. Participants and friends at William Widdowson's farm include, from left to right: Sam White, H. Marples of Huggister Farm, T. Robinson, Mrs Widdowson, Mr Lee Arthur and Mr Renshaw of Woodthorpe, Mr Thorpe, Mr & Mrs Unwin, Mr White Sen., D. Barlow, and Mrs J.T. Handbury.

Careful Attention to all
Printing Orders.

WEDDING CARDS AND CAKE BOXES.

MEMORIAM CARDS AND RIBBONS.

PIPES AND ALL SMOKERS' REQUISITES.

CRAGG BROTHERS,

Proprietor - F. W. CRAGG.

PRINTERS AND STATIONERS.
WHOLESALE AND RETAIL TOBACCONISTS.

17, High Street, Staveley Town,

FOUNTAIN PEN DEPOT.

Large Stock of ENVELOPES, WRITING PADS, STATIONERY, of all kinds.

LOCAL VIEWS, BIRTHDAY CARDS, &c., &c.

HYMN AND PRAYER BOOKS, BIBLES, &c.

An advert for Cragg Brothers, 1930. Mr Frank Cragg provided some of the photographs and postcards used in this book as well as many other pictorial reminders of old Staveley.

Acknowledgements

Being one of the younger generation of Staveleyans I have only known Staveley as it is now, and so I am indebted to all the local people who have taken the time to look out their old photographs and to talk to me about the people and places of their youth. My grateful thanks must also go to Mrs Betty Tansley for her untiring search for items of interest, to Mrs Ida Garner, always a mine of information, to Mrs Doris Brooks for the loan of photographs taken by the late Mr C. Brooks, who had provided invaluable notes and comments on the backs, to Mr Chris Goodlad, who has helped track down many of my postcards, and finally to my mother Jill Matthews for all her help and encouragement.

BRITAIN IN OLD PHOTOGRAPHS

To order any of these titles please telephone 01453 731114

ALDERNEY

Alderney: A Second Selection, *B Bonnard*

BEDFORDSHIRE

Bedfordshire at Work, *N Lutt*

BERKSHIRE

Maidenhead, *M Hayles & D Hedges*
Around Maidenhead, *M Hayles & B Hedges*
Reading, *P Southerton*
Reading: A Second Selection, *P Southerton*
Sandhurst and Crowthorne, *K Dancy*
Around Slough, *J Hunter & K Hunter*
Around Thatcham, *P Allen*
Around Windsor, *B Hedges*

BUCKINGHAMSHIRE

Buckingham and District, *R Cook*
High Wycombe, *R Goodearl*
Around Stony Stratford, *A Lambert*

CHESHIRE

Cheshire Railways, *M Hitches*
Chester, *S Nichols*

CLWYD

Clwyd Railways, *M Hitches*

CLYDESDALE

Clydesdale, *Lesmahagow Parish Historical Association*

CORNWALL

Cornish Coast, *T Bowden*
Falmouth, *P Gilson*
Lower Fal, *P Gilson*
Around Padstow, *M McCarthy*
Around Penzance, *J Holmes*
Penzance and Newlyn, *J Holmes*
Around Truro, *A Lyne*
Upper Fal, *P Gilson*

CUMBERLAND

Cockermouth and District, *J Bernard Bradbury*
Keswick and the Central Lakes, *J Marsh*
Around Penrith, *F Boyd*
Around Whitehaven, *H Fancy*

DERBYSHIRE

Derby, *D Buxton*
Around Matlock, *D Barton*

DEVON

Colyton and Seaton, *T Gosling*
Dawlish and Teignmouth, *G Gosling*
Devon Aerodromes, *K Saunders*
Exeter, *P Thomas*
Exmouth and Budleigh Salterton, *T Gosling*
From Haldon to Mid-Dartmoor, *T Hall*
Honiton and the Otter Valley, *J Yallop*
Around Kingsbridge, *K Tanner*
Around Seaton and Sidmouth, *T Gosling*
Seaton, Axminster and Lyme Regis, *T Gosling*

DORSET

Around Blandford Forum, *B Cox*
Bournemouth, *M Colman*
Bridport and the Bride Valley, *J Burrell & S Humphries*
Dorchester, *T Gosling*
Around Gillingham, *P Crocker*

DURHAM

Darlington, *G Flynn*
Darlington: A Second Selection, *G Flynn*
Durham People, *M Richardson*
Houghton-le-Spring and Hetton-le-Hole, *K Richardson*
Houghton-le-Spring and Hetton-le-Hole: A Second Selection, *K Richardson*
Sunderland, *S Miller & B Bell*
Teesdale, *D Coggins*
Teesdale: A Second Selection, *P Raine*
Weardale, *J Crosby*
Weardale: A Second Selection, *J Crosby*

DYFED

Aberystwyth and North Ceredigion, *Dyfed Cultural Services Dept*
Haverfordwest, *Dyfed Cultural Services Dept*
Upper Tywi Valley, *Dyfed Cultural Services Dept*

ESSEX

Around Grays, *B Evans*

GLOUCESTERSHIRE

Along the Avon from Stratford to Tewkesbury, *J Jeremiah*
Cheltenham: A Second Selection, *R Whiting*
Cheltenham at War, *P Gill*
Cirencester, *J Welsford*
Around Cirencester, *E Cuss & P Griffiths*
Forest, The, *D Mullin*
Gloucester, *J Voyce*
Around Gloucester, *A Sutton*
Gloucester: From the Walwin Collection, *J Voyce*
North Cotswolds, *D Viner*
Severn Vale, *A Sutton*
Stonehouse to Painswick, *A Sutton*
Stroud and the Five Valleys, *S Gardiner & L Padin*
Stroud and the Five Valleys: A Second Selection, *S Gardiner & L Padin*
Stroud's Golden Valley, *S Gardiner & L Padin*
Stroudwater and Thames & Severn Canals, *E Cuss & S Gardiner*
Stroudwater and Thames & Severn Canals: A Second Selection, *E Cuss & S Gardiner*
Tewkesbury and the Vale of Gloucester, *C Hilton*
Thornbury to Berkeley, *J Hudson*
Uley, Dursley and Cam, *A Sutton*
Wotton-under-Edge to Chipping Sodbury, *A Sutton*

GWYNEDD

Anglesey, *M Hitches*
Gwynedd Railways, *M Hitches*
Around Llandudno, *M Hitches*
Vale of Conwy, *M Hitches*

HAMPSHIRE

Gosport, *J Sadden*
Portsmouth, *P Rogers & D Francis*

HEREFORDSHIRE

Herefordshire, *A Sandford*

HERTFORDSHIRE

Barnet, *I Norrie*
Hitchin, *A Fleck*
St Albans, *S Mullins*
Stevenage, *M Appleton*

ISLE OF MAN

The Tourist Trophy, *B Snelling*

ISLE OF WIGHT

Newport, *D Parr*
Around Ryde, *D Parr*

JERSEY

Jersey: A Third Selection, *R Lemprière*

KENT

Bexley, *M Scott*
Broadstairs and St Peter's, *J Whyman*
Bromley, Keston and Hayes, *M Scott*
Canterbury: A Second Selection, *D Butler*
Chatham and Gillingham, *P MacDougall*
Chatham Dockyard, *P MacDougall*
Deal, *J Broady*
Early Broadstairs and St Peter's, *B Wootton*
East Kent at War, *D Collyer*
Eltham, *J Kennett*
Folkestone: A Second Selection, *A Taylor & E Rooney*
Goudhurst to Tenterden, *A Guilmant*
Gravesend, *R Hiscock*
Around Gravesham, *R Hiscock & D Grierson*
Herne Bay, *J Hawkins*
Lympne Airport, *D Collyer*
Maidstone, *I Hales*
Margate, *R Clements*
RAF Hawkinge, *R Humphreys*
RAF Manston, *RAF Manston History Club*
RAF Manston: A Second Selection, *RAF Manston History Club*
Ramsgate and Thanet Life, *D Perkins*
Romney Marsh, *E Carpenter*
Sandwich, *C Wanostrocht*
Around Tonbridge, *C Bell*
Tunbridge Wells, *M Rowlands & I Beavis*
Tunbridge Wells: A Second Selection, *M Rowlands & I Beavis*
Around Whitstable, *C Court*
Wingham, Adisham and Littlebourne, *M Crane*

LANCASHIRE

Around Barrow-in-Furness, *J Garbutt & J Marsh*
Blackpool, *C Rothwell*
Bury, *J Hudson*
Chorley and District, *J Smith*
Fleetwood, *C Rothwell*
Heywood, *J Hudson*
Around Kirkham, *C Rothwell*
Lancashire North of the Sands, *J Garbutt & J Marsh*
Around Lancaster, *S Ashworth*
Lytham St Anne's, *C Rothwell*
North Fylde, *C Rothwell*
Radcliffe, *J Hudson*
Rossendale, *B Moore & N Dunnachie*

LEICESTERSHIRE

Around Ashby-de-la-Zouch, *K Hillier*
Charnwood Forest, *I Keil, W Humphrey & D Wix*
Leicester, *D Burton*
Leicester: A Second Selection, *D Burton*
Melton Mowbray, *T Hickman*
Around Melton Mowbray, *T Hickman*
River Soar, *D Wix, P Shacklock & I Keil*
Rutland, *T Clough*
Vale of Belvoir, *T Hickman*
Around the Welland Valley, *S Mastoris*

LINCOLNSHIRE

Grimsby, *J Tierney*
Around Grimsby, *J Tierney*
Grimsby Docks, *J Tierney*
Lincoln, *D Cuppleditch*

Scunthorpe, *D Taylor*
Skegness, *W Kime*
Around Skegness, *W Kime*

LONDON

Balham and Tooting, *P Loobey*
Crystal Palace, Penge & Anerley, *M Scott*
Greenwich and Woolwich, *K Clark*
Hackney: A Second Selection, *D Mander*
Lewisham and Deptford, *J Coulter*
Lewisham and Deptford: A Second Selection, *J Coulter*
Streatham, *P Loobey*
Around Whetstone and North Finchley, *J Heathfield*
Woolwich, *B Evans*

MONMOUTHSHIRE

Chepstow and the River Wye, *A Rainsbury*
Monmouth and the River Wye, *Monmouth Museum*

NORFOLK

Great Yarmouth, *M Teun*
Norwich, *M Colman*
Wymondham and Attleborough, *P Yaxley*

NORTHAMPTONSHIRE

Around Stony Stratford, *A Lambert*

NOTTINGHAMSHIRE

Arnold and Bestwood, *M Spick*
Arnold and Bestwood: A Second Selection, *M Spick*
Changing Face of Nottingham, *G Oldfield*
Mansfield, *Old Mansfield Society*
Around Newark, *T Warner*
Nottingham: 1944–1974, *D Whitworth*
Sherwood Forest, *D Ottewell*
Victorian Nottingham, *M Payne*

OXFORDSHIRE

Around Abingdon, *P Horn*
Banburyshire, *M Barnett & S Gosling*
Burford, *A Jewell*
Around Didcot and the Hagbournes, *B Lingham*
Garsington, *M Gunther*
Around Henley-on-Thames, *S Ellis*
Oxford: The University, *J Rhodes*
Thame to Watlington, *N Hood*
Around Wallingford, *D Beasley*
Witney, *T Worley*
Around Witney, *C Mitchell*
Witney District, *T Worley*
Around Woodstock, *J Bond*

POWYS

Brecon, *Brecknock Museum*
Welshpool, *E Bredsdorff*

SHROPSHIRE

Shrewsbury, *D Trumper*
Whitchurch to Market Drayton, *M Morris*

SOMERSET

Bath, *J Hudson*
Bridgwater and the River Parrett, *R Fitzhugh*
Bristol, *D Moorcroft & N Campbell-Sharp*
Changing Face of Keynsham, *B Lowe & M Whitehead*
Chard and Ilminster, *G Gosling & F Huddy*
Crewkerne and the Ham Stone Villages, *G Gosling & F Huddy*
Around Keynsham and Saltford, *B Lowe & T Brown*
Midsomer Norton and Radstock, *C Howell*
Somerton, Ilchester and Langport, *G Gosling & F Huddy*
Taunton, *N Chipchase*
Around Taunton, *N Chipchase*
Wells, *C Howell*
Weston-Super-Mare, *S Poole*
Around Weston-Super-Mare, *S Poole*
West Somerset Villages, *K Houghton & L Thomas*

STAFFORDSHIRE

Aldridge, *J Farrow*
Bilston, *E Rees*
Black Country Transport: Aviation, *A Brew*
Around Burton upon Trent, *G Sowerby & R Farman*
Bushbury, *A Chatwin, M Mills & E Rees*
Around Cannock, *M Mills & S Belcher*
Around Leek, *R Poole*
Lichfield, *H Clayton & K Simmons*
Around Pattingham and Wombourne, *M Griffiths, P Leigh & M Mills*
Around Rugeley, *T Randall & J Anslow*
Smethwick, *J Maddison*
Stafford, *J Anslow & T Randall*
Around Stafford, *J Anslow & T Randall*
Stoke-on-Trent, *I Lawley*
Around Tamworth, *R Sulima*
Around Tettenhall and Codsall, *M Mills*
Tipton, Wednesbury and Darlaston, *R Pearson*
Walsall, *D Gilbert & M Lewis*
Wednesbury, *I Bott*
West Bromwich, *R Pearson*

SUFFOLK

Ipswich: A Second Selection, *D Kindred*
Around Ipswich, *D Kindred*
Around Mildenhall, *C Dring*
Southwold to Aldeburgh, *H Phelps*
Around Woodbridge, *H Phelps*

SURREY

Cheam and Belmont, *P Berry*
Croydon, *S Bligh*
Dorking and District, *K Harding*
Around Dorking, *A Jackson*
Around Epsom, *P Berry*
Farnham: A Second Selection, *J Parratt*
Around Haslemere and Hindhead, *T Winter & G Collyer*
Richmond, *Richmond Local History Society*
Sutton, *P Berry*

SUSSEX

Arundel and the Arun Valley, *J Godfrey*
Bishopstone and Seaford, *P Pople & P Berry*
Brighton and Hove, *J Middleton*
Brighton and Hove: A Second Selection, *J Middleton*
Around Crawley, *M Goldsmith*
Hastings, *P Haines*
Hastings: A Second Selection, *P Haines*
Around Haywards Heath, *J Middleton*
Around Heathfield, *A Gillet & B Russell*
Around Heathfield: A Second Selection, *A Gillet & B Russell*
High Weald, *B Harwood*
High Weald: A Second Selection, *B Harwood*
Horsham and District, *T Wales*
Lewes, *J Middleton*
RAF Tangmere, *A Saunders*
Around Rye, *A Dickinson*
Around Worthing, *S White*

WARWICKSHIRE

Along the Avon from Stratford to Tewkesbury, *J Jeremiah*
Bedworth, *J Burton*
Coventry, *D McGrory*
Around Coventry, *D McGrory*
Nuneaton, *S Clews & S Vaughan*
Around Royal Leamington Spa, *J Cameron*
Around Royal Leamington Spa: A Second Selection, *J Cameron*
Around Warwick, *R Booth*

WESTMORLAND

Eden Valley, *J Marsh*
Kendal, *M & P Duff*
South Westmorland Villages, *J Marsh*
Westmorland Lakes, *J Marsh*

WILTSHIRE

Around Amesbury, *P Daniels*
Chippenham and Lacock, *A Wilson & M Wilson*
Around Corsham and Box, *A Wilson & M Wilson*
Around Devizes, *D Buxton*
Around Highworth, *G Tanner*
Around Highworth and Faringdon, *G Tanner*
Around Malmesbury, *A Wilson*
Marlborough: A Second Selection, *P Colman*
Around Melksham, *Melksham and District Historical Association*
Nadder Valley, *R. Sawyer*
Salisbury, *P Saunders*
Salisbury: A Second Selection, *P Daniels*
Salisbury: A Third Selection, *P Daniels*
Around Salisbury, *P Daniels*
Swindon: A Third Selection, *The Swindon Society*
Swindon: A Fourth Selection, *The Swindon Society*
Trowbridge, *M Marshman*
Around Wilton, *P Daniels*
Around Wootton Bassett, Cricklade and Purton, *T Sharp*

WORCESTERSHIRE

Evesham to Bredon, *F Archer*
Around Malvern, *K Smith*
Around Pershore, *M Dowty*
Redditch and the Needle District, *R Saunders*
Redditch: A Second Selection, *R Saunders*
Around Tenbury Wells, *D Green*
Worcester, *M Dowty*
Around Worcester, *R Jones*
Worcester in a Day, *M Dowty*
Worcestershire at Work, *R Jones*

YORKSHIRE

Huddersfield: A Second Selection, *H Wheeler*
Huddersfield: A Third Selection, *H Wheeler*
Leeds Road and Rail, *R Vickers*
Pontefract, *R van Riel*
Scarborough, *D Coggins*
Scarborough's War Years, *R Percy*
Skipton and the Dales, *Friends of the Craven Museum*
Around Skipton-in-Craven, *Friends of the Craven Museum*
Yorkshire Wolds, *I & M Sumner*